MY STORY

MY STORY

BY TOM L. JOHNSON

EDITED BY
ELIZABETH J. HAUSER

AMS PRESS
NEW YORK

Reprinted from the edition of 1911, New York
First AMS EDITION published 1970
Manufactured in the United States of America
International Standard Book Number: 0—404—03593—0

Library of Congress Number: 77—127899

AMS PRESS INC.
NEW YORK, N.Y. 10003

TO THE MEMORY OF
HENRY GEORGE

Acknowledgment is hereby made of the assistance in the preparation of this story of my friend, Elizabeth J. Hauser, without whose co-operation it would not have been written.

Tom L. Johnson.

Cleveland, Ohio,
January 29, 1911.

CONTENTS

CONTENTS

ILLUSTRATIONS

ILLUSTRATIONS

INTRODUCTION

"My Story" was written by Mr. Johnson during the last five months of his life. He did not want to write it. It was undertaken at the instance of some magazine publishers and at the earnest solicitation of a few friends who felt that his own account of his nine years' struggle for a free city ought not to be lost to the world.

All earlier attempts to have Mr. Johnson set down in writing any of his experiences failed. He dismissed such suggestions always with the characteristic comment, "There are so many more important things to do." He was essentially a man of action and he was not willing to give a day or an hour to anything less vital than his work. He was not introspective, seldom reminiscent. Few men, probably, have lived so little in the past as did he. Anything that was unpleasant he resolutely refused to recall; he wiped it off the slate once for all. For him the game always was, "What will happen next?" When a political worker, believed by many if not by Mr. Johnson himself to have been instrumental in Mr. Johnson's last defeat, asked the ex-mayor for an opportunity to talk things over with him, the answer was, "I am willing to talk with you about to-morrow, but I won't talk about yesterday!"

It was therefore not until he knew that fighting was henceforth out of the question for him, that Mr. Johnson consented to write. Then he was willing to do it, not because he might expect to derive any pleasure from it, but because it was the only kind of action left him, and he had been persuaded that his story of the Cleveland fight might be of some use to other cities in their struggles to be free. By sheer force of will he dictated " My Story " after he became so ill that the slightest physical or mental effort was a severe strain. He had been wont to say that he wanted to " die in harness," " just stub his toe and stumble into his grave! " And he did " die in harness." The narrative breathes throughout all the strength, the good cheer, the hope, which animated his working and fighting days.

Big, brave, dauntless, resourceful soul! He *made* his wish come true.

Had Mr. Johnson lived longer he probably would have added nothing of a personal nature to his story. It was with extreme difficulty that he was induced to include the few delightful personal anecdotes which lend such charm to the early chapters. " Those things have nothing to do with the fight against Privilege," he would protest, and he could not be made to understand that anything which appertained solely to himself was of any interest or value.

One is disposed to respect this lack of self-consciousness almost to the point of adding nothing to the narrative. It is because the readers of this book are entitled to an account of the year and three months of Mr. Johnson's life after he left the mayor's office in Cleveland that the last chapter of the volume has been written.

Aside from the preparation of this last chapter the editing of " My Story " has consisted only in dividing the book into chapters and supplying their headings, and, here and there, where some principle or policy seemed to demand emphasis or explanation, in elaborating a little the original statement. When this has been done the elaboration is given in Mr. Johnson's words. Although he was not a writer, it happens that a public address made by him upon the question of Privilege — an address which treats so comprehensively of the cause, the results, and the cure of Privilege, that little or nothing seems to be left to be said on the subject — was taken down and preserved. This address has served as a reference from which to draw such elucidation as has seemed necessary.

For readers who did not know Mr. Johnson, and who cannot read between the lines of " My Story " much which the author has not told, a note of introduction is offered. He has said so little of the overwhelming odds against which he fought and conquered, of the fierceness of the storm which raged about him during the whole of the Cleveland conflict, of the daring and original methods in political work by which he forced achievements possible to every large city! There is humor and sweetness and poise and power to be found in " My Story," but it is the story of a man who never knew what a momentous figure he was. Not the least of his greatness is his unconsciousness of it.

Tom L. Johnson was a pioneer in politics in the doing of things because they were right rather than because they were expedient. He believed in the people, and he addressed himself to them with a sincerity, vigor, and freshness of method as unusual as they are effective. Sometimes he reached them in mass as through his " picture show " of taxation injustices, a device which antedated by many years the present use of picture illustration in all kinds of social problems. Sometimes he made his appeal personally, as when, after sitting in the gallery of the State House and listening to the most violent attacks upon himself and his measures, he would hunt up the author of these attacks, never to say a word in his own defense, but always to try to convince his antagonist of the justice of the legislation in question. An anecdote illustrating his success in this direct method of argument is the following:

A few years ago when the Ohio legislature was providing for one of its periodic investigations of the city government of Cincinnati, a hostile member introduced a bill calling for a similar investigation of Cleveland. On the very heels of this action Mayor Johnson sent a message to Representative (now Senator) John N. Stockwell of the Cleveland delegation telling him that he would arrive in Columbus late that night and asking him to arrange for an immediate interview with the member who had introduced the Cleveland investigation bill.

"I wondered what in the world Mr. Johnson could want of G——," says Senator Stockwell in relating this incident, "but I hunted him up and arranged for the interview. G—— supposed, of course, the mayor was coming to take him to task for his bill. The mayor came, saw G——, told him that what he wanted was his support of some important street railway legislation, explained the measure, convinced G—— of the justice of it, and infused him with so much of his own enthusiasm that that man hustled around the whole of the night seeing other members in the interests of Mr. Johnson's bill, and supported it upon the floor of the house the next day. Mr. Johnson went back to Cleveland without ever referring to G——'s bill to have Cleveland investigated. When I asked him later why he chose G—— of all men to push

his measure and lead in the fight for it, he replied that
he thought G—— was a strong man and as he seemed
to be our most determined enemy he was clearly the most
necessary convert to our measure. He said it would have
been foolish to waste precious time in seeing those who
would be friendly anyway."

Mr. Johnson's fights with Republican legislators were
mild in comparison with his fights with members of his
own party. He was the first political leader in the United
States to ask his supporters to vote against candidates of
his own party and for those of the opposition. In his
campaign for governor he violated all political precedent
when he refused to permit many of the customary expenditures. A rich man, or at least reputed to be rich,
he not only refused to spend money extravagantly, but he
insisted that county committees of the Democratic party
should defray the legitimate expenses of their campaigns.
Seventy-five dollars he demanded from each county in
which he pitched his tent as part of the expense of trans-
porting it. He alienated all the spoilsmen, all the old
line machine politicians, and every State convention found
them in a struggle with him for supremacy. Sometimes
he carried the day and was able to control both platform
utterances and choice of candidates. Between these two
he preferred always to formulate the platform, for, in his
political programme, principles were ever of more importance than persons. And sometimes he lost out, leaving a defeat famous because of the fine spirit in which it
was taken. One of Mr. Johnson's epigrams connects
itself with such a defeat:

At the State convention in 1908, when he was successful
in forcing the adoption of a radical platform, his candi-

date for governor, Atlee Pomerene, was beaten by Judson Harmon. It was a crushing blow. Mr. Johnson had put up a tremendous fight.

"What will Johnson do?" was the query that buzzed over that great audience in the convention hall. Feeling was still at white heat, yet, before there was time for reflection or consideration, before the tumult had subsided, with his friends crestfallen and disappointed at his back, his enemies exultant, and yet already apprehensive, turning, as by a common impulse to look at him, Mr. Johnson spoke, and this is what he said, "I make my fights before nominations, not afterwards."

The soundness of Mr. Johnson's forecast of popular will is seen in many directions to-day. Hardly a progressive measure in evidence in the political thought of the hour but was anticipated and championed by him. Year after year he spent a large part of his time at the State capital urging the passage of measures freeing cities from the grip of franchise corporations. One session he took rooms with members of the Cleveland delegation and spent months about the State House endeavoring to secure juster laws on taxation, laws for municipal ownership and home rule for cities. He was one of the first to agitate for the initiative and referendum and recall, and was an enthusiastic advocate of the short ballot. After he became convinced of the justice of woman suffrage he made several speeches for it, the most notable one in the midst of his mayoralty contest with Mr. Burton. There may be politicians who would do for the woman's cause now what Mr. Johnson did then, but there wasn't another equally prominent public man in the United States who would have done it at that time.

His moral courage, coupled with an intense desire to have social wrongs corrected, caused him often to challenge the authority of those in high places. He had an hour's interview with President Roosevelt during the latter days of the Colonel's administration, and as he was taking his leave, Mr. Johnson said, " The difference between you and me, Mr. President, is this: you are after law-breakers, I am after the law-makers. You would put a man in jail for stealing; I would prevent the theft."

When the trust question was a paramount issue in American politics Mr. Johnson asked William Jennings Bryan, who was a guest in his house, what he would do to solve that problem if he were in a position of real power as President of the United States with a friendly Congress and all the machinery of government to aid him. As Mr. Bryan suggested remedy after remedy, Mr. Johnson showed him how he, a monopolist, a beneficiary of special privilege, could evade, ignore or safely violate such laws as Mr. Bryan was proposing. By practical illustrations he demonstrated the futility of all legislation which does not strike Privilege at its root which is land monopoly.

Mr. Johnson did not hesitate, upon occasion, to go to leading Democratic office-holders in his own State and give them the benefit of his experience with and observation of dishonest party workers. For their own protection and the good of the state he warned these officials against the traitors in their political camps. Such service was not always graciously received, but time usually justified Mr. Johnson's predictions.

To his administration of Cleveland's affairs Mr. Johnson brought, besides his native resourcefulness, all his

training as a big business man. Himself efficient to the
last degree he insisted upon efficiency in others, and every
department of the city government showed results because
of this.

He applied the merit system to the water works and
health departments, though not required by law to do so.
Flat rates were abolished for water service, meters in-
stalled and the cost of water reduced for ninety per cent.
of the consumers. Waste was stopped and in the four
years ending in 1909 over one million dollars had been
saved to water users.

When Mr. Johnson became mayor the city was dispos-
ing of its garbage under the contract plan at an annual
cost of $69,000. When the contract expired the city
bought the plant, and the very first year under municipal
ownership and operation reduced ten thousand more tons
of garbage than under the contract method, and at a cost
of $10,000 less; and this, notwithstanding a reduction in
the hours of employés and an increase of their wages.
Later the collection of ashes, waste paper and refuse was
also undertaken by the city.

In 1900 the electric light monopoly was charging the
city $87.60 a year for each light. By the time Mr. John-
son went out of office, competition of the municipal lighting plant had reduced this cost to $54.96 per light.

Mr. Johnson instituted a building code that was a model
for other cities, established meat and dairy inspection,
barred milk from tubercular cows, saved householders a
million dollars a year by compelling the use of honest
weights and measures, created a forestry department for
the protection of the city's trees, paved several hundred
miles of street, and substituted for the old practice of

sweeping the superior method of cleaning the streets by washing them. He built public bath-houses, comfort stations, and shelter sheds, laid out baseball diamonds, cricket fields and golf links, encouraged band concerts in the parks in summer and skating carnivals in winter, established May Day and Arbor Day festivities.

People were just people to Mr. Johnson and when, soon after his first election as mayor, he deprived the poor of a means of gambling with pennies and nickels by sweeping six thousand slot machines out of the city, he did not neglect to deal a blow to rich gamblers by following this action with a prohibition of pool selling at the Cleveland Driving Park when the time for the fall races arrived.

These many and varied public benefits have been accepted so much as a matter of course that one is disposed to wonder whether the citizens of Cleveland think they have been produced by some automatic agency and without human power.

All of these activities cost money, but Mr. Johnson instituted a purchasing department for the city which saved money by getting a two per cent. discount for the prompt payment of all bills, and established many business economies. The city's assets have increased more than twice as much as her bonded indebtedness. And all of this work was carried on honestly. Cleveland, under Mayor Johnson, was free from graft. No scandal ever attached to the administration. The proof of this assertion was brought out by those who were his enemies. Year after year a hostile State administration sent expert accountants to investigate the city's accounts; unfriendly newspapers did the same thing; franchise corporations employed detectives to hunt for something wrong; all with the same

result! There was no graft. Mr. Steffens was justified
in his estimate of Mr. Johnson, as " the best mayor," and
of Cleveland as " the best governed city in the United
States."

Most of these things Mr. Johnson has ignored in his
story. They were so much a part of the day's work with
him that it would no more have occurred to him to tell
them than to relate that he put on his shoes when he got
up in the morning.

The things he does tell are told simply, and even the
most unpleasant of them without any bitterness. As a
year only had elapsed between the time of his defeat as
mayor of Cleveland and the day he set himself seriously
to the task of telling his story this absence of bitterness
cannot be attributed to the softening influences of time;
nor can it be ascribed to the mellowing hand of age for
Mr. Johnson was not old. Up to his last hour of consciousness he was living ahead of the generation just born,
and there are those who believe that this would have been
so had he lived to be eighty-six years of age instead of
dying as he did at fifty-six.

It must be, then, that even in the heat of the battle
when feeling ran highest he was not affected by it, for not
only had all bitterness vanished when he began to write,
but he had actually forgotten many of his most trying and
cruel experiences.

Contrast his statement that he was hissed but once in
his life and that at a meeting in Brooklyn with this from
the pen of a man who participated in nearly all of Mr.
Johnson's campaigns:

" During his dozen campaigns while mayor it was his habit to
insist upon questions from the audience; he asked for hard ones,

' mean ' ones, he called them; he liked that kind best.   No man
was apparently more vulnerable.   He had been in the street railway business all his life and he opened up his whole life to scrutiny
and gayly acknowledged where acknowledgment was coming,
and answered where an answer was required.   Frequently his
meetings were on the verge of riot; in the east end where feeling
was most vindictive and but a handful of his friends would be
present he would stand on the edge of a jeering, sometimes a
hissing crowd that packed the tent far out to the street lines,
smilingly leaning on the edge of the table until the uproar quieted.
Then he would frequently win the meeting by a simple story or
sweet appeal.   Night after night he met this kind of thing, speaking possibly half a dozen times in from one to three tents and in
as many more halls, and apparently never wearying of it.   He
seemed to court this kind of exposure to attack."

Again, in discussing the Depositors Savings and Trust
Company, he dismisses the relation of other banks to the
Depositors in a single sentence, " A great many of the
local banks were unfriendly, but a few of them acted very
nicely indeed."   That is all, though it is a matter of common knowledge that the organization of the Depositors
was necessary in order to provide the low-fare movement
with a friendly bank and to prevent its transactions from
being made public and thereby circumvented, that it had
constantly to combat rumors against it set in motion by
hostile interests, and that from the very beginning it was
compelled to fight against a combination of the banking
interests of Cleveland to which it finally had to succumb.

He says nothing to indicate that he had any personal
feeling in connection with the strike inaugurated by the
old and still hostile street railway managers directly after
the Municipal Traction Company took possession of the
street railways.   He had had a strike on one of his own

xxii   INTRODUCTION

street railroads but once.   That lasted just ten minutes.
He went in person to the men and told them that he
thought what they were asking for was reasonable and he
was prepared to give it to them.   He had always paid
good wages and had encouraged labor unions among his
employés.   While that Cleveland strike was on he spent
hours of each day in a machine shop working with his
hands on the pay enter fare-box which he had invented and
with which he was preparing to equip the cars.   Did he
resort to manual labor and abandon his mind to the mental
absorption of mechanical problems that the iron might not
enter his soul?   He never told.

So little reference is made to the persecutions and cruel-
ties of the street railway company and the business interests allied with it that the reader whose only source of
information is Mr. Johnson's own story might perhaps
conclude that Cleveland was quite different from Detroit
and Toledo and Chicago and San Francisco and other
cities where the franchises of public service corporations
have been threatened.   But in Cleveland, as in these other
cities, there was organized as if by instinct a sympathetic,
political-financial-social group whose power and influence
made itself known the moment it was touched.   It included the banks and trust companies with their directors.
Banks that did not sympathize with this conspiracy were
coerced by fear into compliance with the will of the
stronger institutions.   Through the banks, manufacturers,
wholesale and retail merchants were reached.   Business
men who openly sympathized with the low-fare movement
were called to the directors' rooms in the banks and advised, sometimes in guarded language, that their loans
might be called or their credit contracted.   Only one bank

of any size dared identify itself with the low-fare railroad
and it was made to suffer some of the stings of ostracism.
Many men who bought low-fare stock had to do it se-
cretly. Contractors, professional and business men were
cowed at meetings of the Chamber of Commerce by the
suggestion that they would lose business; retailers who
voted for Mayor Johnson and let their position be known
were boycotted or threatened with boycott. The professional classes were allied with the business interests. The
lawyers were almost a unit. At one time fourteen of the
leading law firms of the city were employed against the
movement. Many physicians and in a large measure the
clergy were affiliated with this class. There were a few
notable exceptions in both the Catholic and Protestant
churches. Dean Charles D. Williams of Trinity Cathe-
dral, now Bishop of Michigan, never flagged in his devotion to Mr. Johnson or to the cause for which he stood.
The clerks followed in the wake of the business interests
and all who were seeking favor socially, professionally or
commercially, lined up with Privilege.

And there was always a portion of the press to be reckoned with! Two newspapers owned respectively by the
family of one of Mr. Johnson's most powerful political
enemies and by attorneys and stockholders of the street
railway company, persistently misrepresented the people's
movement, and, through paid advertisements, editorially
and otherwise, they made charges of criminality and dishonesty against Mr. Johnson, implying that the movement
was part of his plan to make money, to steal the street
railways of the city for private profit. Brutal cartoons
accompanied their news stories or illustrated their editorial
point of view.

Yet when Mr. Johnson died, a little more than a year after he went out of office, these newspapers joined with thousands of others in proclaiming their belief in his sincerity and honesty. He had made mistakes, they said, but not a shadow of a suggestion of bad faith did they charge up to him.

The newspaper persecution of Mr. Johnson was not confined to Cleveland. A publicity bureau supplied the country papers of the State with material well designed to convince the unthinking and the uninformed that in the Cleveland mayor were reincarnated for the temptation and fall of Ohio all the qualities ascribed to the Satan of the early orthodox church.

To all of this was added the coercive power of social ostracism. It was carried into the clubs and employed against all who distantly believed in or liked Mr. Johnson.

" For the greater part of nine years," writes Frederic C. Howe, " Cleveland was an armed camp. There was but one line of division. It was between those who would crucify Mr. Johnson and all of his friends, and those who believed in him. I doubt if any of the border cities like Washington and Covington during the Civil War were more completely rent asunder than was Cleveland during those years. It is doubtful if the wars of the Guelphs and Ghibellines in the Italian cities were more bitter, more remorseless, more cruel than this contention in Cleveland. If any kind of cruelty, any kind of coercion, any kind of social, political or financial power was left untried in those years to break the heart of Mr. Johnson, I do not know what or when it was."

How he contrived to keep his spirit strong and glad is something one may not hope to comprehend. At one period in the street railway fight when the entire city of Cleveland seemed to have united in a clamor for settlement and when even his most trusted friends and loyal followers were urging concessions which Mr. Johnson's far-seeing vision would not permit him to make, when, for a time, he stood utterly alone, not a word of discouragement, not a sign of irritation escaped him. But when his "boys" finally rallied to his support and a united plan of action was agreed upon once more, the mayor was so happy that a friend, knowing nothing of the occurrence just past, commented upon his gaiety. In explanation he related what had happened. An expression from his listener of admiration at the patience and sweetness of his attitude brought from him this answer: without speaking he took from his inside breast pocket a little worn brown card and handed it to her.

She read:

"The man who is worthy of being a leader of men will never complain of the stupidity of his helpers, of the ingratitude of mankind, nor of the inappreciation of the public.

"These things are all a part of the great game of life, and to meet them and not go down under them in discouragement and defeat is the final proof of power."

"I should like to keep this card long enough to copy the quotation," the friend said, after a moment.

"You may have it," replied Mr. Johnson, "I don't need it any more."

Much of Mr. Johnson's success in public affairs as in his mastery of himself must be attributed to the fact that he did not go into the fight against Privilege with the confusion of ideas and multiplicity of aims which have de-

INTRODUCTION

stroyed the usefulness of so many good, well-intentioned men in similar service. If it be that there are men in whom the sense of justice is more highly developed than it was in Mr. Johnson, in the history of our country, at least, there has been none who has given fuller expression in action to that sense of justice. He was a rich man, made rich by special privilege. He did not blink the fact. When Mr. George's writings opened his eyes to the truth about the established order, he went out to destroy the conditions which make his own class possible.

Inequality of opportunity with its concomitant result, involuntary poverty, was *the social wrong*. To restore equality of opportunity by securing to each worker the product of his own labor, thereby depriving a privileged few from monopolizing rewards which belong to the many, was *the social remedy*. His programme was definite and complete. His philosophy must have been tremendously satisfying, for by means of it he worked out a simple, effective solution to every political problem that might arise, and the answers to his personal problems as well.

That there was a marked development in the noblest qualities in Mr. Johnson's character during the last five or six years of his life none of his friends will gainsay; yet from the very beginning of his interest in social questions there was something different, something extraordinary about him. One of the ablest of American editors, a man who had been closely associated with Mr. Johnson in the earlier days and one who knew him intimately for twenty-five years, said of him a few days after his death, " I don't know how it was, but somehow Johnson never had to reason things out. No matter what the question that came up, no matter how laboriously I might have to study it in order to work my way out, he knew as if by instinct the proper and just solution of it."

Another of the men who was closest to Mr. Johnson from 1901 to 1911 says,

" I can only understand Tom L. Johnson by saying that his qualities were of a different kind than those of other men; his courage, his intellect, his insight, his sympathy, his love were on a something more than human plane.   He saw his mental pictures, reached his decisions, carried his Herculean load for more than forty years because he was endowed with a gift of a different caliber, of another kind than those of any of his contemporaries. There was nothing ordinary about him except his kinship with ordinary people.   He might easily have been a Morgan of finance had he chosen to pursue this field of exploit; he might easily have been one of our greatest inventors, one of our greatest electrical experts.   He was a wonderful mathematician, a great manager of men and things, a political philosopher of the rarest kind with something of the intuitive point of view of Jefferson.   He knew the street railway business from the standpoint of the motorman, the conductor, the manager, the electrician, the financier.   He had been all of these things.   He had mastered the iron and steel business in the same exhaustive way.   For years he arose at five o'clock and began the day with a study of French or some other subject with an instructor, and closed it with the study of some work on political science in which he was interested.   He was an orator of the most effective kind and in quick exchange of repartee or in answering questions, a master.   As a parliamentary leader of the English sort he would probably have been the greatest of his generation, for he not only knew more about more things than any man I have ever met, but he also had a philosophy of life which clarified every question into its logical crystals.   That was one of the rarest qualities of the man.   He did not reason things out; they simply straightened out when they came in contact with his mind. Did a proposition make for liberty? it was approved. Did it make for special privilege in any of its forms? it was wrong. Did legislation open up opportunity, promote personal or political freedom, make it easier for all men to achieve their best? it required no other argument. I have frequently heard him say that if he had the choice of leaving his children with millions or with equal opportunity he would not hesitate which to choose."

No picture of this man would be complete without a view of him at play, for Mr. Johnson played on as gigantic a scale as he worked. Had he chosen to make his play his serious work he would probably have been one of the greatest inventors of his time. He had intended to tell as part of this story, in narrative form and so simply that every layman might understand it, something of his invention which, for want of a better name, was known to his friends as "greased lightning." Even after he was stricken by his final illness and confined to his bed he talked about this and still hoped to be able to dictate it. This was not to be, but we are able to give the story to the readers of Mr. Johnson's book, for Frederic C. Howe, remembering it as Mr. Johnson told it to him, has written it for us. Mr. Howe's assistance not only in the matter of the following story of the invention but in the preparation of this entire introduction has been invaluable.

"Mr. Johnson's most Titanic recreative exploit was what his friends called 'Greased Lightning' or 'Slip-Slide.' One day in the midst of a conference at the City Hall a man waited to see the mayor. When his turn came he said, 'Mr. Johnson, I have an invention out in Chicago — a street railway operated by magnets laid between the rails. It does away with the trolley.' Mr. Johnson replied: 'That interests me. For years I have been thinking of a railway operated by magnets between the rails; but

that does not interest me so much. What I want to do is,to get
rid of the wheels. They are the obstacle to speed. You cannot
go much faster than the present rate of speed because when you
do the wheels fly asunder from the rapidity of the revolutions.
Now there must be a way of running a train without wheels and
that is what I am most interested in. We ought to be able to
travel three or four hundred miles an hour but we can't do it
so long as we are dependent on wheels.'

" He finally went to Chicago and saw the invention. Shortly
after his return trucks loaded with great square timbers and pieces
of steel drew up in front of his mansion on Euclid avenue. The
area ways to the basement floor were opened up and the unwieldy
freight was pushed into the basement. Electrical machinery followed. Then Mr. Johnson picked out the best electrician he could
find in the city and explained his idea. It seemed too absurd for
trial but they went to work. Day after day and month after
month in the early morning and late at night he worked in the
cellar with these strange appliances for solving the problem of
rapid locomotion. He jokingly told his friends what he was planning to do. They laughed at his monster plaything which covered
the floor of the cellar and extended as a track for ninety feet from
one end to the other. It was given the derisive name of ' Greased
Lightning.' There were no wheels above the tracks, only a rough
car on steel shoes like flat bottomed skates. Below and between
the tracks were steel magnets. That was all, with the exception
of powerful electrical devices connected with similar machinery in
the back yard. The underlying idea in non-technical terms was
to propel the car by a series of magnets laid between the tracks,
which would act in succession, the current being cut off as the car
passed over the one below it. This was the propelling power.
But this power was downward. There was nothing to relieve
the friction of the shoes on the tracks, nothing to lift the car so
that the forward movement would be possible. Finally the day
was set for the trial. Powerful currents were turned on and by
the carefully studied electrical formulas the car should have moved

forward. Instead of that the magnetic power under the car was so strong that it crushed the structure to the earth. ' Greased Lightning' failed to move.

"For weeks Mr. Johnson studied the problem. He went over his calculations. They were theoretically correct. Of that he was sure. He had his processes proved up by his mechanician. Then he threw away the road bed, the car and the appliances which had cost thousands of dollars and reversed the arrangement.

"A structure was built across the top of the cellar and consisted of a series of magnets that were energized at the proper time to lift the car and carry it forward. At the top of the car were shoes which were made to fit loosely between upper and lower tracks located on the elevated structure. To the shoes were attached light contact fingers made of a spring bronze which touched the tracks slightly in advance of the shoes. The car when not in motion would hang by the shoes upon the lower track. The contact fingers would be in tight contact with the same. The instant the controller was turned on the current would pass through the contact fingers energizing lifting magnets sufficiently to lift the car and the shoes from the bottom track. If, however, it were lifted sufficiently for the contact fingers to touch the top track the current in the lifting magnet would be reduced so as to float the car practically half way between the two tracks. Thus the car theoretically would float in the air and when the magnets designed for forward propulsion were energized it would move forward in proportion to the speed at which these magnets were energized.

"This is a description of what he planned to do as explained to my non-technical mind. It was finally completed, after many delays, and the current turned on. ' Greased Lightning' actually moved. The car was propelled forward and backward as rapidly as it was safe to permit in the short ninety feet of track in the cellar. It was interesting to watch the loading of the car, for as each additional passenger stepped on there would be a slight downward movement until the contact finger touched the lower rail when it would immediately resume its former position.

"The car in motion was necessarily absolutely noiseless and without the least vibration. With eyes closed, at the slight rate of speed at which it was necessary to move in the cellar, the occupant could not tell whether the car was in motion or not. Had the speed been greater the only difference would have been the feeling of the air current.

"Mr. Johnson was satisfied that he had demonstrated the correctness of his long study of the subject. If the device was theoretically correct it must be practically correct, he argued. But he had no time and not sufficient money to build a large model. That would require hundreds of thousands of dollars. It would also revolutionize locomotion and scrap the railroads of the country. For, as he said, with 'Slip-Slide' one could go from Chicago to New York in four or five hours; from New York to Philadelphia in half an hour. There was an end of space; an end of the tenement and the slum. Here was a means of making the ends of America touch one another.

"He went to Schenectady and interested the General Electric Company. They were incredulous. But they sent three expert electricians to Cleveland. They spent weeks there studying the device. They checked up every process in the reasoning and finally reported that the project was scientifically sound and correct. The General Electric was still unconvinced so they sent their chief electrician to Cleveland. After investigation he, too, was convinced that space was annihilated. He so reported to the company. Then there were conferences between Mr. Johnson and the company. Contracts were drawn for the building of a model and the trial of the project.

"It was practically agreed that the General Electric was to furnish the money for an experiment on a large scale; a two-mile track was to be built at Schenectady. The General Electric was to have certain rights of manufacture and Mr. Johnson certain selling rights, but before the contract was signed it was found that the proposed experiment would cost at least half a million dollars. The company decided that it would not be justified in expending so large an amount on an experiment, and it was then proposed that a number of individuals join in financing the experiment on some equitable basis of division of final profits. This arrangement was never completed, for at about that time the panic of 1907 interfered and Mr. Johnson was immersed in his political fight to the exclusion of all interests of a personal nature. Negotiations were stopped, no further progress was made on the invention which Mr. Johnson fully believed would have practically annihilated space and joined the two sides of the continent more closely together than Boston and New York now are."

With all his resources, all his interests, all the dominating traits of character which were his, Mr. Johnson was as dependent on his friends for happiness as a little child is dependent on its mother for care. His play like his work had to be shared. Friends were the supreme necessity of his life. When reduced fortunes compelled him to give up the spacious mansion on Euclid avenue where he had lived for years in luxury, that had been generously shared with friends and kinsfolk, it is inconceivable that the sacrifice cost him no pang. Yet he made it smiling, and more than once was heard to say, "It is worth losing money to find friends. I know now who my real friends are." And they had to be *real* friends; for he who gave friendship in such royal measure demanded genuine affection and plenty of it in return. "I cannot stand the counterfeit," he often said.

What history will do with the name of Tom L. Johnson we do not know. But this we know, that it was this human quality in him, this love of his kind, that sent him into the people's fight and kept him in it to the end. It was this which made him turn aside from money-getting, this which made him forego the keen pleasures of me-

chanical pursuits, this which made the loss of wealth and
of what men call success, the loss of health, yes, of life
on earth itself, seem of small account to him.   And because he loved much, he lived much.   No one who reads
his story can fail to realize that he lived more in almost
any ten years of his adult life than it is given to most men
to live in a long, long lifetime; nor can they fail to see
that his living was a complete and constant giving—a giving of that greatest gift within man's power to give —
HIMSELF.

ELIZABETH J. HAUSER.

"The man who is worthy of being a leader of men will never complain of the stupidity of his helpers, of the ingratitude of mankind, nor of the inappreciation of the public.

"These things are all a part of the great game of life, and to meet them and not go down under them in discouragement and defeat is the final proof of power."

FOREWORD

THE greatest movement in the world to-day may be characterized as the struggle of the people against Privilege.

On the one side the People — slow to wake up, slow to recognize their own interests, slow to realize their power, slow to invoke it. On the other, Privilege — always awake and quick to act, owning many of the newspapers, controlling the election and appointment of judges, dictating to city councils, influencing legislatures and writing our national laws.

What is Privilege?

Privilege is the advantage conferred on one by law of denying the competition of others. It matters not whether the advantage be bestowed upon a single individual, upon a partnership, or upon an aggregation of partnerships, a trust — the essence of the evil is the same. And just to the extent that the law imposes restrictions upon some men and not on others, just to the extent that it grants special favors to some to the exclusion of others, do the people suffer from this evil.

These law-made restrictions and benefits are many, but substantially all may be grouped, in the order of their importance, in the following five classes: land monopolies, taxation monopolies, transportation monopolies, municipal monopolies and patent monopolies.

The greatest of all governmental favors or special privileges is land monopoly, made possible by the exemption from taxation of land values.

The special privileges growing out of conditions created by our local, State and national tax systems are so far-reaching and disastrous in their effects that one might devote a volume to the discussion of this division of Privilege, and then not begin to compass the question.

Under transportation monopolies come the governmental favors to railroads and to those enterprises dependent upon the railroads, such as special freight lines, sleeping-car companies, express and telegraph companies.

Municipal monopolies consist of rights and special privileges in the public streets and highways which in the nature of the case cannot be possessed by all the people and can be enjoyed only by a few. Under this head come the franchises which our cities grant to street railways, to water, gas, electric light and telephone companies, and in these lie the chief sources of corruption in municipal life.

Patent monopolies are the last distinct survival of a policy which once had a very much wider application and which in every other case has been abandoned because it was recognized to be unsound. At one time it was common enough to reward public service of almost any kind by the grant of a trade monopoly. Soldiers in war were tempted by the prospect of such a grant and often got it as the result of a victory. Statesmen were tempted and were often rewarded in the same way for services to the State, or services to their party. Now this is universally recognized to be an error.

Patent monopolies cut off from us the opportunity to take immediate advantage of the world's inventions. They exert upon many men an influence as baneful as the

most corrupt lottery by tempting them from regular work
and useful occupations. They interfere with the natural
development of invention.

Useful inventions come naturally and almost inevitably
as the next necessary step in industrial evolution. Most
of them are never patented. The patents that are granted
interfere with this natural development. If inventors
must be rewarded it would be better to pay them a bounty
than to continue a system productive of so much evil.

And so by securing in different ways " special privileges
to some " and denying " equal rights to all," our governments, local, State and national, have precipitated the
struggle of the people against Privilege.

It matters not what the question — whether a water or
gas franchise, a street railway monopoly, a coal combination, an ordinary railroad charter, or the grabbing of the
public domain — the issue between them is always the
same.

Owners and managers of public-service corporations
may change; so may their methods. They may respect
public opinion or scorn it; they may show great consideration for their employés or treat them as machines; their
policies may be liberal or the reverse; they may strive for
all the traffic will bear, looking to dividends only, or they
may share their profits with the public.

What of it?

So, too, political parties may change.

And what of that?

A Republican boss or a Democratic boss is equally useful to Privilege. It may seek legislative power through
dealing directly with corrupt bosses, or it may find the
control of party machinery by means of liberal campaign

contributions the more effective; again it may divert the attention of the people from fundamental issues by getting them to squabbling over nonessentials.

This is often demonstrated when the contest is made to appear to be between two men, though in reality both are committed in advance to obey the wishes of Privilege. Superficial moral issues are especially serviceable in this particular line of attack.

But it is on the judiciary that Privilege exercises its most insidious and dangerous power. Lawyers whose employment has been entirely in its interests are selected for the bench. ·Their training, their environment, their self-interest, all combine to make them the most powerful allies of monopoly. Yet this may be, and often is, without any consciousness on the part of the judges themselves that their selection has been influenced by an interest opposed to the public good.

Thus unwittingly men, otherwise incorruptible, become the most pliable agents of Privilege and the most dangerous of public servants. No mere change of political names or of men can correct these evils. A political change will not affect judges with their judge-made laws, and so long as Privilege controls both parties, a political change will not affect the legislative bodies which create judges. An effective recall of judges would furnish the machinery to correct many abuses, and this step can be taken without waiting for the economic changes which must afford the final and fundamental relief.

For it is to *economic change,* and not to political change, that the people must look for the solution of this problem. Not *lawbreakers,* but *lawmakers* are responsible for bad economic conditions; and these only indirectly, for it is business interests controlling lawmakers that furnish the great motive force in the protection of Privilege.

The economic change that will correct these political abuses is one that must remove the prizes which Privilege now secures from the People.   It must reserve to the public the ownership and management of public-service utilities so that they shall be regarded no longer as private loot, but as public rights to be safeguarded and protected.

That good, law-abiding corporations and good, well-meaning men cannot correct these wrongs without changing the economic conditions which produce them, has been proved times without number, and only serves to emphasize the fact that the real fight of the people is not to abolish lawbreaking, but to put an end to that lawmaking which is against the public good.

It is true that the contest looks like an unequal one; that the advantage seems to be entirely on the side of Privilege; that its position appears invulnerable.

Is there then no hope?   Let us see.

The people's advance guard has been routed often, and will be time and time again.   New recruits must come to the front.   As the firing lines are decimated the discontented masses must rush forward to fill the gaps in the ranks.   Finally, when *we are fighting all along the line,* public opinion will be strong enough to drive Privilege out of its last trench.

Agitation for the right, once set in motion, cannot be stopped.   Truth can never lose its power.   It presses forward gaining victories, suffering defeats, but losing nothing of momentum, augmenting its strength though seeming to expend it.

Newspapers controlled by the Interests cannot stop this
forward movement, legislatures must yield to it, the courts
finally see and respect it and political parties must go with
it or be wrecked.

What more striking example could be cited than the
disintegration of the Republican party as shown at the
1910 election, following so closely upon the almost un-
paralleled vote for its candidate for President?

Big Business, corrupt bosses, subservient courts, pliant
legislatures and an Interest-controlled press may block,
delay, apparently check its progress, but these are only
surface indications. The deeper currents are all headed
in the same direction, and once fairly started nothing can
turn them back.

It is because I believe that the story of my part in this
universal movement helps to illustrate the truth of this
proposition that I have decided to tell it.

I am going to show how Privilege fights in the city,
the State and the nation, but I shall deal more largely with
the city since it is here that the abolition of privilege must
begin.

In the main, the things I shall tell about Cleveland are
the things that might be told about any city or state. The
source of the evil; the source of the good; the source of
the shame and corruption; the contest between opposing
economic interests; the alliance among those identified
with the franchise corporations on the one hand, and the
unorganized people on the other, is the same everywhere.

Cleveland's experiences are the experiences that other
cities will have in their efforts to be free. Privilege may
not be quite as irresistible for them as it was for us, because the people have been gathering strength, party lines

are being broken and knowledge of the meaning of Privilege is spreading.   Privilege no longer asserts itself with the arrogance of unlimited and unchallenged power as it did a few years ago.   The pressure of right is reaching into the higher places.   It is disintegrating the classes which have ruled.

The influences which operated to arouse my interest in the struggle of the people against Privilege are significant only as they show one of the many ways in which our minds are made to meet and grasp these great problems, for, while really sincere investigators arrive at last at the same conclusion, nearly all of us travel different roads to get there.

MY STORY

I

A MONOPOLIST IN THE MAKING

I WAS born at Blue Spring near Georgetown, Kentucky, July 18, 1854. My father, Albert W. Johnson, and my mother, Helen Loftin, met while attending different schools at the latter place and here they had been married August 4, 1853.

My mother was born in Jackson, Tenn., the same little town from which my fellow disturber of the public service peace, Judge Ben B. Lindsey of Denver, came.

My earliest recollections are of events connected with the war, though an incident which happened the year before seems very clear in my mind. Just how much of it I actually remember, however, and how much of it is due to hearing it often repeated I cannot say. But what happened was this: Joe Pilcher and I were playing on the floor with a Noah's Ark and a most wonderful array of little painted animals. These toys were made by the prisoners in the penitentiary at Nashville, where my mother had purchased them for me on our way South to our summer home, a plantation in Arkansas. After infinite pains and hours of labor my playmate and I had arranged the little figures in pairs, according to size, beginning with the elephants and ending with the beetles, when one of the young ladies of our household, dressed for a party, crossed the room and with her train switched the lines to hopeless entanglement in the meshes of the long lace curtains, two of the animals only remaining standing. Joe, who was somewhat my senior, burst into tears, while I smiled brightly and said:

" Don't cry, Joe; there are two left anyhow."

My mother never tired of telling this story and its frequent repetition certainly had a marked influence upon my life, for it established for me, in the family, a reputation as an optimist which I felt in honor bound to live up to somehow.   I early acquired a kind of habit of making the best of whatever happened.

In later life larger things presented themselves to me in exactly the same way.   Nothing was ever entirely lost. There was no disaster so great that there weren't always " two left anyhow."   My reputation for being always cheerful in defeat — a reputation earned at such cost that I may mention it without apology — is largely due to this incident, trivial though it may seem.

I remember the beginning of the war very well and am sure that from this time my recollections are actual memories, not family traditions.

As his first service to the Confederacy my father, a slave owner and cotton planter, organized a military company at Helena, Ark., of which he was Captain.   Becoming Colonel in command of a brigade under General T. C. Hindman a little later, one of his first duties was to execute the order to destroy all cotton likely to fall into the hands of the enemy.   Though he was opposed to this policy he enforced the order with rigid impartiality, compelling my mother, who had managed to hide some cotton in the cane-brake, to bring it out and have it burned as soon as he discovered her secret. The burning of this cotton made a great impression on my mind, especially the sorrow of the negroes who stood around the smouldering bales and cried like children at sight of the waste of what had cost them such hard work to raise.

Shortly after this we moved to Little Rock and it was while we were living there that my mother shot a burglar who was trying to get into the house through a bedroom window. I recall this incident vividly. I can see the bed which my mother and the baby, Albert, occupied — with its white mosquito bar cover — in one corner of the room; against the opposite wall the bed in which my brother Will and I slept; the form of a man trying to climb through the window, and my mother's upraised arm as she discharged a pistol at him. She didn't hurt him much, but when he was captured in a similar attempt a few weeks later, the burglar admitted that he had gotten the wound in his leg from Mrs. Johnson.

My mother was not only courageous and self-reliant, but remarkably independent in thought and in action. She cared so little for what people might think or say that having made a decision she acted upon it without further ado. If my own disregard of the things " they say " is an inheritance from my mother I am more grateful for it than for any other characteristic she may have given me. With all her independence, however, she was one of the most tactful persons I have ever known. She had a genius for getting on well with people even under the most trying circumstances.

The stirring events of her young wifehood and motherhood afforded plenty of outlet for her energy, and in later and calmer times she found new means of expression. She studied French and music after she was forty, and she remodeled and built so many houses just for the enjoyment she got out of the planning that house building became almost a steady occupation with her.

General Hindman and my father quarreled over a court martial. Some young soldiers had stolen away one night and visited their homes in the vicinity of the camp. They were brought back and charged with desertion. Father insisted that they were not deserters, that they were just homesick boys who would have returned of their own free will, and he refused to conduct the trial on that account. Because of this quarrel he left Hindman to join General John C. Breckinridge's command near Atlanta.

In two light wagons and a barouche the family and several servants, old Uncle Adam standing out most clearly in my memory, started on that journey. We crossed the Mississippi river at Napoleon and just as we landed on the Mississippi side a Yankee gunboat came into sight. If we had been a few minutes later, or the gunboat a few minutes earlier, my father undoubtedly would have been taken prisoner. We went to Yazoo City, thence in our vehicles across the State of Alabama, arriving at Atlanta by Christmas — the first Christmas of the war.

I do not remember just how long we stayed in Georgia, but certainly more than a year, and most of that time at Milledgeville. One morning, much to my delight, I was permitted to hold in my arms the one-day-old son of the family with whom we were boarding. That baby is now William Gibbs McAdoo, famous for his successful promotion of New York City's underground railways.

When we left Georgia, we went north, through the Carolinas — most of the way by our own conveyances — to Corner Springs, Virginia, and later to Withville. While living at the former place I often saw detachments of Southern troops march by our house in the morning, and companies of Union soldiers pass in the afternoon of the same day. At Withville I had a terrible attack of typhoid fever, the first illness of my life. From Withville we went to Natural Bridge, where we spent a year or so, leaving here for Staunton just at the close of the war.

Though my father had served in the Confederate Army throughout the whole of the conflict he was a great admirer of Lincoln and very much opposed to slavery, and many, many times, even while sectional feeling was most bitter, he told me that the South was fighting for an unjust cause. My own hatred of slavery in all forms is doubtless due to that early teaching which was the more effective because of the dramatic incidents connected with it. Father's sympathies were with the North but loyalty to friends, neighbors and a host of relatives who were heart and soul with the South kept him on that side. Like so many of these he was now penniless, and I having attained the advanced age of eleven years commenced to look for something to do.

Immediately after Lee's surrender one railroad train a day commenced to run into Staunton, and I struck up a friendship with the conductor which was to prove not only immediately profitable to me, but which probably decided my future career. One day he said to me,

"How would you like to sell papers, Tom? I could bring 'em in for you on my train and I wouldn't carry any for anybody else, so you could charge whatever you pleased."

The exciting events attending the end of the war naturally created a brisk demand for news and I eagerly seized this opportunity to get into business. The Richmond and Petersburg papers I retailed at fifteen cents each and for " picture papers," the illustrated weeklies, I got twenty-five cents each. My monopoly lasted five weeks. Then it was abruptly ended by a change in the management of the railroad which meant also a change of conductors.

The eighty-eight dollars in silver which this venture netted me was the first good money our family had seen since the beginning of the war, and it carried us from Staunton, Virginia, to Louisville, Kentucky, where my father hoped to make a new start in life among his friends and relatives.

The lesson of privilege taught me by that brief experience was one I never forgot, for in all my subsequent business arrangements I sought enterprises in which there was little or no competition. In short, I was always on the lookout for somebody or something which would stand in the same relation to me that my friend, the conductor, had.

Up to this time I had had practically no schooling, though my mother had managed to give me some instruction. Mathematics came to me without any effort whatever, this aptitude for figures evidently being an inheritance from my father and grandfather. My turn for mechanics came to me from my mother. She taught me to sew on the sewing-machine and I remember my great pride in a dress skirt which I tucked for her from top to bottom.

Our migrating days were not yet over, for being able to borrow some money in Louisville my father took us all back to Arkansas where he attempted to operate the cotton plantation with free labor. The experiment was a complete failure, a disastrous flood being one of the contributing causes.

Our next move was to Evansville, Indiana, where my father engaged in various enterprises and where I got my one and only full year of schooling. I passed through three grades in that year and was ready to enter High School when we again moved back to Kentucky — this time to a farm some eighteen miles from Louisville.

We were extremely poor and sending me to school in town was out of the question. I do not recall that our poverty or my lack of educational advantages had any depressing influence upon me. What helped most to make up for my meager schooling was my habit of observation and my investigating turn of mind — not to call it curiosity. I went about with an eternal Why? upon my lips. It was this doubtless which made life so interesting that I wasn't greatly impressed by the material condition of the family; also I had no silly theories about work and no so-called family pride to deter me from doing anything that came my way to do.

It never disturbed me in the least to sweep out an office and I liked the extra five dollars a month which this job paid me. It did surprise me very much, however, when some of my well-to-do friends and relatives would drive by and appear not to see me when I had charge of a gang of laborers in the street. My father and mother were quite as free from any class feeling as I was.

One of my jobs in Louisville was in the office of a

rolling-mill. When my mother went in to see about getting this job for me she had to wear a crocheted hood because she had no money with which to buy a hat or a bonnet. I spent more of my time in the mechanical department of the mill than in the office for it was that end of the business which interested me most.

Young as I was, I soon realized that this kind of enterprise offered no particular advantage. There was no conductor here to hand out something which wasn't his to give, and a few months later I welcomed an opportunity to get into the street railroad business in which I was to continue for most of my life. This appealed to me as a non-competitive business, depending upon the special privilege of public grants in the highway, though I did not analyze it at that time. The public side of the question meant nothing to me, of course; in fact it never occurred to me that there *was* a public side to it until I became familiar with Henry George's philosophy a good many years later.

I remember how offended I was when I first read his fascinating words and realized that the things I was doing were the things this man was attacking. Attracted to his teachings against my will I tried to find a way of escape. I didn't want to accept them; I wanted to prove them false. But this is running ahead of my story.

II

THE MONOPOLIST MADE

It was the first of February, 1869, that I went to Louisville to take my job in the rolling-mill and it was at about this time that Bidermann and Alfred V. du Pont bought a street railroad in Louisville. These brothers were grandsons of Pierre Samuel du Pont, one of the physiocratic economists of France, associate of Turgot, Mirabeau, Quesnay and Condorcet to which group " and their fellows " Henry George inscribed his *Protection or Free Trade,* calling them " those illustrious Frenchmen of a century ago who in the night of despotism foresaw the glories of the coming day." Pierre du Pont, after narrowly escaping the guillotine, came to this country during the Reign of Terror and established on the Brandywine the du Pont powder works known as the E. I. du Pont de Nemours Powder Company, the concern that now manufactures practically all the high explosives in the United States.

The du Ponts were friends of our family and gave me an office job in connection with their newly-acquired street railroad. I lived with the family of my uncle Captain Thomas Coleman in Louisville and a lively family it was with its nine daughters and two sons. Though these girls were my cousins and I was but fifteen years old I fell in love with one after another of them until I had been in love with all except the few who were either too old or

9

too young. The associations of this home and the influence of that splendid woman, my aunt Dullie Coleman, and her daughters saved me from the temptations that ordinarily beset the country boy in the city.

My salary was seven dollars a week and my duties were varied. I collected and counted the money which had been deposited by the passengers in the fare-boxes, made up small packages of change for the drivers (the cars had no conductors), and in a short time took entire charge of the office as bookkeeper and cashier. I sat up until eleven o'clock every night for a month learning to "keep books." At the end of that time a trial balance had no terrors for me.

This was of course before the introduction of electricity in street railway operation and the cars were drawn by mules. How I hated to see horses and mules go into the street car service where they would be ground up as inevitably, if not quite as literally, as if put through a sausage machine! It was this feeling of pity for the defenseless creatures that first interested me in cables and electric propulsion.

From the very first it was the operating end of the business that appealed to me. My liking for mechanics was stimulated by my environment and I was soon working on inventions, some of which I afterwards patented. From one of these, a fare-box, I eventually made the twenty or thirty thousand dollars which gave me my first claim to being a capitalist.

The fare-boxes in use up to that time were made for paper money. Mine was the first box for coins, paper currency having just been withdrawn from circulation. It held the coins on little glass shelves and in plain sight

TOM L. JOHNSON AT SEVENTEEN

A. V. DU PONT   BIDERMANN DU PONT

until they had been counted. Since any passenger as well as anyone acting as a spotter could count the money there wasn't much likelihood that either the drivers or the car riders would cheat. This box is still in use.

In a few months I was secretary of the company, and at about the end of my first year of employment my father came in from the farm and the du Ponts made him superintendent of the road. He continued in this position until he was appointed chief of police of Louisville, several years later. Then I became superintendent, holding the job until 1876 when I embarked in business for myself.

I may say, with all propriety, that Bidermann du Pont, the president of the road, found in me a hard working and efficient assistant, but I cannot say that I never occasioned him any anxiety, for my restless, eager nature was constantly seeking ways of expression — which ways were not always either dignified or safe. For instance, one night when a lot of our cars were lined up on Crown Hill, waiting to carry the crowds home from a late entertainment in a summer garden, I challenged the drivers to join me in taking one of the cars down the hill as fast as it would go. The plan was — to start a car with as much speed as the mule team could summon, when it was fairly started the driver to drop off with the team, the rest of us to stay on for no reason in the world except to see " just how fast she would go." The drivers weren't very keen to accept my challenge, but finally four of them decided to do so. After several starts we got up a rate of speed rapid enough to suit us and away we went. As the car tore madly down the hill I recalled the railroad track at the bottom and the curve in our track just beyond but there really wasn't time to think about what might

happen if the car and a train should reach the crossing
at the same instant; for just then we shot over the railroad track, hit the curve which didn't divert the car from
its straight course, and landed half-way through a candy-
shop. The company paid damages to the shop-keeper,
and what Mr. du Pont thought of the episode I never
knew for even after the matter had been adjusted he never
mentioned it to me.

A little while after this when there were some new
mules in the stables waiting to be trained to car work,
I decided to hitch the most refractory and unpromising
team to a buggy and " break them in." A little driver
named Snapper joined me in this enterprise. With much
difficulty, and the assistance of some dozen darkeys, we
got the mules into harness and hooked up to an old, high-
seated buggy. I had the reins, Snapper took his place on
the seat beside me and we were off. It wasn't long before
I knew to a dead certainty that those mules were running
away.

We had a clear stretch of road before us, however, and
I reflected that they'd have to stop sometime and trusted
to luck that we'd be able to hang on until they did. But
presently, just ahead of us, there appeared a great, covered wagon, with a fat, sun-bonneted German woman on
the seat driving. She was jogging along at a comforta-
ble pace, all unconscious of the cyclone which was approaching from behind. To get around her wagon was
impossible, but here was my chance to stop our runaway!
I steered the mules straight for the wagon, one on one
side, one on the other, and the pole of the buggy caught
the wagon box fairly in the middle. In the mix-up Snapper and I fell out, the mules dashed on with some rem-

nants of the wreck still attached to them, and the old lady was the most surprised individual you ever saw in your life. She wasn't hurt, and neither were we, nor was the wagon much harmed.

The president of the road was as silent on this foolhardy adventure as he had been on the candy-shop scrape, but Mr. Alfred du Pont took me severely to task for it, saying that while he did not object to my breaking mules he did object most seriously to having me break my neck.

I had not been in the street railroad business long before I determined to become an owner. I didn't want to work on a salary any longer than I could help. My fondness for girls in general and girl cousins in particular culminated in my marriage, October 8, 1874, to a distant kinswoman of my own name, Maggie J. Johnson, when she was seventeen and I was twenty. At twenty-two I purchased the majority of the stock of the street railways of Indianapolis from William H. English, afterwards candidate for vice-president of the United States in the Garfield-Arthur and Hancock-English campaign.

I went to Indianapolis to see Mr. English in the hope of interesting him in my fare-box. He said to me,

" I don't want to buy a fare-box, young man, but I have a street railroad to sell."

My business dealings with him were so unpleasant and the charges which my lawyer (afterwards Governor Porter of Indiana) brought against him in a law suit so severe, that the petition embodying them was used by his Republican opponents as a campaign document. That fight with Mr. English was my first great business struggle, and it was a fight for a privilege — for street railway grants in the city of Indianapolis.

I had some money, but not enough for my purchase. Mr. Bidermann du Pont, though he had no faith in my business associates and though the road was in a badly demoralized state, loaned me the thirty thousand dollars I needed with no security whatever except my health, as he himself expressed it. That loan meant a lot to me, but the confidence which went with it meant more, for Mr. du Pont was the first business man to give me any encouragement.

When I made my final payment to him some five or six years later I told him that my money obligation was now cancelled, but that a life-time of friendship for him and his could not discharge my greater obligation for his faith in me.

My father went with me to Indianapolis and became president of the company. When a friend asked him:

" If you are president of the road, what is Tom? " he replied, " Oh, Tom's nothing! He's just the board of directors."

As this board of directors, I speedily realized that our enterprise would be a failure unless we could free ourselves from Mr. English's persecutions. He was old enough to be my father, and his attitude towards me was arrogant. He was the most influential man in Indianapolis and not above threatening us with his power over the city government unless we coöperated with him in every way, especially in getting tenants for his houses of which he owned about two hundred, and which he rented to employés of our road and to other workingmen.

Mr. English was a typical representative of the powerful agent of special privilege of that day. He was president of one of the principal banks of the city.

The people's money goes into the banks in the form of deposits. The banker uses this money to capitalize public service corporations which are operated for private profit instead of for the benefit of the people. How incongruous that the people's own savings should be used by Privilege to oppress them!

Mr. English's great asset was his domination of the local city government through which he controlled the taxing machinery of the city, thereby keeping his own taxes down at the expense of the small tax-payer.

When I bought into the railroad he turned the office of treasurer over to me as his successor and at the first meeting of the board of directors we passed resolutions stating that his accounts had been audited and giving him a receipt for his stewardship. When I objected to this because I had not seen the books he said it was a mere matter of form and that he would turn them over to me immediately after the meeting. It was eleven months before I ever got a look at those books and then my right to them had been established by a lawsuit. After going through the books I forced Mr. English to make several restitutions of very large amounts of money to the company. Once we had a disastrous fire and he immediately notified the insurance companies that the damages must be paid to him. We had to consent to this or expose ourselves to expensive and annoying litigation.

He kept us in constant hot water. We had paid ten per cent. of the purchase price in cash and given notes running through a period of ten years for the remaining ninety per cent. His reason for selling to us in the first place seems to have been to rid himself of some partners whom he did not like. He evidently expected to make us very sick of our bargain, to benefit by whatever payments we made and finally to get the property back into his own hands unencumbered by undesirable partners.

I did not propose to be frozen out in this manner, however, and was able to borrow enough money from F. M. Churchman, an Indianapolis banker, to purchase our own notes at fourteen cents on the dollar. It happened that Mr. Churchman was not on friendly terms with Mr. English and was the more willing on that account to help me. He and his friends were interested in the gas company and were familiar with the business possibilities of public service corporations. He seemed impressed with my ability to make the railroad pay which, by economy and careful management, it soon commenced to do. We never felt quite safe from Mr. English even after we had paid him off and had acquired the minority stock, but in Mr. Churchman and his friends we had strong and influential allies.

As I look back on those days now there seems to have been no limit to my energy, my ambition, or my capacity for hard work; but then, as in all my later life, I took a great deal of recreation. I couldn't have worked so much, if I had played less. I was fond of baseball, billiards and horseback riding and bicycling and automobiling were to come in their time; but after all I loved my work more than anything else, especially the mechanical side of it — the experimenting and inventing — and that was really my greatest recreation.

III

BUSINESS AND POLITICS

I NOW began to branch out in street railway enterprises
on my own account and in 1879 — just ten years after my
entrance into the business as an office boy — I became a
bidder for a street railway grant in Cleveland. Mark
Hanna was a director and Elias Simms the president of a
company which was after this same grant.

Captain Simms, as he was called, was an ex-steamboat
man and a dredging contractor, a very considerable figure
in the community. He was well to do, having made a
great deal of money out of dredging contracts which he
secured through his hold on the city councils. He openly
complained of the methods of his friends in the council
somewhat after this fashion: "All councilmen want is
money. Just have to go around with my pocketbook in
my hand all the time."

Largely because of his councilmanic control he became
interested in street railways. He knew nothing about the
business itself but relied for success on his ability to get
grants. He was much more prominent in street railroad
matters than Mr. Hanna at this time, Hanna being very
much younger and having other business interests.

The law stipulated that new grants should go to the bidder offering the lowest rate of fare, but included also a
provision (of which I was ignorant) for extensions to existing lines.

17

The bid of the Hanna-Simms company provided for a five-cent fare, while mine offered six tickets for a quarter, whereupon the council threw out all the bids and made the grant to Mr. Hanna and his associates as *an extension to their lines* at the five-cent fare.

So that was the way it was done, was it?

Well, I was only twenty-five and willing to learn.

I now purchased the Pearl street line on the west side and subsequently got my various grants *as extensions to that line,* though when I bought it, it was under lease to Hanna and Simms and I didn't get possession for over eighteen months.

Most of my operations in Cleveland were based on grants already in existence which I purchased from people who did not know their real value.   This city looked like a good field to me for it then had eight street railroads operated by different companies and owned by bankers, politicians, business and professional men who had been successful in various undertakings, but without a street railroad man in the entire list.   I thought my knowledge would give me some advantage there.

Cleveland is built on two plateaus some fifty or sixty feet above the level of Lake Erie.   Each of these plateaus runs down a sheer bluff into a valley through which the Cuyahoga river flows.   The river is less than 200 feet wide, but bridges three-quarters of a mile long are required to span the valley and bring the plateaus onto a level.   Before these plateaus, known as the West Side and East Side, were connected by a viaduct the Simms-Hanna horse-cars traveled down the steep hill on the west side, across a short river bridge and up the hill on the east side.

TOM L. JOHNSON AT TWENTY-SIX

"Just ten years after my entrance into the business as an office boy I became a bidder for a street railway grant in Cleveland."

The viaduct was completed by the time I got possession of the Pearl street line.

At this time all the car lines, except the Pearl street, which had its terminal on the west side, ran to the center of the city only. It cost two fares to go from one side of town to the other, passengers going east or west being obliged to change at the public square since there were no through lines. A very short ride, if it necessitated using two lines, cost ten cents also, while the authorized fare for the entire system (covering the city and extending half a mile beyond the city limits) was sixteen cents. Cleveland was not unlike other cities in this respect. Most of them had several private companies and the people who were obliged to use the various lines had to pay several fares.

One of my early street railway discoveries was that the best way to make money was to operate a through line at a single fare, and to supplement this by the transfer system where more than two lines were involved. In these days when this principle of operation is in such general use it is hard to believe that it was not always recognized, but I believe I was the first to introduce this plan of operation which I developed early in Indianapolis.

The Pearl street line had its terminal at the West Side Market House from which point to the center of the city it operated over the Hanna-Simms tracks. Passengers from the Pearl street cars were obliged to change to Mr. Hanna's cars at the Market House and to pay an additional fare. Failing to get permission to operate our cars over the Hanna-Simms tracks we established an omnibus line and carried our passengers without extra fare from our terminal to the heart of the city in buses. This half mile of Mr. Hanna's track which lay between the end of the Pearl street line and the viaduct was what prevented our cars from running to the center of the city.

When the viaduct was completed the city laid car tracks over the bridge though it had no legal right to do so. The State legislature not having delegated to the city the right to build, own or operate a street car line, it had no right to lay tracks even on its own property. If the street railroad company which was empowered by law to build these tracks had done so instead of permitting the city to do it, the whole street railway situation in Cleveland would have been changed and my operations would certainly have been eliminated.

To permit the city to build these tracks over the bridge was the greatest blunder Simms and Hanna ever made for it was the city ownership of this three-quarters of a mile of track that gave the city so much power in the street railway controversy which occurred years later. These tracks terminated at the beginning of four tracks in Superior street, which was free territory and which led to the heart of the city. The three-cent-fare contest running through my nine years as mayor might have resulted in final defeat for the people but for this mistake on the part of the railroad company. I say mistake on their part advisedly, for I never attributed the laying of those tracks on the viaduct to any foresight of the city council. They built wiser than they knew.

City ownership of tracks, the city's right to allow companies the use of tracks, short-lived grants have always been the most powerful weapons in the hands of the public for resisting the aggressions of street railway monopolies. Cleveland had all three of these advantages.

The story of that contest belongs to a much later period, but I may say here that it might have been very different if Mr. Hanna had not become absorbed in national politics. If his chief interest had centered in street railway operations in Cleveland the city would have had to contend against some sources of corruption which were fortunately lacking in our nine years' war, for Mr. Hanna regarded politics as merely a business asset. In the early days I cared nothing for the political side of the game. My interest was in developing street railway systems relying on my knowledge of the business for success. But with Mr. Hanna and his kind street railroads were a side issue, and from the time I came into contact with him practically everything I did in the street railway business became a political question. Indeed, it was a case of playing politics or getting out of the business.

My first contests with Mr. Hanna were on the west side, but later we extended our operations and our fighting to the east side. First and last we had many bitter struggles but never any personal disagreements. I always had perfect confidence in Mr. Hanna's keeping his word in any transaction and he never disappointed me.

We ran our buses about a year, Mr. Hanna's company fighting every move we made, and then it happened that they wanted to renew a franchise which included that pivotal half mile of track. By this time the contest between us had become a matter of public interest and had been the chief issue in several councilmanic elections. The town was making it so hot for the council that in spite of Mr. Hanna's tremendous personal influence and his powerful backing, the councilmen refused to grant the renewal except on condition that we be permitted to operate our cars on his tracks.

In Mr. Hanna's eyes our victory was a reflection on the management of Captain Simms, the president of the company, or at least a sign that Simms's power was waning, and it led to a quarrel between them. Simms was then more prominent in street railway circles than Hanna, and our success was regarded more particularly as a victory over him than over Hanna. The quarrel resulted in Hanna buying out Simms and his other partners. No doubt Hanna reasoned that if there was fighting to do in the future he would do it himself.

In the meantime I had purchased the Jennings avenue line, a narrow gauge railroad on the west side running through a low-lying section known as the " flats," and this gave me control of two of the eight street railway companies of the city. My next move was to try to get a grant empowering me to build east side lines to be operated across the city in connection with the Pearl street and Jennings avenue lines for a single fare.

Mr. Hanna and all the other street railroad interests in the city were lined up solidly against this proposition. They contended that we could not possibly make our venture pay, that because of the length of the haul we were virtually offering to carry passengers for two and a half cents, whereas the actual cost to the company was three cents per passenger.

The real strength of the Hanna forces lay not in their arguments but in their influence with the council. Councilmen known to be on our side were spirited out of town on various pretexts. One, a railroad conductor, was suddenly sent back on his run one night to keep him away, and thus the steam railroads were drawn into the contest. Henry Everett, manager of one of the rival companies, went to Indianapolis and tried to organize against us there a fight which would divert my attention from the Cleveland situation. He failed to accomplish anything beyond giving me some extra work and a good deal of care.

Mr. Hanna was present at the council meeting every Monday night and so was I. The contest went on for a long time. By and by the odds seemed to be in our favor. Two councilmen, Crowley and Smith by name, who had always voted with the Simms-Hanna interests, lined up on our side. I could not understand why.

Finally, it occurred to me that possibly Simms might be able to throw some light on the subject. One night I hired an old public hack and drove over to his home on the west side. In response to my knock he came to the door himself — in his shirt sleeves and chewing tobacco as usual.

" Come in, Johnson, come in," he said, showing no signs of surprise or any other emotion at the sight of me.

He gave me a chair near the stove, and taking another, sat down to listen to what I had to say. I came to the object of my visit at once, asking him to explain about Crowley and Smith. He was impassive, non-committal, almost silent for a long time, but finally in disjointed sentences I got the following from him:

" You're a smart young feller, Johnson. Beat me, didn't ye? Yes, ye beat me. Folks might say I ain't very smart. Everybody knows Hanna's smart, though. Takes more'n a fool to beat Hanna. If you beat Hanna, nobody'll say that any damn fool could beat Simms. Ye beat me; I want ye to beat Hanna."

So with the votes of Crowley and Smith we did beat Hanna, but without a vote to spare. Our ordinance got just the nineteen votes necessary to pass it.

Could anything show more forcibly than this incident does the game of politics as it was played in Cleveland then and as it is played in other cities? Think of a single man being able to control the votes of two councilmen to satisfy a desire for personal retaliation or revenge! Think of men elected to public office with no more conception of their obligation to their constituents, the community, than to permit themselves to be so used!

Taken all in all, that was the biggest street railroad fight of my life, and its innumerable and annoying details severely taxed my optimism many times; but after all, I had the best of it, for besides being possessed of the enthusiasm that went with my temperament and my youth (I was not yet twenty-eight), I had the popular side of the contest in my favor. Looking back upon it now, I realize that that was the real reason for my success, although at the time I actually attributed it to my own business sagacity.

That venture turned out to be the most profitable of any of my street railroad enterprises. My competitors' prophecies that it would not pay failed dismally. Of course one of the immediate effects of my securing the franchise was to compel the other companies to follow our example and operate through lines at a single rate of fare.

That street railroad fight begun in Cleveland in 1879 was no mere battle but the beginning of a thirty years' war, though certainly none of us then engaged in it had the slightest idea what was to come. Yet, I have always thought that Mr. Hanna anticipated many of the possibilities of the great struggle which was to follow, for it was after my first victory over him in the matter of gaining the right to operate over his lines that he telegraphed me in Indianapolis proposing a partnership and a consolidation of our interests. I wired my refusal.

When I met him the next time I was in Cleveland, Mr. Hanna asked me why I had declined his proposition, pointing out as advantages to such an arrangement *his* acquaintance and influence with bankers and *his* familiarity with the political end of the game and *my* knowledge of and experience in the street railroad business itself. My answer was that we were too much alike; that as associates it would be a question of time, and a short time only until one of us would " crowd the other clear off the bench; " that we would make good opponents, not good partners.

I never have had any occasion to modify that opinion.

As Mr. Hanna and I fought in Cleveland, so do other individuals, other interests fight in other cities. And so long as the street railways of our cities are operated by private interests so long will this unholy warfare continue. I had no conception of the character of the struggle I was engaged in then, but I know now that the cure for this evil with all its possibilities of terrible consequences to men individually and to society collectively is the municipal ownership of street railways.

A large proportion of the political evils of our cities is due to private ownership of public utilities. Private ownership lodges the power to grant franchises and special privileges in some council, legislature or other public body or official. Just as soon as a man becomes the owner of

stock in a public-service corporation, he has an interest
absolutely opposed to the interests of the city.

The more " liberal " the terms of the franchise the
worse the bargain for the city and the public.   The class
which by reason of its position should be our best citizens
is best served by the worst city government.

The merchant, the manufacturer, real-estate dealer and
mechanic are all benefited by whatever will tend to reduce
the cost of car fare, gas, water, garbage collection and
taxes, while the owner of stock in a street railway, gas
or water company is interested to have the cost of these
services as high as may be.   Lawyers, bankers, merchants,
all are excluded from active participation in city politics
by this conflict of interests.   The community is thereby
deprived of the service of many of its ablest men.

Private ownership not only operates to exclude a comparatively small group of able men from public service,
but it extends its influence to that larger body — the electorate, the people as a whole.   By owning or controlling
newspapers it is possible for the franchise corporations
to mislead public opinion.   They make a daily, hourly
business of politics, raising up men in this ward or that,
identifying them with their machines, promoting them
from delegates to city conventions to city offices.   They
are always at work protecting and building up a business
interest that lives only through its political strength.   The
watered securities of franchise corporations are politics capitalized.

Regulation by city or commission will not correct these
evils.   The more stringent the regulation, the more bitter
will be the civic strife.   Only through municipal ownership can the gulf which divides the community into a small

dominant class on one side and the unorganized people
on the other be bridged; only through municipal ownership can the talent of the city be identified with the interests of the city; only by making men's ambitions and pecuniary interests identical with the welfare of the city can
civil warfare be ended.

Municipal ownership will work betterment in service,
reduce its cost to the people and purify politics by ex-
tinguishing a powerful interest hostile to good government.

IV

THE TRAINING OF A MONOPOLIST

BECOMING a monopolist at the age of eleven when a railroad conductor gave me a corner on the sale of newspapers is without doubt the thing which made me look out for a business in which there was little or no competition, and the accident of being taken into a street railroad office was what caused me to select that particular line of non-competitive enterprise as my field.

One isn't conscious of the significance of these events at the time but as a man looks back over his life he can put his finger on the few experiences which are responsible for his most profound convictions and which have determined his general line of conduct.

My experiences with William H. English impressed upon me the necessity of looking very sharply to my own interests in all future enterprises, but the relation between his business and the municipal government of Indianapolis passed entirely over my head. I was very young and not in the least conscious of the connection between business and politics. It was reserved for Mark Hanna to teach me that.

When I read Henry George I came to a realizing sense of the menace of Privilege, and what I saw at Johnstown, following the flood of 1889, caused me to realize the menace of charity — a fact not so commonly recognized, I believe, as the dangerous power of Privilege and not al-

28

JOHNSON COMPANY WORKS

Taken during early history of company when Mr. Johnson was connected with it

RECENT PICTURE OF JOHNSON COMPANY WORKS

Town of Moxham, Seventeenth Ward of Johnstown, Pa.

ways correlated with it in the mind of the student of.social conditions.

It was a new invention which led to my going into business in Johnstown. I had invented a girder groove rail, or thought I had. Subsequent developments showed that a similar rail had been made earlier in England. Mine was a steam railroad T rail with a street railroad wearing surface. Attempts to manufacture these rails from iron at Birmingham, Alabama, and Louisville, Kentucky, had failed so completely as to cripple the concerns that had made the experiments. There were insurmountable mechanical difficulties in using iron, and our failures led us to look for a firm which would manufacture them for us from steel. We proposed making these rails for the market as well as for use in our street railways.

Just as I thought I had invented the rail, so my associate, Arthur J. Moxham, thought he had invented the best process for rolling them. Both the rail and the manufacturing process, therefore, were protected by patents, not very strong patents, to be sure, but they served as a good business bluff and kept others out of the field.— Special privilege again! Not typified by a friendly train conductor this time, but by the patent laws of the United States! — In due time we were so strongly entrenched in a business way that we didn't need patent protection.

We selected the Cambria Iron Company at Johnstown, Pennsylvania, as the concern which should manufacture our rails. We wanted to make the best possible terms with them. Realizing our importance as customers, they were eager to meet us half way. We exchanged courtesies at a lively rate. Mr. Moxham and I were frequently entertained by them at the club and invited to the houses of the officials to dinner and other social affairs. I managed to get out of these engagements whenever possible, leaving the social responsibilities to Mr. Moxham who was admirably qualified for them. He was a delightful entertainer. It was when our negotiations had reached a critically important stage that, returning from a dinner at the home of one of the Cambria officials one night, he found me playing checkers with the bootblack at the club. This was too much! If I would leave the social amenities to him, I might at least so conduct myself in his absence as not to scandalize the community and jeopardize our interests. He scored me roundly for my exhibition of bad taste, " if not disgraceful conduct." When he was at the height of his indignation. I broke in with my defense:

" But Arthur, you don't know what a hell of a good game of checkers this boy plays! "

Happily the checker game didn't interfere with our negotiations, and presently the day on which we were to sign the agreement came round. We approached the conference in fear and trembling, for in our minds there had arisen the question of how long the contract should run. We wanted a short contract but were perfectly sure the Cambria people would hold out for a long one. To our surprise D. J. Morrell, the president, suggested a contract terminable at the will of either side on three months' notice. This was exactly what we wanted but I couldn't refrain from asking Mr. Morrell why his side proposed such terms. His answer taught me a lesson which I never forgot.

He said that in making contracts with the public for franchises or public rights or grants, one should strive for a long time contract or one in perpetuity if possible, since public interests in contest with private rights were rarely successful; but that between private interests long contracts were foolish, since the contract never survived the mutual desires of the contracting parties; that if either side wished to terminate the contract it was always possible to find a way to do so.

" The greatest strength of private contracts," said he, " is not expressed in words or legal phrases but is in the fact that such a contract pays."

In his long experience, he said, he had found private contracts profitable to one side only, usually productive of so much bad blood as to prevent favorable modifications, and not worth the paper they were written on.

He had there a glimpse of a great truth which had come to him through observation and actual experience and not by abstract reasoning or philosophizing.

A. V. du Pont, the elder of the du Pont brothers already referred to, with Mr. Moxham, myself and a few smaller stockholders now established at Johnstown a plant for manufacturing curves, frogs and switches out of the girder rail which the Cambria people were making for us.

At the same time I was interested in many other enterprises. Our street railway operations were going well and making money. My inventions were paying. Some Chicago bankers, interested in street railroads in their own city, had bought our Indianapolis railroad, assuming the bonded indebtedness and giving me one check for about eight hundred thousand dollars, nearly half of which came to me as my individual profit, the rest going to my father and the other stockholders. This had enabled me to pay all my debts and embark in new enterprises with a surplus.

I was one of a group of men which purchased the Sixth street railroad in St. Louis. We were opposed by all the other street railways and our line was kept out of the center of the city for a long time. Some years later after the introduction of electricity in operating we sold this road at a handsome profit.

Richmond, Virginia, was the first city to operate its cars with electricity and in 1889 A. V. du Pont and I went down there to investigate the practicability of this kind of operation. Firmly convinced that we should find the new power inadequate when it came to taking cars up hill, the first thing we saw was cars climbing Richmond's steep streets as easily as they glided along the level ones. Our report to the street railway companies in which we were interested in several large cities was quite different than we had expected it would be.

At about the time I went into the St. Louis enterprise I purchased a street railway franchise in Brooklyn which later became involved in litigation and was tied up in the courts for a long time. Eventually I got my principal and interest back but no profits. Before the litigation I had sold a lot of bonds in this enterprise to some Louisville people. When the court proceedings threatened protracted delay I bought back all these bonds at a higher price than the purchasers had paid for them. I was under no legal obligation to do this, of course; and my reasons for doing it were purely selfish. First, I couldn't endure the thought of having persons who had invested because of their faith in me lose, and second, it was better for my future credit to retain their confidence. Perhaps

TOM L. JOHNSON AT THIRTY-TWO

"Protected now by special grants in the highway, by the tariff and by land monopoly
my training as a monopolist had gone far."

I myself thought I was acting generously, so frequently are motives inspired by business interests mistaken for personal virtues.

Once or twice in my life I have been forced to take over the management of a street railroad that didn't pay, but in these cases I had no hand in the original acquisition of the properties. I never made an unfortunate street railroad investment.

Our contract with the Cambria people proved so profitable that we presently decided to build our own rolling-mill. Though this decision cost the Cambria an excellent customer, they coöperated with us in every way in building our plant which was situated in the center of a large level tract of land in a new suburb known as Moxham. We had purchased all the land in that locality which was suitable for building purposes, and our holdings reached quite to the edge of the great perpendicular bluffs which enclose the valley. We placed the mill with a view to profiting by the increased land values which would follow the growing up of the community around it, and we made money out of both.

Protected now by special grants in the highway, by the tariff, by patents and by land monopoly my training as a monopolist had gone far. No wonder I liked my business. It was not the money making end alone that appealed to me; I liked the whole game, but the fact that I was getting rich and seeing my associates prosper may have been my greatest stimulus.

V

THE LESSONS JOHNSTOWN TAUGHT

OUR mill was completed and ready for occupancy when the Johnstown flood occurred, May 31, 1889, and in an hour wrought such havoc as no imagination can picture, havoc which must be seen to be believed possible. The property losses of our firm were very small for though our old plant was in the path of the flood and was swept away, it had been practically abandoned, much of the machinery and stock having been removed to the new mill.

We had built a steam railroad which ran from Moxham into Johnstown and for some time had been trying to get possession of the city's street railways too. It was not until after the flood, however, and in consequence of the general demoralization of that business along with all other activities, that the owners were willing to sell. Then they were only too glad to get rid of the property, and they may have had small regard for the business sagacity of anyone who would buy a railroad when cars, shops and tracks had been washed away, and when what was left of the latter was covered by a seemingly hopeless mass of debris.

We made no money out of the strap-hangers or other passengers in the first days of operating in Johnstown for the street cars like our steam railroad ran free. So with the groceries, meat markets and other shops. It

34

wasn't a case of " After us the deluge," but " The deluge
after us," and " us " was everybody who had anything
the community could use.   There wasn't much talk about
the sacred rights of property around Johnstown just then
as I remember it.

When the first shock of the disaster was over the dazed
people realized that there was no responsible head to which
they could look for relief, guidance or protection, for that
little city was made up of eleven boroughs, each with its
own set of councilmen, its burgess and its miniature city
government.   In times of comparative peace there was
no getting together of these powers because of petty jeal-
ousies, continual bickerings and contested rights.   The
hopelessness of expecting anything from this quarter now
was perfectly apparent to all.   So a public mass meeting
was called, at which it was decided to elect a Dictator —
one in whom all powers, legislative and executive, should
be vested.   The choice fell upon Mr. Moxham, and a
most fortunate choice it was, for so wisely did he admin-
ister the affairs of that afflicted community that his authority was never once questioned.

Think of being called upon to feed, clothe and house a
destitute and panic stricken population of thousands, to
search out and care for the bodies of unnumbered dead, to
clear away the wreckage of a razed city, and withal to
maintain order, insure public safety and provide against
further calamity.   This was the task which faced Johnstown's elected dictator, himself a British subject, not an
American citizen.   Here was indeed " work that called
for a man," and I shall never cease to be proud of the
splendid way in which Mr. Moxham responded to that
call.

The first thing he did was to assign a duty to every man available for work of any kind.

It was but natural that he should look to the leading citizens, the men who stood high in business circles, those who were prominent in the churches and in the social life of the community for the most intelligent and spontaneous coöperation; but these failed so utterly to meet the emergency that their defection was a matter of general comment. They ran away from responsibility.

But if the calamity brought out the weakest and worst elements of character in this class, it had quite the opposite effect on those in the humbler walks of life. The men who were accustomed to work with their hands were not found wanting. All that was big and brave and strong and good in their characters came uppermost. And in that crisis when native worth — not artificial attributes — was the test of patriotism, or citizenship, or brotherhood, or whatever name you choose to call it by, the positions of the two classes of society in Johnstown were reserved.

One man who stood out like a giant was Bill Jones, known to the world because of his association with the early development of Andrew Carnegie's enterprises, but deserving to be known for his own sterling worth. He had been connected with the Cambria Iron Company at one time and directly after the flood he came on from Pittsburgh with a great body of men, extensive camp equipment and tools of various kinds and went to work. In his rough and ready way he got right at the essential things and brought the kind of relief that money couldn't buy.

One day when he and I were going through the devastated district on horseback, a man so begrimed with

dirt as to be unrecognizable hailed him with a hearty,
" Hello, Bill! "   Jones dismounted to exchange greetings
with his unknown friend and said, " You'll have to tell me
who you are."   The man answered,

" I'm Pat Lavell," and then they embraced like two
brothers.

There was a pause, for Bill Jones was hesitating before
putting that hardest of all questions: " How did it go
with you? "— the question so apt to bring a story of un-
thinkable disaster in reply.

" Lost everything," answered Lavell, " my home, my
savings,— everything; but," and in spite of the grime his
face lighted up with the brightest look I ever saw, " I'm
the happiest man in Johnstown, for my family's all right."

They say at some of the fine London hotels that Bill
Jones didn't cut much of a figure when he visited the
English metropolis.   When I hear this I like to call up in
my mind the image of Bill at Johnstown, and I wish I
could make everybody else see the picture of that man tri-
umphant.   I cherish the memory of my acquaintance with
Bill Jones as one of the great privileges of my life.

Somehow the value and importance of " leading citizens " to a community has never impressed me much since
then.

I reached Johnstown from Cleveland the day after the
flood, arriving just a few hours after Mr. du Pont, who
had come on from Cincinnati, where he happened to be
when the news of the disaster reached him.   We were
both immensely relieved to find our partner, Mr. Moxham,
all right.   We three men were all smokers, but it had not
occurred to Mr. du Pont or to me to bring an extra large
supply of cigars, for even if we had been thinking of our

own comfort, which we were not, we did not know that it was impossible to get tobacco in Johnstown, nor had we anticipated the difficulties in getting supplies of any kind from Pittsburgh or any other place in the outside world.

Mr. Moxham and I got together early and took account of stock and hit upon a plan which would prevent the tobacco famine from affecting Mr. du Pont for several days at least. We planned that when we got together each morning, preparatory to separating and going about our respective work for the day, that one of us would say, "Well, how many cigars have we among us?" Mr. Moxham and I would produce ours, being careful not to let Mr. du Pont know that we had no large reserve supply in our rooms; he would of course produce his and then we would divide them equally among us. Arthur and I would put ours into our pockets, remarking casually that we didn't care to smoke then but would do so later. The plan worked all right. Mr. du Pont, all unsuspecting, smoked his cigars and never knew that we carried ours around in our pockets and added them to the common store the next morning. It was the greatest source of comfort to both of us that our elder partner did not have to be deprived of his cigars, but we never dared tell him of the deception we practiced upon him, for while we considered it a good joke and enjoyed it hugely we knew he wouldn't have forgiven it.

The work delegated to me was the removal of the bodies of the victims of the disaster. No words can describe the horror and reluctance with which I approached this grewsome task. The sight of the first few bodies recovered moved me to tears. But before we had gone far I had lost all feeling of shrinking or even of sadness and went about it in a seemingly heartless manner. It was the stress of the cruel situation, the absolute necessity for getting the awful work done which made this possible.

The natural buoyancy of my nature soon asserted itself and as there was nothing else out of which any fun could be had, I " made fun " of the free operation of our street cars, which continued for some sixty or ninety days. I told my partners that this method of operating was the most perfect device I ever had encountered for getting rid of the evils arising from the collection of fares. I insisted that it could not be improved upon; that it did away with all possibility of dishonesty or carelessness on the part of the conductors and the general public; in fact, that it was a cure-all. They retorted that they preferred the disease even in its most virulent form to so drastic a remedy.

Whether my hope of some day seeing the people riding on free street cars had its birth before this time or was due to the Johnstown object lesson I cannot say. But certain it is that that experience convinced me that free cars were not only possible but practicable. When I seriously advocated them some years later the objection I met oftenest was that people would spend all their time riding. Even if I had not been able to refute this by citing Johnstown where nothing of the kind happened, I should still have answered that people would no more ride aimlessly hour after hour on free cars than they now ride aimlessly on free elevators.

Have you ever really thought what free cars would mean?

Wouldn't the greatest advantage be the removal of franchises which are to-day the prizes that Big Business strives for, bribes for, and even corrupts whole communities to acquire?

Did you ever hear of anybody trying to get a fire department franchise?

How would free car service be paid for? How is free elevator service paid for? The owners of buildings provide it without pay? Oh, no, they don't. In apartment houses the tenants pay for elevator service in their rent. And in office buildings the tenants seem to do the same thing, but they don't really. You and I pay for the elevator service. It is charged to us in the bills rendered by our doctors, our lawyers, our plumbers, our dressmakers, our tailors, our milliners, our contractors, albeit it isn't separately itemized.

Well, wouldn't you rather pay it that way than to fish in your pocket for a nickel or three cents or a penny every time you enter an elevator? I would.

Free street car rides would be paid for in the same way,— not by some public benefactor, some mysterious agency which gives something for nothing — but by the car riders themselves. And they would find the item in their rent receipts.

To meet the problem of a community with no money was not easy, but we were presently confronted with the graver problem of a community with too much money. The greatly exaggerated reports of the loss of property and of human lives, the first press dispatches placing the number of the latter at ten thousand, brought a correspondingly great volume of relief.

That curious inconsistency which makes human nature quite complacent in contemplating the annual slaughter of infants in our great cities, the physical, mental and moral crimes involved in the employment of little children in industry, the menace to the race in over-working and underpaying women, and the terrible social consequences of forced unemployment of great numbers of men, but which moves it to frantic expressions of sympathy by the news of an earthquake, a fire or a kidnapping, caused the American people to empty their purses and their children's savings banks for the benefit of Johnstown.

When it was known that three millions of dollars had been sent in, the town quit work and it seemed as if every inhabitant was bent upon getting a share of the cash.

The hungry were fed, the naked clothed, the homeless housed, widows pensioned; charitable acts, every one, and made possible by a generous charity fund. But these expenditures didn't exhaust it. They hardly made an impression on it.

Roads were repaired, bridges rebuilt, the river widened, cemeteries laid out, monuments erected, hospitals established; public work every bit of it with no legitimate claim on a charity fund. But still there was money left!

Three million dollars doesn't sound like much when you say it, so familiar have we become with figures which represent the fortunes of the one hundred men whom Senator LaFollette named by name for the enlightenment of his professedly skeptical colleagues, but when you take three million dollars and go out to buy things with it, real material things, it turns out to be a very great deal of money.

When we had managed to use perhaps a million of the fund a meeting was called to decide what should be done with the rest of it. The situation was extremely serious. The flood of gold threatened as great disaster, though of a different nature, as the flood of water had caused. The residents couldn't be induced to work and workmen had to be brought in from the outside, thus further taxing the capacity of the already overcrowded houses.

The Governor of the State, James A. Beaver, frightened us by counseling delay and investigation of individual cases. Others urged indemnification for losses. This was clearly as improper a use for a charity fund, a fund given to relieve actual suffering and immediate distress, as the public work had been.

Surely no body of men assembled in conference was ever faced by a more unique situation. At this meeting I shocked everybody by advising that the money be converted into silver dollars, since it could not be returned to the donors, loaded into wagons, hauled out and dumped into the streets where the people might literally scramble for it. It was now absolutely certain that nothing could be done until we got rid of it, and this plan had the merit of speed to recommend it anyhow, and I wasn't at all sure that it wouldn't result in about as full a measure of justice as any plan that could be devised after protracted investigation. Mr. Moxham and I were for any plan that was quick.

In the end the committee reimbursed losers, giving each a certain percentage of estimated losses. Before the people were completely demoralized the money was all given away or appropriated, and then the town went to work, went back to the sober pursuit of every-day affairs, and life assumed a normal aspect once more.

Lest some reader of the foregoing paragraphs think I condemn the motives which prompt charity let me disclaim that! It is not generous impulses, not charity itself, to which I object. What I do deplore is the short-sight-

edness which keeps us forever tinkering at a defective
spigot when the bung-hole is wide open. If we were wise
enough to seek and find the causes that call for charity
there would be some hope for us.

In Johnstown it was a defective dam used for the recreation of the well-to-do. A great reservoir of water in
which fish were kept to be fished for by the privileged
members of the South Fork Hunting and Fishing Club of
Pittsburgh. This property, comprising some five hundred
acres, had been acquired by purchase. Originally a part
of the State canal system it had passed into the hands of
the Pennsylvania Railroad Company when the latter purchased the canal in 1857–58, and became private property
in 1875 when Congressman John Reilly bought it. He
later offered it for sale at two thousand dollars, when it
was purchased by the originator of the Club above mentioned and two other Pittsburgh gentlemen.

It was suspected that the dam wasn't safe. I myself
had gone to look at it one day the summer before it broke
and had speculated on what might happen to us in the
little city eight miles down the valley in case the dam
should give way. The innocent cause of the catastrophe
when at last it did come was some leaves which clogged
the spill-way. Citizens living in the vicinity wanted to
remove the wire grating which held the leaves back and
caused the water to go over the breast of the dam, but
were refused permission to do so, refused, forsooth, because some of the privately-owned fishes swimming around
in the privately-controlled pool might escape — might be
swept over the confines of their aristocratic dwelling and
eventually be caught with a bent pin attached to a cane
pole, instead of being hauled out of the sacred waters, in

which they had been spawned, by that work of art known as a high class rod and reel equipped with a silk line and a many-hued artificial fly.

Yes, the Johnstown flood was caused by Special Privilege, and it is not less true that Special Privilege makes charity apparently necessary than it is that " crime and punishment grow on one stem! " It is cupidity which creates unjust social conditions sometimes for mere pleasure — as in this case — but generally for profit. The need of charity is almost always the result of the evils produced by man's greed.

What did charity do for Johnstown? It was powerless to restore children to parents, to reunite families, to mitigate mourning, to heal broken hearts, to bring back lost lives. It had to be diverted to uses for which it was not intended. *As charity* it had to be eliminated, as we have seen, before the people could save themselves.

Materially Johnstown was benefited by the flood, just as so many other communities have been by similar catastrophes. And material prosperity seems so important that we have acquired a habit of saying, " Oh, the fire was a good thing for Chicago or London," " The flood was a good thing for Johnstown," etc., etc. But is it not true that when human lives are lost the price paid for material benefits is one that can't be counted? We must leave this out of the reckoning then when we say that the flood was a good thing for Johnstown.

The town went forward as one united people now no longer divided by separate borough governments, and on the wreckage of the former city built up a great manufacturing community which to-day numbers more than fifty thousand souls.

It was a marvelous thing to witness such utter destruction and in so short a time such complete reconstruction, and the spectacle made a profound impression upon me. When I became mayor of Cleveland twelve years later I was faced by problems of a different character, but problems due to the same root cause from which Johnstown's difficulties came. And many, many times when these problems seemed hopelessly entangled I reasoned with myself that there must be a way out, since in Johnstown under apparently greater disadvantages we had always found a way.

In Cleveland we made progress by slow and painful degrees. No completed picture presented itself here as in Johnstown, but, leaving out the element of time, the cases were, to my mind, so similar as almost to parallel each other.

The problems which had to be met in Johnstown and which are being met in Cleveland have their counterparts in all other communities, and sooner or later will present themselves for solution. Just as surely as we meet these problems with remedial measures only, with charitable acts and time-serving expedients,— just so surely will great catastrophes in some form or other overtake us.

If we will seek out and remove the social wrong which is at the bottom of every social problem, the problem will vanish. Nothing could be simpler. If, on the other hand, the cause is not eradicated the problem will persist, multiply itself and all the evils that go with it, until one day that particular catastrophe which goes under the dreadful name — *revolution* — occurs.

It was at our Johnstown plant during the panic of the early nineties that we hit upon a device for supplying the shortage of currency which has since been so widely used in times of similar stress.   There were plenty of orders for our product — street railroad rails — but the buyers couldn't pay cash.   We called our employés together and explained the situation to them.   We told them we were unable to command enough currency to pay the full amount of their wages, but that if they were willing to accept a small percentage in cash and the remainder in certificates that we should be able to continue to operate the mill; if they could not agree to such an arrangement we should have to shut down.

The law specifically prohibited the payment of wages in anything but money — a provision intended to protect working men from exploitation by " the company store," an institution we never had in connection with any of our industries.   To avoid violating the law therefore we should have to hand over to each employé his full pay in currency with the understanding that he was to present himself immediately at another window in the office and buy an agreed upon percentage of certificates.

We were selling rails for such cash payments as we could get and accepting the purchasers' bonds for the remainder.   We proposing to do for our men just what our customers were doing for us.   The bonds were to be held by a joint committee of company representatives and working men and against these bonds the certificates were issued.   Our employés decided to accept our proposition, and our coöperative enterprise, for that is what it was, proved entirely satisfactory.   The certificates passed at nearly par and we experienced no serious legal embarrassment, nor was there any misunderstanding of our motives.

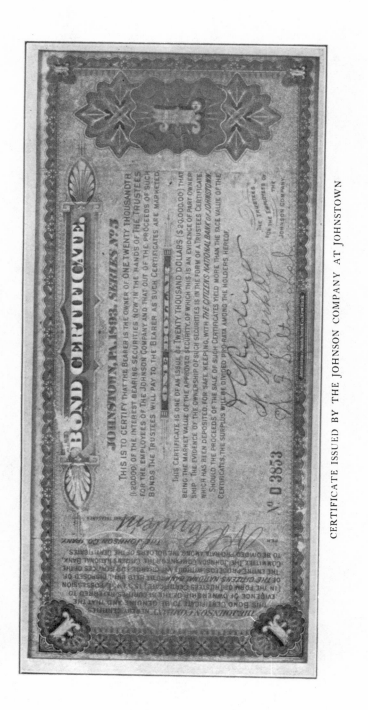

CERTIFICATE ISSUED BY THE JOHNSON COMPANY AT JOHNSTOWN

In a way these certificates corresponded to clearing house certificates, at that time forbidden by law, but since partially legalized — which is to say that certain national banks now have legal authority to issue clearing house certificates. It's curious that what is right and lawful for some banks is wrong and unlawful for others. But necessity knows a law that isn't written on statute books and will continue to force the use of clearing house certificates or similar expedients from time to time until we are wise enough to arrange our money-issuing machinery with a view to taking care of business in hard times as well as in good times.*

* Appendix.

VI

MY interest in Privilege, as this record has shown, was all on the privileged side. The unwisdom of the public in making grants of the highway, or the question of municipal ownership would have been as incomprehensible to me as the Greek alphabet. I had acquired my various special privileges by perfectly legitimate methods according to my own standards. Most of my street railway operations were based upon franchises already in existence which I had purchased from the owners. Very few of my grants had come through city ordinances passed for my benefit. I had had comparatively little contact with politics in any way. I had sometimes contributed to the campaign funds of both political parties and was therefore indifferent as to which side won. I was absolutely interested in business, in the great business opportunities before me, in the sure prospect of continuing to make money,— and I was looking for a conductor all the time. I knew now that there were many guises in which he might appear, and my training had fitted me to recognize him in almost any of them.

When I was securely established as a business man, and at the very height of my money-making career the incident which was to change my whole outlook on the universe occurred. It came about through the intervention of a conductor too — but not the kind I was looking for — just

48

a prosaic railroad train conductor running between Cleveland and Indianapolis.

I still owned my Indianapolis interests and was traveling between that city and Cleveland frequently. When on one of these trips a train boy offered me a book called *Social Problems*. The title led me to think it dealt with the social evil, and I said as much, adding that the subject didn't appeal to me at all. Overhearing my remarks, the conductor urged me to buy the book, saying that he was sure it would interest me, and that if it didn't he would refund the half dollar I invested in it. So I bought it, and I read it almost without stopping. Then I hastened to get all the other books which Henry George had written up to that time. I read *Progress and Poverty* next. It sounded true — all of it. I didn't want to believe it though, so I took it to my lawyer in Cleveland, L. A. Russell, and said to him:

" You made a free trader of me; now I want you to read this book and point out its errors to me and save me from becoming an advocate of the system of taxation it describes."

The next time I went to Johnstown I talked with Mr. Moxham about it. He said he would read it. For months it was the chief subject of conversation between these two men and myself. Mr. Moxham read it once, carefully marking all the places where, in his opinion, the author had departed from logic and indulged in sophistry. He wasn't willing to talk much about it, however, saying he wanted time to think it over and read it once more before he discussed it with anybody. By and by he said to me,

" I've read *Progress and Poverty* again and I have had

to erase a good many of my marks, but I don't want to talk about it yet."

And then in due course of time there came a day when he said,

" Tom, I've read that book for the third time and I have rubbed out every damn mark."

Long before this I had become convinced that Mr. George had found a great truth and a practical solution for the most vexing of social problems, but Mr. Russell wasn't yet ready to admit it. Some time later he and Mr. Moxham and I were obliged to go to New York together on business, and we spent our evenings in my room at the hotel smoking and discussing *Progress and Poverty*. Mr. Russell's avowed intention was " to demolish this will-o'-the-wisp." Every time he stated an objection either Mr. Moxham or I would hold him up to explain exactly what he meant by such terms as land, labor, capital, wealth, etc. As fast as he correctly defined their meanings his objections vanished one by one, and that trip worked his complete conversion and was brought about by his own reasoning, and not by our arguments. The effect of all of this upon me was to make every chapter of that book almost as familiar to me as one of my own mechanical inventions.

It was in 1883 that I became interested in Mr. George's teachings — the year my family took up their residence in Cleveland, though previous to this time my wife and our two children, a son and a daughter, both of whom were born in Indianapolis, had spent some time with me at the Weddell House, where I lived when I was in the city.

I continued in my business with as much zest as ever, but my point of view was no longer that of a man whose chief object in life is to get rich. I wanted to know more about Mr. George's doctrines. I wanted to ask him questions, for I had not outgrown the why, what and wherefore habit of my childish days.

My business took me often to New York and on one of those trips in 1885 I went to call upon Mr. George at his home in Brooklyn. I was much affected by that visit. I had come to a realizing sense of the greatness of the truth that he was promulgating by the strenuous, intellectual processes which have been described, but the greatness of the man himself was something I felt when I came into his presence.

Before I was really aware of it I had told him the story of my life, and I wound up by saying:

"I can't write and I can't speak, but I can make money. Can a man help who can just make money?"

He assured me that money could be used in many helpful ways to promote the cause, but said that I couldn't tell whether I could speak or write until I had tried; that it was quite probable that the same qualities which had made me successful in business would make me successful in a broader field. He evidently preferred to talk about these possibilities to dwelling on my talent for money-making. He suggested that I go into politics. This seemed quite without the range of the possible to me, and I put it aside, but said that I would go ahead and make money and devote the profits largely to helping spread his doctrines if he would let me.

One of the first things I did, and it makes me smile to

recall it, was to purchase several hundred copies of Mr. George's new book, *Protection or Free Trade,* and send one to every minister and lawyer in Cleveland.

Why do converts to social ideals always select these most unlikely of all professions in the world as objects for conversion in their campaigns in behalf of new ideas?

I had not yet discovered that it is " the unlearned who are ever the first to seize and comprehend through the heart's logic the newest and most daring truths."

That first meeting with Mr. George was the beginning of a friendship which grew stronger with each passing day and which, it seemed to me, had reached the full flower of perfection when I stood at his bedside in the Union Square Hotel in New York City the night of October 28, 1897, and saw his tired eyes close in their last sleep.

Mr. George was about forty-six years old, I thirty-one, when we met and from the very first our relations were those of teacher and pupil.

My first participation in any organized activity was to attend a meeting of a voluntary committee called at the home of Dr. Henna in New York in August, 1886, to consider how our question could be made a political one. Among that little group besides Mr. George and Dr. Henna, were Father McGlynn, William McCabe, Louis F. Post and Daniel DeLeon. A short time afterwards a second meeting was held at Father McGlynn's rectory, but before we had formulated any specific plans Mr. George was called upon to become the candidate of the labor unions of New York for mayor, and so without our volition our object was accomplished. I was active in this campaign as also in the state campaign the following year, when, against his judgment, Mr. George was put forward as the United Labor Party candidate for secretary of State.

Mr. George persisted in his belief that my greatest service to the cause lay in the political field, and every time I urged my inability to speak as a reason against this, he answered that I couldn't tell because I had not tried.

And so one night early in the year 1888 I tried, the occasion being a mass meeting in Cooper Union. Of this attempt Louis F. Post generously wrote some years later, " He spoke for possibly five minutes, timidly and crudely but with evident sincerity, and probably could not have spoken ten minutes more had his life been the forfeit," but his private assurance to me was that it was without exception the worst speech he had ever heard in all his days. I am sure he has never heard anything to match it since. I know I never have.

But this unpromising beginning didn't discourage Mr. George and it made the next trial a little easier for me; and by and by I was speaking with him at various public meetings. I recall one especially large and successful one in Philadelphia.

Some five or six years later, perhaps, in a great meeting in Chickering Hall, New York, my part on the programme was to answer any questions which might be put by the audience. This was usually done by Mr. George, and though I had tried my hand at it several times before this was the first time I had attempted it when Mr. George was present. When the meeting was over we left the hall together and walked some blocks before a word was spoken. I had gotten on very well in my own estimation, but Mr. George's continued silence was raising doubts in

my mind.   When he did speak, he laid his hand on my
arm and said,

"I am ready to go now.   There is someone else to answer the questions."

With Mr. George and Thomas G. Shearman of New
York, I went before the Ohio legislature and advocated
a change in the tax laws.

In the winter of 1895–96 a newspaper called the *Recorder* was started in Cleveland.   At Mr. George's suggestion Louis F. Post, then of New York, came to Cleveland and went onto the paper as an editorial writer.   Hop-
ing that the *Recorder* might prove a truly democratic
organ and thinking it might become self-supporting if it
did not have too hard a struggle at the start, I, volun-
tarily, at first without Mr. Post's knowledge, and later,
against his advice, made good the weekly deficits.   First
and last I contributed eighty thousand dollars to this enterprise.   Regarding this purely as one of my contributions
to our cause I took no evidence either of debt or ownership consideration.   An effort to throw the paper against
Mr. Bryan was prevented by Mr. Post.   In 1897 I was
pretty badly hit by the panic and had to withdraw my
financial assistance with only a week's warning.   Mr.
Post left the *Recorder* at about this time and the paper
was obliged to abandon the regular newspaper field, though
it continued as a kind of court calendar.

In the readjustment I was compelled to pay an additional twenty thousand dollars, the courts maintaining that
I was a stockholder.   I did not mind having put in the
eighty thousand, but I always considered the enforced payment of that additional twenty thousand a great injustice.

Subsequently Mr. Post established *The Public* in Chicago. To this truly democratic weekly journal it has been my privilege to give some support.

In such ways as these I was helping Mr. George's cause and it was my ambition to become able to do all the outside work, the rough and tumble tasks, leaving him free and undisturbed in his most useful and enduring field of influence, that of writing. It was my privilege to be partly instrumental in making it possible for him to write his last book — a privilege for which I shall never cease to be profoundly grateful.

A warm friendship sprang up between my father and Mr. George and the latter built a house at Fort Hamilton, Brooklyn, next to my father's and my brother Albert's and very near the summer home of my family at the same place. Together my father and Mr. George selected family burial lots adjoining each other in Greenwood Cemetery and overlooking the ocean. Here as time goes on members of our respective families are gathered to their final rest.

I was with Mr. George a great deal in the Fort Hamilton days when his home was the headquarters of the single tax movement in this country. Sometimes he went with me on bicycling excursions, and we used to laugh a good deal about one business trip he made with me. I invited him to go, telling him that I should not be very busy, that we could take our wheels and have some time to visit. It was a western trip. We stopped at a good many towns, I had interviews with several men in each place and, as was my custom, I made no discrimination between night and day when it came to settling business matters, or taking trains. To me it was rather a leisurely journey. We got in a few spins on our bicycles and of course we visited on the train. Mr. George said nothing to me about the character of the trip, but when he got home his comment to Mrs. George was,

" Well, if Tom calls this trip one when he wasn't very busy, he needn't invite me to go on one when he is."

In Mr. George's last campaign for mayor of New York in 1897 I was his political manager. It was during that campaign that I was hissed in a public meeting, the first and only time in my life that that ever happened to me. It was at a meeting in Brooklyn in a large hall or an opera house. As I stepped forward to the middle of the stage to begin my speech a slight hissing came from the house, but it was overbalanced by the applause. A few moments later when I had gotten fairly started it came again, this time loud and insistent and from a group of men seated in the front and near the center of the balcony. I stopped, looked towards them and called out, " Well, what is it? What don't you like? Tell me; maybe I can explain." No answer, but more hisses.

" Oh, you don't know what you are hissing for? You were just told to do it," I continued. " Well, come on, give us some more of it. I like it, it makes me feel good," and I coaxed for more hissing, making the sound of the tongue against the teeth used to urge a horse to greater speed. But I got no response now and the meeting was not disturbed again.

The group of hissers had evidently been sent to the meeting with instructions to break it up, but their courage failed them. When the meeting was over they followed me out and while I was waiting for the private trolley car in which I was traveling that night, a great husky workman standing near me on the sidewalk exclaimed in loud tones, " Well,

HENRY GEORGE

did you see the big —— —— —— throw the con into them!"

Intending to pay me a compliment, he called me a name which Southerners and Westerners usually consider sufficient provocation for a quarrel, and my heart stood still for a moment, for my brother Albert was just behind me and I fully expected him to reach past me and hit the man who had spoken. I reached one arm behind me and got hold of my brother and put my other hand on the man's shoulder and said, "Come, my friend, help me to persuade these fellows to go with me to my next meeting," and then I invited the group of men who had tried to stop my speech to get into my car and go with me. Completely bluffed by this time they all slunk away.

When the question of Mr. George's candidacy was being discussed by some of his friends and advisers and it had been decided that he should run, someone suggested that the campaign might cost him his life. He was not yet sixty years of age, but the hard lines of his life had told upon him, and his friends knew his physical strength could hardly measure up to the demands of a heated political struggle. When the suggestion that his life might be the forfeit was made, Mr. George straightened suddenly in his chair, his eyes brightened, and with his whole heart evidently in his answer he said:

"Wouldn't it be glorious to die that way!"

His body was weaker, but the same intrepid spirit was in the man as when he had made his first campaign for mayor of New York ten years before. Then when William M. Ivins had approached him on behalf of Tammany Hall and the County Democracy, offering him a seat in Congress sealed, signed and delivered if he would withdraw from the mayoralty contest Mr. George said, " If I cannot possibly be elected as you say, why do you want me to withdraw? " And to Mr. Ivins's reply, " You cannot be elected, but your running will raise hell! " Mr. George rejoined that he did not want to be elected, but he did want to raise hell. It is this, this disregard of self-interest, this indifference to one's personal fate, this willingness to " raise hell " for the sake of a cause or to give one's life for it that the world cannot understand. And it is because the world has never understood that men like Henry George in all the ages have had to pay so big a price for just the chance to serve.

VII

A MAN of thirty-four at the high tide of a successful business career, learning every day to utilize special privileges to increase his wealth, and satisfying his natural aptitude for mechanics by working on inventions, tied up with numerous partners in big enterprises of various kinds, is somewhat bewildered as to just what his future course of action should be when his civic consciousness first asserts itself — at least this was my case. To all outward appearances, I went along much as before for some time after my conversion to Mr. George's social philosophy. Then chance sent me off into a new field — one I had not the remotest intention of entering, though nearly all my progenitors of whom there is any historical record had been in it before me. Richard M. Johnson as vice-president of the United States had attained the highest office of any of these, the political activities of the other members of the family taking them into various southern State legislatures, to Congress and making governors of a few.

It was in the year 1888 while I was up the lakes on a fishing trip that I was nominated for Congress by the Democrats of the twenty-first congressional district of Ohio. In spite of my association with Mr. George and his ambitions for me — or rather for the cause through

me — I was still very indifferent to matters political.   I
had never voted — a fact let me hasten to add which I
never advertised in any of my political campaigns!   The
nomination was a complete surprise to me and I did not
learn of it until after the convention had adjourned.   I
don't know to this day why I was nominated.   Of course
my street railroad battles had brought me somewhat into
the public eye and I think the Democratic managers believed that I would be a good spender.   Mr. George
urged me to accept, and after careful consideration I
decided to do so.

This district was so strongly " protectionist " in sentiment that even the Democrats who had represented it
had been protectionists; so the local managers advised me
to be very careful in framing my letter of acceptance,
saying that if I were not too radical they believed I might
win.

With this warning in mind I *was* careful — to state my
position exactly — and I did it in the following sentences:

" I am, as you all know, in personal belief a free trader and
advocate making, as soon as it can be lawfully done, a radical
change in the present system of taxation by which change the
burden shall be shifted from the products of labor where it now
bears heaviest onto the monopoly of natural opportunities to labor.
This, I am well aware, is for the future and not yet in present
issue.   However reluctant and personally diffident I have been
and am to enter this campaign of principle as a candidate, I will
do everything in my power to bring about a discussion that
will demonstrate to the people that in freedom and not in restric-
tion rests the true solution of the great problem of justice to all
in bearing common burdens and of special privilege to none at the
expense of any others."

This letter of acceptance was my platform and it was probably at once the briefest and most radical platform put forth in that district since the adoption of protection. I was beaten by the Republican nominee, Theodore Burton, by about five hundred votes.

Two years later I was again a candidate for Congress; this time of my own volition, for I had become fully convinced that the most practical way to serve the cause to which I had committed myself was to bring the question into politics. W. W. Armstrong, editor of the Cleveland *Plain Dealer,* was also a candidate for the Democratic nomination, but after a contest I carried every ward in the city except one, and lost that by only a few votes. Mr. Burton, who had beaten me two years before, was a candidate for reëlection and telegraphed a challenge to debate with me the issues of the campaign.

The committee was preparing a letter declining when it occurred to them to consult me about it. I told them I should certainly accept, that I was willing to get off the ticket if that was their wish, but I wasn't willing to run before I had been hit. They received my decision with many misgivings. As the challenged party I claimed the right to name the terms of the contest, and in the final arrangement it was agreed that each side should make five ten-minute speeches in each debate.

In the two years which had elapsed since my first effort in Cooper Union, I had increased my time limit to ten minutes, and for that space I could talk like a whirlwind, though I probably could not have spoken longer at one stretch to save my life. Mr. Burton is a lawyer, a scholar, a master of English, a practiced speaker, if not an orator, but his style is deliberate and it was next to impossible for him to get fairly started under eleven minutes. We had four debates in public halls in various parts of the city with crowded houses at every meeting. The principal subject of discussion was the tariff. I went to the first of those engagements with an outward show of cheerfulness and confidence that I was very far from feeling, but I had no serious apprehensions after the first night. The ten minute rule saved me, and I won the election.

Mr. Burton refused to run against me two years later, and when he was the opposition candidate for mayor of Cleveland fifteen years afterwards he declined absolutely to debate with me in person.

Colonel O. J. Hodge was the congressional nominee of the Republicans in 1892 and now it was I who issued the debating challenge. Though Colonel Hodge was accustomed to public speaking, having been a member of the Ohio legislature and speaker of the house of representatives, he refused my challenge, giving as his reason that I would pack the meetings against him, whereupon I proposed admission by ticket only and volunteered to give him all the tickets. Still he declined. One evening during the campaign I drifted into one of his meetings. A general invitation was extended to the audience to come forward and meet the candidate. I went up with the rest, was recognized by the crowd and importuned to speak. The audience was very cold when I commenced, but before I had spoken many minutes I felt a growing sympathy among them. Colonel Hodge and I left the meeting together and as we drove down town in my buggy he said I had served him a mean trick to come in and capture his meeting and wind up by carrying him off bodily. I was

TOM L. JOHNSON BETWEEN THIRTY-SIX AND THIRTY-EIGHT

"I had become fully convinced that the most practical way to serve the cause to which
I had committed myself was to bring the question into politics."

again successful and elected to Congress for a second term.

My congressional experience was a good school, and I felt that in a way it took the place of college in my life. It gave me an acquaintance with men of many types from all over the country, broadened my outlook, enlarged my vision, and increased my sense of responsibility. As Mr. George spent a great deal of time with me in Washington, I might carry the simile further and say it was like going through college attended by a private tutor. It is needless to state that his advice and assistance were invaluable to me. He took an active part in the distribution of all literature which went out under my frank.

John DeWitt Warner of New York, and Jerry Simpson of Kansas, both of whom were fellow members in my first term, were wholly committed to the single tax, and in my second term our little circle gained another adherent in the person of Judge McGuire of California. We four, with two others, Harter of Ohio, and Tracey of New York, had the pleasure of voting for the first outright single tax bill ever acted upon in a parliamentary body — a measure drawn by Judge McGuire.

Besides these gentlemen there were about twenty other members who were more or less familiar with the question, every one of whom admitted privately that Mr. George's arguments were unanswerable, but very few of whom would commit themselves publicly. They took much the same attitude on this question that Speaker Reed charged the Democrats with taking on the famous "Reed rules." In conversation with Mr. Reed one day when I remarked that I believed in his rules, he laughed and answered:

" Oh, yes, lots of Democrats say that to me, but I notice none of them says it publicly on the floor of the House."

I replied that I had already said it publicly in my own district, for when my Republican opponent had tried to make the Reed rules an issue in our debates my answer had been that I didn't know much about them, but what I did know I liked. It was manifestly silly to go to the expense of electing and maintaining members of Congress and then to permit them to be considered absent when they chose to refuse to answer to their names in roll-call. "Well, I'll watch you," said Mr. Reed.

At the very first opportunity I expressed my approval on the floor of the House and Mr. Reed and I enjoyed the situation more than some of my colleagues did. The latter complained frequently throughout my two terms that I embarrassed them. On the tariff matter, for instance, they said they could answer the ordinary objections of Republicans very well, but they couldn't answer a Republican who pulled one of my speeches out of his pocket and said, "Well, here's a member of your own party, Johnson of Ohio, who not only says the Democrats haven't kept their party pledges but that they haven't even tried to keep them."

I was an enthusiastic bicyclist, as I have already said, and Mr. George and I frequently took long trips together on our wheels. I taught Jerry Simpson to ride a bicycle and I can positively deny the basis of the tradition which came to be associated with his name in the popular mind. Jerry did wear socks.

My acquaintance with Mr. Harrison, who was President during my first term in Congress, dated back to the time when he had been our lawyer in Indianapolis, and my acquaintance with Mr. Bryan, who was one of the young members, had its beginning here.

My committee appointments could not by any stretch of the imagination be considered important. The Committee on the District of Columbia got pretty busy shortly after my appointment to it, however, and in less than five months we succeeded in having a resolution adopted providing for an investigation of the taxing methods of the District. This committee had discovered among other things that the assessment of land values was seventy-six million dollars when it should have been more than three hundred million; that small residence property was discriminated against, while vacant lots and valuable property were favored. The resolution stated these facts and authorized a select committee of three to inquire into the method of assessing land values. This committee consisted of Joseph E. Washington of Tennessee, James Wadsworth of New York, and myself as chairman.

As our work proceeded and the investigation went on more and more interest was taken in it by landowners who were paying less than their share of taxes. Towards the end of it they became thoroughly aroused. Assessors who coöperated with us at first and seemed to be in sympathy with the movement were soon won away or frightened away. It had some effect on the assessment which followed, but the greatest result was that it was the first time any comprehensive report had been made showing specifically the low assessment of valuable property, the high assessment of small homes and the utter futility of all attempts to tax personal or intangible property.

So far as I know this was the very beginning of a line of inquiry that has gone on extensively in this country since, is the heart of the Budget fight — the big question in English politics at the present time,— has been applied in parts of Australia, in New Zealand and in Western Canada, and is to-day a recognized part of the taxing systems in these places. It was the first authoritative expression of any public body on this subject, and coming from a committee of Congress had a good deal of weight. There is no doubt that the tax laws of the future will be framed on the principles embodied in this report.

Its recommendations were based on this central truth, that a tax on the value of land is the only just tax. Analysis shows that the rental value of land does not arise from any expenditure of labor or investment of capital by the owner of the land. The value which the owner of the land may create by the expenditure of labor and capital is a value which attaches to buildings or improvement. The value which attaches to the land itself comes from the growth of the whole community. It was this growth and improvement of the community which made some land in the District of Columbia worth over three millions of dollars an acre. If the owners of this land had left it idle, if they had been absentees or idiots, this value would have attached to the land to the same extent and in the same manner. It came from a growth of population and general improvement and was primarily due to the fact that that particular place had been selected as the site of the national capital. Thus everyone who adds even temporarily to the population and business of Washington or any other city does something to add to the value of the land, something to increase *a fund which may be taken to defray all the expenses of government* without levying any tax on legitimate property or improvement, or which will in any way increase the cost of living. Every resident must directly or indirectly contribute to the rental value of land. In this way every resident, yes, every sojourner, may be said, in what he pays for the use of land, even though it be for a single night's lodging, to pay a just tax sufficient to provide for the legitimate expenses of the local government and to make the most ample public improvements. But if individual land-owners are permitted to put the proceeds of this tax in their pockets, and taxes are then levied that fall on use and consumption, the body of citizens is really taxed twice. " The first and paramount consideration in taxation should be equality of burden," and only by taking the rental value of land in taxes can such equality be secured.

VIII

THE MONOPOLIST IN CONGRESS—*Continued*

DURING my first term in Congress it occurred to me that the " leave to print," so generally employed by members to include in their speeches statistics, long quotations, etc., might be used to great advantage in spreading our propaganda. I saw no reason why I should not arrange with some of my colleagues to ask leave to print certain portions of Mr. George's book *Protection or Free Trade,* as a part of our various speeches on a tariff bill. So I approached the following named members and laid my plan before them : William J. Stone of Kentucky, Joseph E. Washington of Tennessee, George W. Fithian of Illinois, Thomas Bowman of Iowa and Jerry Simpson of Kansas. It was agreed among us that each should ask leave to print a specific part of the book, so that the speeches of the six would comprise the entire treatise. The speeches were made between March 11 and April 8, 1892, and when the whole was in print in the *Congressional Record* it was simply a matter of restoring the original sequence to make the completed volume ready to frank and send out.

I had 100,000 copies printed in pamphlet and announced that I would mail them to all applicants at one cent per copy. This issue was made in May, 1892, and so great was the demand that by November 1 of that year 1,062,000 copies had been printed of which 1,024,000 were distributed before the presidential election and the rest afterwards. Nearly all of these were sent out on application, and most of them addressed to individual sub- scribers. In some instances political clubs subscribed for thousands of copies, sometimes providing me with the names and addresses of persons to whom they were to be sent; sometimes having them sent in bulk and attending to the distribution themselves. The free traders of the country raised a fund for this work, and we printed a second edition which was retailed at two cents a copy. The sales did not of course cover the cost and the deficit was met by this voluntary fund. We purchased the type and paid for the press work and binding by private sub- scription. The government through the franking priv- ilege, furnished the postage, but the postage only.

Now the Republican committees had been wont to em- ploy this method of distributing campaign literature, and had sent out tons of pamphlets containing protectionist falsehoods and misleading statistics on economic questions of all kinds — sometimes in such a way that the govern- ment paid for the printing as well as the postage. This is one of Privilege's established methods for distributing its propaganda, but when we presumed to invoke the same means to spread a great truth the hue and cry was raised all over the country. What was a perfectly proper action on the part of the enemy was a " low-down political trick " when I did it. The newspapers gave the impres- sion that I had shamefully abused my privileges and had by the exercise of black magic or similar means hoodooed a trusting and innocent national government. This im- pression I never was able to correct.

Have you ever noticed how a story which involves
scandal is played up by the press? That is because it is
" news." But a refutation of the scandal is never
" news; " consequently it either never gets into the papers
at all or is published in small type in the " Letters from
the People " department, which department is popular
only with the persons who have written the letters.

There were many amusing incidents connected with the
distribution of *Protection or Free Trade*. Republican
congressmen would come to me, often with wry faces, and
hand over requests for the pamphlets accompanied by
small remittances. Others were good natured about it,
and it was a common thing to be accosted after this fashion, " Say, Johnson, one of my constituents wants fifty
copies of that damn book of yours. I hate to have 'em
circulating in my district but I don't see how I can get out
of sending them."

The first national political convention I ever attended
was the Democratic Convention which nominated Cleveland at Chicago in June of 1892, to which I was a district
delegate. The committee on resolutions of which Senator Vilas of Wisconsin was chairman was controlled by
protection Democrats, and the tariff plank which they
were about to report was a pitiful straddle on the question. I thought it was worth while to test the temper
of the convention on a more radical plank and I got Colonel Henry Watterson of Kentucky and Honorable
Ben T. Cable of Illinois to coöperate with me to this end.
We consulted with Lawrence T. Neal of Ohio, a member
of the resolutions committee and found him willing to
bring in a minority report. Among us we framed the
following plank:

We denounce Republican protection as a fraud, a robbery of the great majority of the American people for the benefit of the few. We declare it to be a fundamental principle of the Democratic party that the federal government has no constitutional power to impose and collect tariff duties, except for the purpose of revenue only, and we demand that the collection of such taxes shall be limited to the necessities of the government when honestly and economically administered. We denounce the McKinley tariff law enacted by the Fifty-first Congress as the culminating atrocity of class legislation; we endorse the efforts made by the Democrats of the present Congress to modify its oppressive features in the direction of free raw materials and cheaper manufactured goods that enter into general consumption and we promise its repeal as one of the beneficent results that will follow the action of the people in entrusting power to the Democratic party. Since the McKinley tariff went into operation there have been ten reductions of the wages of the laboring man to one increase. We deny that there has been any increase of prosperity to the country since that tariff went into operation, and we point to the dullness and distress, the wage reductions and the strikes in the iron trade as the best possible evidence that no such prosperity has resulted from the McKinley Act. We call the attention of thoughtful Americans to the fact that after thirty years of restrictive taxes against the importation of foreign wealth, in exchange for our agricultural surplus the homes and farms of the country have become burdened with a real estate mortgage debt, $2,500,000,000, exclusive of all other forms of indebtedness; that in one of the chief agricultural states of the West there appears a real estate mortgage debt averaging $165 per capita of the total population, and that similar conditions and tendencies are shown to exist in other agricultural exporting states. We denounce a policy that fosters no industry so much as it does that of the sheriff.

I dictated the first sentence with the exception of the word *Republican,* being content with denouncing protection, without designating any special brand, but Mr. Neal inserted " Republican." He couldn't get one other member of the committee to join him in signing his minority report.

Immediately after it was presented to the convention the permanent chairman, William L. Wilson of West Virginia, recognized Colonel Watterson, who supported it in a characteristic speech. The fight was now on. Mr. Cable and I busied ourselves among the delegates urging them to vote for the Neal report, and I kept as close as possible to Chairman Wilson too. Delegate Lamb of Indiana asked a number of times how many names were signed to the minority report but his question wasn't answered, and the convention didn't know that it bore one lone signature.

At the close of the debate the chairman recognized me. The convention had grown restive and disorderly and I knew that if I didn't get the attention of that audience of fifteen thousand with my first words I couldn't get it at all. I spoke for three minutes and was hoarse for three weeks. The minority report was carried by a vote of 564 to 342. The whole thing was done in less than thirty minutes, Neal, Watterson and I being the only ones who had spoken in favor of it. We had no specific arrangement with Chairman Wilson though he was in sympathy with our efforts. The plank was adopted because the majority of the delegates present preferred it to the one presented by the resolutions committee, and the action brought consternation to Senator Vilas who had paid little attention to the Neal plank thinking it couldn't possibly prevail, as also to the other managers who were as downcast as our little coterie was jubilant. As we left the hall

William C. Whitney, Cleveland's representative in the convention, said to me,

"I would rather have seen Cleveland defeated than to have had that fool free trade plank adopted."

The "fool free trade plank" caused Mr. Cleveland much distress of mind too. Mr. George and I went to Buzzard's Bay to talk it over with him. We might as well have stayed away so far as getting Mr. Cleveland to express himself was concerned. He talked but he didn't say anything. He was pleasant and friendly, bore us no ill will for our part in making his platform declare for free trade, but when we came away he had not divulged his views on the question. In his letter of acceptance he made use of the term, "impossible free trade" as a sop to the other side.

In his book *Our Presidents and How We Make Them,* Colonel A. K. McClure says it was only the masterful management of William C. Whitney that held that convention for Cleveland, and Cleveland himself believed he owed his nomination to Whitney and said so to us on the occasion quoted. I told him that Mr. Whitney deserved no more credit for the action of the convention in this regard than he would for pushing a load of hay that was already well started down a hill.

The repudiation of its platform pledges by the Republican party in the last session of Congress is history repeating itself. Change the name Republican to Democrat and substitute 1894 for 1909 and you have the story of Democratic legislation on the tariff, following the campaign already alluded to in which a million copies of *Protection or Free Trade* were circulated. The Wilson bill was more viciously protectionist in some of its features than the McKinley law which it succeeded for it took sugar off the free list, and when I protested against it saying that if I did not know better I should be obliged to suppose that " the gentleman from Maine " and his fellows of the minority had hypnotized the majority and written the bill for them, and were making a pretense of opposing it in order to induce Democrats to accept a Republican measure under the delusion that it was a Democratic one, Mr. Reed replied,

" On the contrary I called the attention of the committee to that very bad break the first time I got a look at the bill."

The McKinley bill and the Wilson bill seemed to be based on opposite principles, but in reality the only difference was that McKinley *graciously gave the manufacturers what they desired,* while Wilson *put them to the inconvenience of fighting to get the things they wanted.* But neither of these bills nor any subsequent tariff bill has been framed in the interests of the consumer.

We are constantly hearing it said that the manufacturers get what they want because they have a lobby, and the reason the consumers come short is because they have nobody to represent them at Washington. Nobody to represent them! If Congress were true to the principles of democracy it would be the people's lobby.

I predicted the defeat of the Democracy as the result of our failure to stand by our party pledges. The prediction was fulfilled. I went down with the rest of the ticket and Mr. Burton was again elected to represent the twenty-first district of Ohio. I don't want to give the impression that I considered myself a political prophet; I didn't. The fulfillment was just an exception to Colonel Ingersoll's rule in which I believed then and believe even more strongly now, viz., that in politics there is nothing so uncertain as a sure thing. The fact that I ran several thousand ahead of my ticket must surely be construed as an evidence of the approval of the people of my district of my consistent stand on my platform promises.

When the Wilson bill was under discussion and I moved an amendment putting steel rails on the free list a great howl went up. How could I, a manufacturer of steel rails, seriously make such a proposal? It was in vain that I assured the members of the House that I was not representing my stockholders in Congress but that larger constituency which would be benefited by free trade. When I said quite frankly that I was a monopolist and that so long as I continued in business I should take advantage of all the class legislation enacted by Congress, but that as a member of Congress I should work, speak and vote against such class legislation I was accused of insincerity. That cry of " insincerity " has followed all my public work. I had made my money by monopoly, therefore my opposition to monopoly could not be genuine.

An impecunious writer, a poor labor agitator, an obscure soap-box orator was insincere in his opposition to the system because he had nothing at stake; I, a beneficiary, was insincere because I had everything at stake. An amusing encounter which I once had with a representative of the Chamber of Commerce in Cleveland illustrates this very point admirably. This man was objecting to my stand on some people's measure and wound up by saying, " You can't be right on this. You have too much money." " Well, what about Peter Witt? " I retorted, naming an advocate of the same measure who was poor, and he replied, " He has too little." " Will you tell me," I said, " just what amount of money a man may have before he can be right? " That is the way Privilege reasons.

Now I never professed unselfish motives. I got so much more happiness, so much more satisfaction out of life in promulgating the social theories I learned from Mr. George than I ever got from making money that it was no sacrifice for me to give up the one for the other. But I was still engaged in some big money-making enterprises while I was in Congress and I was more than willing to use the knowledge I had gained in business to confound the advocates of Privilege.

I fought hard to have steel rails put on the free list and knowing Mr. Dalzell of Pennsylvania, as the member most interested in the iron and steel schedule I gave him several days' notice of what I intended to do, and in the debate yielded him part of my time.

I reasoned that if I contended for free trade in this particular branch of industry with which I was so familiar and in which I was personally interested; it would clear the way for a similar fight on all other free trade amendments. It could not be charged that I was for free trade in every district but my own nor in every industry except the one in which I was myself engaged.

When I spoke of the steel-rail pool Mr. Dalzell surprised me by denying its existence. He said there *had been* a combination between certain steel rail men, which had been broken up by the refusal of a large number of firms to go into it, and that it had fallen of its own

The Lorain Steel Company, Lorain, Ohio, U.S.A.

NOW THE NATIONAL TUBE COMPANY: BUILT BY MR. JOHNSON

weight but that there was no condition in it for keeping up prices, etc., etc., and that now this pool was no more. Mr. Dalzell was like that secretary of the interior of a later day who went out to investigate the beef trust and came back to Washington from Chicago with the statement that there was no beef trust. He had asked the Armours and they had said, " No." And so Mr. Dalzell had asked the rail manufacturers whether there was a steel-rail pool and they had said, " No."

For answer I picked up from my desk a paper which I said was a copy of an agreement proving the existence of the pool. Mr. Dalzell said he was bound to accept my statement, but that he deprecated trusts as much as I did. I retorted that as a business man I didn't deprecate trusts, I joined them,— but that as a member of Congress I neither represented nor defended them. I said that if it were true as our Republican members were urging that protection was a good thing for labor then Pittsburgh ought to be a very paradise for working men, but the actual fact was that a few days before Mr. Carnegie had sailed for Jerusalem he utilized the tariff to reëstablish the steel-rail pool and pay other manufacturers to shut up their works and throw their men out of employment; then came a general cut in wages in all his great establishments; and *then* he announced himself ready *to give as much as five thousand dollars a day to feed the unemployed of Pittsburgh.* Privilege doesn't have to bribe congressmen when it can fool them.

Of course steel rails weren't put on the free list, and of course the steel-rail pool continued until the necessity for such combination was done away with, when the various concerns represented in them passed into a common ownership.

This merging of various enterprises into one wasn't brought about so much by the necessity for protection against laws which forbade combinations in restraint of trade, as by the necessity for the mutual protection of the pool members against each other. It was a matter of common knowledge on the inside that their agreements were ruthlessly broken. I have known members of labor unions to starve to carry out *their agreements*.

While the Wilson bill was under consideration I received a letter from some Cleveland cloak manufacturers requesting me to vote for a specific duty in addition to an ad valorem duty on ladies' cloaks. The letter had been prepared by politicians and newspaper men for the express purpose of putting me in a hole with my constituents. They knew perfectly well that I wouldn't promise to vote for the duty, but they thought my answer would give them the opportunity they wanted of coming back at my free trade talk with a protectionist argument which would make me ridiculous. I learned that the big protectionists of my district were fairly hugging themselves in joyful anticipation of the sorry spectacle I would make. They were about to silence me forever in that district at least on the subject of free trade.

I explained the matter to Mr. George and he framed a letter in reply, which was given wide publicity as part of my speech on the Wilson bill. That letter was one of the finest pieces of writing Mr. George ever did, and if anything deserves a place in this story it does. It was as follows:

CLEVELAND, Ohio, Dec. 29, 1893.

To Joseph Lachnect, Emil Weisels, Joseph Frankel and others, tailors and tailoresses in the employ of Messrs. Landesman, Hirscheimer & Co., cloak manufacturers of Cleveland.

Ladies and Gentlemen:

I have received your communication and that from Messrs. Landesman, Hirscheimer & Co., to which you refer, asking me to vote against the Wilson tariff bill, unless it is amended by adding to the duty of 45 per cent. ad valorem, which it proposes, an additional duty of 49½ cents per pound.

I shall do nothing of the kind. My objection to the Wilson bill is not that its duties are too low, but that they are too high. I will do all I can to cut its duties down, but I will strenuously oppose putting them up. You ask me to vote to make cloaks artificially dear. How can I do that without making it harder for those who need cloaks to get cloaks? Even if this would benefit you, would it not injure others? There are many cloak-makers in Cleveland, it is true, but they are few as compared with the cloak-users. Would you consider me an honest representative if I would thus consent to injure the many for the benefit of the few, even though the few in this case were yourselves?

And you ask me to demand, in addition to a monstrous ad valorem duty of 45 per cent., a still more monstrous weight duty of 49½ cents a pound — a weight duty that will make the poorest sewing-girl pay as much tax on her cheap shoddy cloak as Mrs. Astor or Mrs. Vanderbilt would be called on to pay on a cloak of the finest velvets and embroideries! Do you really want me to vote to thus put the burden of taxation on the poor while letting the rich escape? Whether you want me to or not, I will not do it.

That, as your employers say, a serviceable cloak can be bought in Berlin at $1.20 affords no reason in my mind for keeping up the tariff. On the contrary, it is the strongest reason for abolishing it altogether. There are lots of women in this country who would be rejoiced to get cloaks so cheaply; lots of women who must now pinch and strain to get a cloak; lots of women who cannot now afford to buy cloaks, and must wear old or cast-off garments or shiver with cold. Is it not common justice that we should abolish every tax that makes it harder for them to clothe themselves?

No; I will do nothing to keep up duties. I will do everything I can to cut them down. I do not believe in taxing one citizen for the purpose of enriching another citizen. You elected me on my declaration that I was opposed to protection, believing it but a scheme for enabling the few to rob the many, and that I was opposed even to a tariff for revenue, believing that the only just way of raising revenues is by the single tax upon land values. So long as I continue to represent you in Congress I shall act on the principle of equal rights to all and special privileges to none, and whenever I can abolish any of the taxes that are now levied on labor or the products of labor I will do it, and where I cannot abolish I will do my best to reduce. When you get tired of that you can elect someone in my place who suits you better. If you want duties kept up, you may get an honest protectionist who will serve you; you cannot get an honest free trader.

But I believe that you have only to think of the matter to see that in adhering to principle I will be acting for the best interests of all working men and women, yourselves among the number. This demand for protective duties for the benefit of the American working man is the veriest sham. You cannot protect labor by putting import duties on goods. Protection makes it harder for the masses of our people to live. It may increase the profits of favored capitalists; it may build up trusts and create great fortunes, but it cannot raise wages. You know for yourselves that what your employers pay you in wages does not depend on what any tariff may enable them to make, but on what they can get others to take your places for.

You have to stand the competition of the labor market. Why, then, should you try to shut yourselves out from the advantages that the competition of the goods market should give you? It is not protection that makes wages higher here than in Germany. They were higher here before we had any protection, and in the saturnalia of protection that has reigned here for some years past you have seen wages go down, until the country is now crowded with tramps and hundreds of thousands of men are now supported by charity. What made wages higher than in Germany is the freer access to land, the natural means of all production, and as that is closed up and monopoly sets in wages must decline. What labor needs is not protection, but justice; not legalized restrictions which permit one set of men to tax their fellows, but the free opportunity for all for the exertion of their own powers. The real struggle for the rights of labor and for those fair wages that consist in the full earnings of labor is the struggle for freedom and against monopolies and restrictions; and in the effort to cut down protection it is timidly beginning. I shall support the Wilson bill with all my ability and all my strength.

Yours very respectfully,

TOM L. JOHNSON.

Day after day passed. No answer came from Cleveland. It was my turn to be amused now for the reply never did come.

One of the principal movers in the matter, an experienced newspaper man connected with the leading Republican daily in my district, told me some time afterwards that he had wasted reams of paper and burned much midnight oil in a fruitless attempt to answer. "But," said he, "I'm just as much a protectionist as ever only it won't work on ladies' cloaks."

IX

CHANCE was responsible for my tent meeting campaigning. Once in one of my early Congressional campaigns when I wanted to have a meeting in the eighteenth ward in Cleveland there was no hall to be had. A traveling showman had a small tent pitched on a vacant lot and someone suggested that it might be utilized. It had no chairs but there were a few boxes which could be used as seats. Very doubtful of the result we made the experiment. It cost me eighteen dollars, I remember. After that I rented tents from a tent man and finally bought one and then several.

The tent meeting has many advantages over the hall meeting. Both sides, I should say all sides, will go to tent meetings — while as rule only partisans go to halls. Women did not go to political meetings in halls in those days unless some especially distinguished person was advertised to speak, but they showed no reluctance about coming to tent meetings. In a tent there is a freedom from restraint that is seldom present in halls. The audience seems to feel that it has been invited there for the purpose of finding out the position of the various speakers. There is greater freedom in asking questions too, and this heckling is the most valuable form of political education. Tent meetings can be held in all parts of the city — in short the meetings are literally taken to the people.

It was not long after I got into municipal politics in Cleveland before the custom of tent meetings was employed in behalf of ward councilmen as well as for candidates on the general ticket, and they too were heckled and made to put themselves on record. The custom of heckling is the most healthy influence in politics. It makes candidates respect pre-election pledges, forces them to meet not only the opposition candidates but their constituents.

But the greatest benefit of the tent meeting, the one which cannot be measured, is the educational influence on the people who compose the audience. It makes them take an interest as nothing else could do, and educates them on local questions as no amount of reading, even of the fairest newspaper accounts, could do. I do not believe there is a city in the country where the electorate is so well informed upon local political questions, nor upon the rights of the people as opposed to the privileges of corporations, as it is in Cleveland. Detroit and Toledo probably come next. The tent meeting is largely responsible for this public enlightenment of the people of Cleveland.

The one disadvantage of the tent is that it is not weather-proof. And yet it was seldom indeed that a meeting had to be abandoned on account of rain. Great audiences came even on rainy nights and our speakers have frequently spoken from under dripping umbrellas to good-natured crowds, a few individuals among them protected by umbrellas but many sitting in the wet with strange indifference to physical discomfort.

At first my enemies called my tent a " circus menagerie " and no part of my political work has been so persistently cartooned; but when they employed tents somewhat later they called theirs " canvas auditoriums." The adoption of the tent meeting by these same enemies or their successors may not have been intended either as an endorsement of the method or as a compliment to my personal taste, but I can't help considering it a little of both.

In my 1894 canvass for Congress at the first meeting held in a new tent, an incident occurred which brought me into contact with one of the bravest and most resourceful fighters against special privilege that it has been my good fortune to know.

The meeting had proceeded only a few minutes when about a third of the audience set up a call for " Peter Witt," and the name was cheered lustily two or three times.

I had never heard of Peter Witt, but ten minutes later in response to my customary invitation for questions an angry, earnest man, with flashing eyes and black locks hanging well down on one side of his forehead, rose in the center of the tent and shaking a long finger at me put a question in the most belligerent manner imaginable. I knew that the man the audience had been cheering for stood before me. I disregarded his question and asked with all the friendliness I could summon,

" Are you Mr. Witt? "

With scant civility he half-growled, half-grunted an affirmative answer, and I continued,

" Since you seem to have so many friends here, and in a spirit of fair play, I would be glad to share the platform with you. I do not like to see you at the disadvantage of having to speak from the audience."

There were mingled shouts of " Come on, come on! " and " Speak where you are! " from the crowd, and the angry young man was literally forced to come forward.

"Chance was responsible for my tent meeting campaigning."

The time consumed and the difficulty encountered in stumbling over camp chairs through the crowd and up onto the platform worked a change in Mr. Witt's manner. Fully half his steam had escaped and there wasn't much of his venom left when I grasped his hand. So little of kindness had come his way that he was not prepared for the warm reception and cordial introduction to the audience which I gave him.

Peter Witt was an iron molder by trade and the things he had suffered because of the brutalities of our industrial system had made him hate the system and long to free his fellow workers from its baneful power. His reward for his struggles, his sacrifices and his passionate devotion to the common good had been — to use one of his own expressions —" the blacklist of the criminal rich and the distrust of the ignorant poor."

Believing the Populist party offered more hope of relief than any other political organization he had allied himself with it, and I afterwards learned that the demonstration in my tent meeting was a preconcerted plan on the part of the Populists to capture that meeting. They didn't capture the meeting, nor did we capture the Populist orator for not during that campaign did Witt let up in his fight against the Democratic ticket, nor would he admit any change of feeling towards me personally. But he has fought with me, not against me, in every campaign I have since been in, and one of the strongest friendships of my life commenced that night when I welcomed Peter Witt to my platform. His sphere of influence has widened since then, and also his circle of friends, for many men, at first repulsed by his seeming bitterness, coming later to understand his sterling qualities, his sturdy honesty, his unswerving fidelity to principle, became his friends. Among them he may count some high priests of Privilege for these are human like the rest of us and being human they admire rugged honesty and genuine courage more than anything else in the world.

The year after I left Congress I got rid of my street railway properties in Cleveland and a brief history of the last days of my operations there is necessary to an intelligent understanding of the street railway war which occupied Cleveland's attention during most of my nine years as mayor.

In the latter part of March, 1893, the Everett road, the lines operated by the Andrews and Stanley interests and our company consolidated. In April of the same year Mr. Hanna took in the cable road. All the street railroads of the city were now in these two companies. The newpapers called the first the Big Consolidated, and the second the Little Consolidated which common parlance soon shortened to the Big Con and the Little Con; and when the Big Con and the Little Con consolidated ten years later, in 1903, the Concon was the result.

The Big Con controlled sixty per cent. of the business and the Little Con forty per cent. In the organization of the Big Consolidated I sided with the Andrews-Stanley crowd in electing Horace Andrews president of the company. The Everett interests would have liked to elect Henry Everett to that position. My brother Albert was a member of the board of directors of which I was chairman.

In the first days of the consolidation when we who had been fighting each other so long were in daily communication and occupying the same offices a good many amusing things happened. Mr. Everett and a man who had been associated with him were having a quiet little meeting every day, for instance, and seemingly getting a great deal of pleasure out of some figures they were examining. By and by I became curious to know what these daily meetings were about and when I asked Mr. Everett he showed me with great glee figures which proved that their property had appreciated in value much more than mine since the consolidation. The increased earnings were coming from their lines, not ours. He was quite jubilant about it.

" Aren't all the companies sharing equally in the profits of consolidation? " I asked.

" Why, of course," he answered.

" Then," I said, " I don't see how you have got it on us any. Your lines are making the profits for the others. I guess I'll take your figures and show 'em to my people so they can see just how good a deal I made."

That phase of the matter had actually never occurred to him. He didn't get any enjoyment out of comparative figures after that.

There was always a good deal of antagonism between Mr. Everett and me, and as we held the balance of power either of us could make the other uncomfortable by voting with the Andrews-Stanley crowd, as I did when I helped elect Mr. Andrews president, instead of voting for Mr. Everett.

Once the Everett interests planned as a joke that at the annual meeting they would see that my election as a director was made by a smaller vote than that given for any other officer. They thought it would be great fun to let me in by the barest majority, thus making it appear that I was *persona non grata* on the board.   Somehow the plan leaked out and I learned of it.

The day of the meeting came.   I was on hand with my votes, about one-third of the whole number.   When the votes were counted I had received more than anybody else.

When it dawned upon the other directors that I had cast all my votes for myself and none for anybody else, they made me pay for my fun by giving them a big dinner. I put up a dummy ticket too with Mr. Everett's name at the head and distributed a few of my votes on this ticket. The newspapers the next day in reporting the meeting said that " the Everett ticket was badly beaten " and it would have taken more than a dinner to appease the indignation this caused.

One day Mr. Hanna came to me and said, " Well, Tom, now that you've all consolidated, you and I might as well take up some old matters of dispute between us and get them settled."

" Certainly! " I answered, " that's a good idea.   By our consolidation agreement all disputes are to be referred to the president, so all you have to do is to see your friend Horace Andrews."

Mark Hanna's methods were to those of Horace Andrews as quicksilver is to winter molasses.   He knew it and he knew that I knew it.   He gave me one look and delivered himself vigorously of two words by way of reply.   I understood his language.   I am quite sure those differences he spoke of haven't been adjusted to this day.

I sold all my Cleveland street railway interests in 1894 and 1895 and never afterwards had any pecuniary connection with street railroads in that city.

X

THE LESSONS OF MONOPOLY

THE thing I have referred to as my civic consciousness was deepening. My congressional experiences had confirmed me in my belief that political corruption was a secondary symptom and political remedy but an opiate which might disguise the symptom for an hour, or a day; that crime and vice and misery were for the most part consequences of involuntary poverty, and involuntary poverty the result of law-made privilege whereby some men get more than they earn while the vast mass of mankind earns more than it gets. More and more I realized that it was the existence of this legalized privilege in society which creates a Riverside drive in New York, a Lake Shore boulevard in Chicago, a Euclid avenue in Cleveland, and at the same time an East Side in New York, a Canal street in Chicago and a slum district in Cleveland.

I was thinking a lot about these things by the time I left Congress and my business associates commenced to complain of my philosophy, saying it was at variance with their interests, and that to put it into operation would hurt them. This feeling gradually extended from friends and immediate associates to an ever enlarging group, gathering bitterness as it spread until the time came when I was looked upon as a public enemy by Big Business.*

* Appendix.

The attitude of the Cleveland Chamber of Commerce while I was mayor clearly illustrates this. My position on any question was all they had to know about it to determine what stand they should take. If I was for it, they were against it. If I was against it, they were for it. But this never troubled me. When I started out in my fight against Privilege I saw the road I had to travel, the obstacles I should have to overcome, the personal abuse I should encounter. These things and more I foresaw and they all came along on scheduled time.

In the meantime my own business enterprises were growing though I was seriously thinking of getting out of all of them. Our rail-mill at Johnstown becoming inadequate for our increasing business we decided to enlarge it and add blast-furnaces and blooming-mills thus making it a complete steel plant beginning with the ore and ending with the finished rail. There wasn't room for so much expansion in Johnstown, nor was that the best point for assembling raw material and distributing the finished product. The improved blast-furnace practice had carried the economic point of assembly nearer to the mines, so the lake region now had the advantage over Pittsburgh as a place of location for such industries as ours.*

Our experts reported the largest tract of land and the best harbor available at Lorain, Ohio, so we purchased there seven square miles at the mouth of the Black river. This gave us ample space for the mill and left plenty of land to be influenced by increased values.

We built the mill in terrifically tight times and had been running about a year and a half when the Federal Steel Company, the present United States Steel, was be-

* Appendix.

ginning to be formed. Our financial embarrassment was so great that we sold out to the Federal, but too early to reap the large benefit, later developments showing that a year's delay would have meant many millions more of profit.*

In addition to our land speculation, we built a street railroad ten miles long from Lorain to Elyria, and we retained both the land and the railroad when we sold the mill.

My brother Albert and R. T. Wilson of New York, a man high up in the business and financial world, had purchased the street railways of Detroit, an old broken-down horse car system with a few worn-out electrically equipped cars. When I was defeated for Congress they knew I would soon be free for business again and came to me with a proposal that I undertake the management of this road on a profit-sharing basis. I didn't want to do it, told them I was thinking of quitting business, but they insisted. What finally induced me to accept was not so much the pecuniary reward which the undertaking promised, as the chance to build unhampered by lack of funds a modern street railroad in a growing city. This looked like something worth doing. I consented to it on certain conditions and that enterprise was the beginning of a second plunge into big business undertakings.

Hazen S. Pingree was mayor of Detroit and though I had never met him I admired him greatly. He was promoting a three-cent-fare line for the city through Henry Everett, one of my old enemies. Privilege was putting up a fight against Pingree which in its essential features

* Appendix.

was much the same as the fight I was to encounter later as mayor of Cleveland.

I stipulated to Mr. Wilson and my brother that I was not to be expected to try to defeat the mayor's three-cent-fare project except by improved facilities on our lines; that is, I was to so remodel our railroad that it should have the advantage on its merits, rather than to go before the city council and engage in a scramble and put a lot of obstacles in the way of the Everett grant. Neither the mayor nor Mr. Everett knew anything of this agreement of course. The latter had no reason to expect any quarter from me in any contest, and there were plenty of influences at work to prejudice Mayor Pingree against me. The newspapers added to this prejudice by saying that I was coming to Detroit to hypnotize him and nothing made him so mad as that.

His attitude at our first meeting was very hostile. When he had stated two or three ultimatums of street railway policy to which I agreed he was greatly surprised but still skeptical. As we proceeded to tear up old tracks and rebuild the road complying with the mayor's suggestions as to construction, doing the very things the city had been unable to compel the former owners to do and asking no favors in return the mayor commenced to melt a little. We spent six million dollars in cash on that railroad and the result was the best electrically equipped street railroad in existence anywhere. The credit for this was largely due to A. B. du Pont, the engineer in charge. Mr. du Pont is a son of my early employer Bidermann du Pont.

When some of the councilmen who were known to be friends of the old system — the one purchased by Mr.

Wilson and my brother and comprising all the lines then in existence — told the mayor I had advised them to vote with him for the three-cent grant and had advised against imposing any hardship on Everett and his friends, he was thoroughly mystified.

When we met he asked me in his frank manly way to explain my attitude. I told him the city needed additional street railway facilities, it was evident our company couldn't get any concessions and that the new company ought to have them; that my reason for wanting the grants made to the new company on as fair a basis as possible was purely selfish, for it would be only a question of time until the old company would acquire them. To impose unfair conditions in the new grants would be simply putting burdens on our own backs when these lines came to be absorbed by ours.

This amused the mayor and he called my attention to a provision in the grant which said that if the new company should consolidate with or sell out to the old the grant became void. I replied that notwithstanding that provision or any other they could frame into words nothing could prevent us from acquiring the other railroad. This rather staggered Mr. Pingree and in his childlike way he said,

" Mr. Johnson, explain that to me, won't you? "

" I will not consolidate with the new company or make any attempt to buy," I answered, " but some day I will have a friend of mine down in New York or West Virginia or somewhere else, whom I shall call Smith for convenience, acquire the stock of the railroad by purchase; and, Mr. Mayor, if you attempt to put in a provision to prevent my Smith or some other Smith from doing this, you will simply defeat your own ends, for railroad stocks to be useful must be saleable."

It gradually dawned on him that he didn't have much safety in his safeguard provision and he said to me then what he said to me many, many times afterwards,

" I have here a clean sheet of paper. You tell me how to write this grant so that you can't get it."

I said there was only one way and that was for the city to acquire the three-cent line, own and operate it; then we could neither consolidate, purchase nor have Smith purchase it. All my subsequent observation and experience have not enabled me to work out any better answer than that. The mayor said that though he believed in municipal ownership he was doubtful of the powers conferred by the state laws in this direction and he feared the inauguration of such a project would arouse the opposition of the business interests and defeat it.

The city gave Everett the grant. Everett built the road. We completed remodeling the old lines before his was done and when he operated for three cents we did the same. We weren't in need of money. Our enterprise was financed and we could stand the contest. Everett had yet to raise the money for his project. It was a foregone conclusion that with our better laid-out system our line would first cripple, then acquire the three-cent road. In eight months this was accomplished and I announced it to the mayor one day by inviting him to take a ride in a private trolley-car and telling him, at the moment we stepped onto the car on the Everett line, that this property had just passed into the hands of a friend of mine named Smith.

We at once raised the fare on the old lines, the three-cent fare continued on the other and to this day these two lines are operated with two rates of fare. It has never been possible to raise the fare on the three-cent lines.

It was Mayor Pingree's promotion of that three-cent-fare line for Detroit that first impressed me with the practicability of this rate of fare. The company's loss is so slight compared to the gain to the public that where the traffic is dense people should insist upon the lower fare.

Before I got through with the Detroit enterprise Pingree and I became warm friends. One night after a supper together in my room we talked for a long time over our cigars. An ordinance was pending granting our lines a double track privilege where there was now a single track. He said,

" Of course, Johnson, I'm going to veto that ordinance if it passes; but I don't know why. The people out that way all want it; it seems like a necessary improvement, but I'm against it. I wish you'd tell me what's wrong with it."

I said there wasn't much wrong with it, but that if I were a member of the city council I'd see Tom Johnson in the hot place before I'd vote for it. Next day at a committee meeting Pingree made a speech against the ordinance and when he said, " If I tell you what a man said to me last night not one of you will dare to vote for this measure," I suspected what was coming. He repeated my exact words and appealed to me to verify them, which of course I did. The ordinance didn't get a vote, not one.

If anybody but Pingree had done that I should have resented it. He hadn't promised not to use my words against me, but I never dreamed that he would.hold me up to public ridicule in that fashion. Yet I couldn't resent it in him. He said afterwards that he was in a mighty tight place and that he had to do it because he didn't know what else to do.

Later I coöperated with him in trying to sell the whole street railway system to the city. Popular clamor and opposition to Pingree defeated this. It was claimed that the price was too high and that I was getting the advantage of the mayor. The public did not know that I had agreed to reduce the cost to the city by such share of the purchase price as would come to me as my profit. It would have been useless to tell this. Nobody would have believed it. I suppose there are people who will not believe it now. But the citizens later had the humiliation of seeing the property which our company had offered to the city for fifteen millions sold to other private interests for twenty-five millions. Then Detroit realized the chance it had missed and couldn't avoid seeing that I was more interested in municipal ownership than I was in personal profits — a fact that Pingree knew all the time. But any attempt on our part to have made the public believe this would have brought ridicule upon us, so I allowed myself to be misunderstood.

Pingree was charged with being a political boss, but he wasn't one, for a political boss is a man whose word is his capital and it must be absolutely good. Pingree was a political idol. He was always in a fight and always on the popular side. Thoroughly honest and trustworthy except when he was in a political contest, then as he said of himself he never hesitated to promise the same place to more than one man. Once before a whole roomful of

HAZEN S. PINGREE

people he stated that he was out of ammunition, for he had promised every job at least twice.

After Pingree became Governor I twitted him once on one of his public messages, saying:

" That's a nice message, that is! There isn't a democratic line in it." Instantly he came back with this:

" Well, I'll have you know I'm a Republican Governor."

At another time when someone complained that the Governor had advanced different arguments on the same public question on two different occasions, he replied:

" You are the most unreasonable damn fool I ever saw. Of course the second argument isn't like the first one, but I'll have you understand I've changed secretaries in the meantime."

One of the last things Pingree did was to collaborate in the writing of a book about the Boer War which he dedicated to me. It was never published, but the manuscript with his inscription was sent to me after his death.

XI

MORE LESSONS OF MONOPOLY

WHILE they were still interested in Detroit, my brother, with Mr. Wilson and some others, acquired the Nassau street railroad franchise in Brooklyn, N. Y. I had nothing to do with this at first, but all concerned in the ownership wanted me to take an active part in the management and as soon as I was somewhat free from pressing matters in Detroit I joined them.

A very troublesome suit was pending in which it was charged that a lot of Brooklyn councilmen had made this Nassau grant ostensibly in good faith, but in reality to someone who represented them. The enterprise was taking on such proportions that it was well worth while to employ the most skillful legal talent obtainable, and our people engaged Samuel B. Clark and Elihu Root as their attorneys. Joseph H. Choate was later called in to assist them.

After the case had been well worked up by these lawyers, Albert Johnson and Mr. Wilson, the prospective purchasers, put the whole thing up to me for a decision. In view of the fact that the grant was clouded and that litigation was likely to continue for some time would I advise them to make the investment? I replied that I would; that few street railroad grants were free from crookedness, but to prove the case was another matter. I didn't believe it could be proved, so my advice was to build. Mr. Root's characteristic comment on this, I remember, was, " No matter what the decision, Johnson, you can't avoid being either a good prophet or a good adviser."

The case was dropped after the first court decision against the politician who had brought the suit, and in the meantime work on the railroad was progressing. Before finishing its own line the Nassau acquired the Atlantic avenue system and established the first five-cent fare from Brooklyn Bridge to Coney Island. Previous to this the fare had been about twenty-five cents. The five-cent fare was really the beginning of the great popularity of Coney Island and it changed the character of its patronage. People who had been accustomed to go there three or four times in a season, now went several times a week and took their families. The crowds steadily increased, and five-cent lunches became more popular than seventy-five-cent dinners.

At this time there were four surface street railroads in Brooklyn, the Brooklyn Rapid Transit being the largest, the Nassau system next. In addition to these surface lines there were an elevated road and a municipally owned and operated line on Brooklyn Bridge. The municipal line was a mile and a half long from the Park Row terminal on the New York side to the Brooklyn terminal near the business center of the city. The fare for this mile and a half was two and a half cents. This was the first case of municipal ownership of a city transportation line in this country and was the most efficient so far as the public was concerned of any line in existence before or since.

The management was vested in the Bridge authorities

appointed by the two cities. Now here was a commission appointed by two notoriously corrupt city governments yet performing its various duties with absolute fidelity to the public. Why? Because the enterprise was operating under the daily observation of the persons most interested in it. Between a privately operated enterprise and one publicly operated the people will always insist upon a higher degree of efficiency in the latter. This was strikingly illustrated in the case of the Municipal Traction Company's operations in Cleveland a few years later. The people soon become disheartened and give up the fight in trying to get good service from a private company.

And between two public enterprises, one under the eye of the people and the other removed from their observation, the one they have closest contact with will be held to higher standards. For example, witness the placid indifference with which the ordinary citizen regards a one hundred thousand dollar robbery of customs receipts, and by contrast his virtuous wrath if by chance his postman happens to be late three days in succession. He doesn't mind being robbed indirectly and at long range, but he *will* have his mail delivered at the same time each day or know the reason why. What's the postoffice for anyway?

The history of the city ownership and operation of those tracks on the Brooklyn Bridge if properly studied will completely answer the objections raised by opponents of municipally owned and managed street railways.

The cheapest fare between New York and any part of Brooklyn at this time was seven and one-half cents, the city getting two and one-half, as has been stated, and the sur-

face lines five cents, though to any of the suburbs of
Brooklyn it cost more than that.

The Nassau people urged the building of a surface line
across the Bridge on the roadway, giving two surface
tracks in addition to the two elevated tracks already in
use. All four of the surface car systems wanted to cross
the bridge if any one of them was going to do so and
they chose me to represent them in an effort to get a franchise. I was instructed to procure a franchise for not less
than twenty years. I made my application to the Bridge
authorities. They said they would not think of granting
a franchise for more than ten years at the longest.

I reported. All the companies except ours demurred.
The others hesitated about spending so much money for
so short a grant. I told them I would try again, but that
I felt it was so important to get a five-cent fare into operation between New York and Brooklyn in view of the
rapid growth of the latter city, that I was in favor of accepting the ten-year grant. I was accordingly instructed
to go ahead and get it; but when I had my next interview
with the Bridge officials they said they had changed their
minds and didn't think they cared to make a grant for
so long a time as ten years. I went back to my people
then and reported that for my own company I was going
to take anything I could get; that if the grant was a public benefit it would continue; if it wasn't it ought to end.
I don't think the last argument made much impression on
them, but the prospect of seeing our cars running over
the bridge with a through fare of five cents, while passengers from all other lines would have to change at the
bridge and pay seven and one-half cents did, and it moved

them to agree to take for their companies anything I could get for ours.

Of course I wasn't very particular whether they moved or stayed. A grant that would take us over and leave them behind wouldn't be a bad thing for the Nassau. Finally on behalf of the four companies I accepted a grant that could be terminated by telephone or other message from the Bridge authorities. This grant, which we sometimes referred to as our " ten minute franchise," was really just as good a grant as any company ought to have, and in this case it proved very lucrative, although it destroyed the city's street railroad, which property was finally operated by the Elevated Company. The real weakness in the city's case was that it had already given away all the surface road and elevated rights in Brooklyn. If all these facilities could have been operated by the city by the same efficient public management that had prevailed on the Bridge for so long, a most admirable municipal system would have been the result.

The surface tracks were laid across Brooklyn Bridge and completed December 18, 1897, and my brother Albert ran the first car over them on the last night of that year.

In 1898 E. H. Harriman became interested in acquiring the Nassau property. He was not so large a steam railroad operator at that time and really wanted the Nassau road for the Brooklyn Rapid Transit Company. He was chosen as the expert negotiator for his side and I served in the same capacity for ours. We had a long and bitter contest and the result many times appeared very doubtful. I got to know him very well and our relations, though hostile at first, became more than friendly

MORE LESSONS OF MONOPOLY 103

and led to Mr. Harriman's suggesting more than once that
I join him in a wider field.

The final scene in these negotiations is worth describing,
as it illustrates so admirably the degree of confidence in
which large business interests hold each other. There
were seven main holdings representing the Nassau and its
purchases and each of these in turn was split up among
various ownerships. It was necessary to change the personnel of many boards of directors and to change the
character of many kinds of securities, and if a hitch should
occur in any of these steps it would prove very embarrassing. Nobody had sufficient confidence in anybody
else to allow this to be done by piecemeal. It had to be
done all at once or not at all.

After months of negotiation a time was fixed for the
transfer of the property, the delivery of certified checks,
stocks and bonds, the reorganization of many boards of
directors, changes of officers and many important transactions that had to be done ostensibly in a certain sequence
of time, but in reality instantaneously on account of the
total lack of confidence among the distinguished gentlemen involved in the enterprise.

A room in the Empire Building was engaged for the
day or as much longer as it should be needed. Banks
and trust companies had been notified. All securities and
certified checks had been previously presented to and
initialed by the party who was to receive them, so that in
the final exchange this work of verification was saved.
Representatives of the banks and trust companies, the
lawyers of the various interests, the numerous boards of
directors, the delegates generally of the enterprises involved, and a handsome important-looking man named

Vorhees, were finally all assembled in this one room. Here around a great circular table sat the leaders of the seven interests with their associates grouped back of them, — as fine a band of pirates as ever cut a throat or scuttled a ship.

Much time was lost in the last three hours in settling an unforeseen dispute which arose late in the proceedings. Finally the lawyers announced that all was ready. Then there was a sort of roll call in which all papers which were to be exchanged were called aloud and checked off. This done, Mr. Vorhees suddenly became the most important figure in the room. Looking wise, saying nothing and knowing less, he executed a contract agreeing to buy all of this property, involving some thirty million dollars, and then another in which he sold everything he had just bought. He performed very much the office that a stock exchange does when it enables people to make big trades while concealing the identity of the principals and preventing their meeting, thus obviating possible litigation. He looked so handsome, his manner was so impressive and his compensation so moderate that I hesitate to apply a harsh name to him. Yet he was in truth a legal dummy. But he was important, fully as important and knew quite as much about what was taking place as the policeman who guarded the door. For the brief space of a few seconds Vorhees was the owner of a thirty-million-dollar property, but of course the door was locked. It was not locked because of Vorhees, but because of the high regard in which the gentlemen doing this business held each other. It had been announced that nobody would be permitted to leave the room until every interest had received and acknowledged what it was entitled to, and the announcement was accompanied by the locking of the doors.

The currents and counter-currents represented in that transaction were not known to any one person, certainly not to the brokers or to the lawyers. Nobody knew all the subdivisions of ownership. The way we did this business was the only practical way in which it could have been carried out.

No one had any interest now in what he had had, the whole interest centered on what he was to get. After the reorganization of the boards of directors, the selection of new officers for the various companies, the delivery of certified checks and securities, there was another roll call and each was asked, " Have you received what your interest is entitled to? " After everybody had answered in the affirmative the doors were opened and Mr. Vorhees departed with the thanks of his colleagues for his great courtesy and the masterful manner in which he had conducted the transaction.

For our securities I received quite a handful of certified checks of one hundred thousand dollars each in denomination. These I had previously presented at the bank to ascertain that they were genuine and all I had to do in the final accounting was to examine my own initials on them.

Banks and trust companies remained open long after midnight to receive our deposits and lock up our important papers. The transfer was now complete. Some of us knew what effect the transaction would have on certain stocks and improved our opportunities by judicious stock purchases the minute the stock exchange opened in the morning.

While I was interested with a lot of people who were accustomed to deal in rather big transactions, and during a time of great business depression, I received a call from Mr. Wilson one night long after midnight. He came to my room at the Waldorf in New York and asked me to forgive him for waking me, but said he was in a state of terrible depression and felt that he must have me talk to him and cheer him up. We chatted for some time on various topics and when I had finally succeeded in getting him into a more tranquil frame of mind, I asked him why he didn't give up business since it worried him so excessively. He was worth many millions and with his simple tastes couldn't spend his income.

"Yes, yes," he said, "I ought to stop business. I know it and I've tried it. My family seems to get some enjoyment out of life and I ought to. But I can't — not away from the office. I have stayed away for weeks at a time as a trial, and then I get so blue that I have to rush back. Then after I've been at the grind awhile I am overwhelmed with the awfulness of it all, as I was to-night when I had to come down here to see you."

"Well," I answered, "if you will play the game, you've got to take the thumps." He answered that he saw no relief in any course he could now take.

That incident set me to thinking seriously of my half-formed resolution to give up business. I asked myself whether it was possible if I continued in it that I should come to be possessed with the insanity of it as this unhappy old man was. Would it become a habit with me, like a drug? Would I find myself powerless to give it up, as the gambler is powerless to stay away from his games? I was young and strong and I dearly loved the stimulation that went with the fight. But I decided that I must get that stimulation some other way. I knew I "was as other men" and I foresaw that in the end business would control my destiny; that I should not rule it, but that it would rule me. No, much as I enjoyed the game, I wasn't willing to take the thumps, and having reached this decision I threw all my energies into my efforts to get out of the various things I was engaged in. This sounds easier than it was, and I never did get out entirely, but from the night of that old financier's visit I never lost sight of the fact that I must give up the money-making game. I retired from the Nassau and Detroit interests at about the same time, and it was within a few months of this that we sold the Lorain mill.

I was now prepared to devote myself to the advancement of the principles advocated by Mr. George. I wanted to see those principles put into practice. My temperament and training made it impossible for me to take up the academic promotion of the question, and my future activities were as greatly misunderstood and criticized by some of the doctrinaires of the George school, as by my political enemies. I "got it" both going and coming.

I understood pretty thoroughly the lessons which Privilege teaches before I took up the question on the other side; I had some idea of what the fight would cost me, but I embarked in this new field from purely selfish motives. I was seeking happiness and I chose the line of least resistance. All my public doings are to be accounted for in this way.

XII

ELECTED MAYOR OF CLEVELAND

CHANCE plays a much greater part in most men's lives than they are willing to admit. It was certainly chance that made me a monopolist, chance that put a copy of one of Henry George's books into my hands and opened my eyes to the great gulf that is fixed between the beneficiaries of Privilege and its victims, chance that sent me to Congress, chance that brought me into contact with Mayor Pingree and his three-cent-fare crusade, chance that sent old Mr. Wilson to my room at the Waldorf that winter night and caused me to give up the game of business for the game of life, and again it was chance that made me a candidate for mayor of Cleveland.

As soon as I had completed the sale of the Lorain steel plant and of the Nassau and Detroit street railways, my brother and his family and I, with my family, went to Europe to spend the summer. I came home to attend as a delegate the national Democratic Convention at Kansas City, where Mr. Bryan was nominated for the second time.

Knowing that I never accepted the " sixteen to one " doctrine some people were disposed to question the consistency and propriety of my support of Mr. Bryan in 1896, and to excuse it in 1900 on the ground that the money question was a dead issue.*   I worked with those

* Appendix.

108

who accepted Mr. Bryan's doctrine because I believed that the free silver fight was the first great protest of the American people against monopoly — the first great struggle of the masses in our country against the privileged classes. It was not free silver that frightened the plutocratic leaders. What they feared then, what they fear now, is free men. The money question was not a dead issue in 1900 and so long as Wall street interests dictate our financial policies the money question cannot die.

On January 8, 1901, I spoke at a Jackson Day banquet in the Kennard House, Cleveland, and announced that I was now practically free from business and intended to devote my life to politics. I said that I would not be a candidate for any office, but would fight in the ranks for the principles of democracy. A little more than a month later I was nominated for mayor. On February 1, a delegation of fifty Democrats called on me at my home and presented me with a petition signed by 15,682 names asking me to become a candidate. It would have been cowardly for me to refuse to run simply because I had publicly announced that I had no intention of doing so.

Harris R. Cooley was one of that delegation and made a speech. Mr. Cooley was the pastor of the Cedar avenue Disciple church of which I was a member, and together we had been through a church fight, in which the issue was the admission to membership of persons who had been baptized other than by immersion. It isn't necessary to state which side we were on. We carried our point.

When I became mayor it seemed the most natural thing in the world that I should appoint as director of charities this minister whom I had known so long and whom I knew to be so well qualified. Yet to this day and in the face of the international fame which Mr. Cooley won in his nine years' administration of Cleveland's correctional and charitable institutions I am sometimes asked how I happened to appoint a " preacher " to so important an office.

The newspapers so persistently called me " Tom L. Johnson of New York " then that it was seldom that even the smallest item of news in connection with my activities got into the papers without it being made to appear that I was simply pretending that Cleveland was my residence (although I had never missed voting there since my first race for Congress), and my interest in politics for other than personal reasons was scouted on all sides. First the newspapers insisted that I wanted to go to Congress again and when this finally had to be dropped because I refused to consider a nomination, then they were sure it was the United States Senate on which my ambitious eyes were fixed. How they did ring the changes on that! All the newspapers in Cleveland joined in circulating these reports.

I was by no means an acceptable candidate to all the Democrats, most of those holding office being especially opposed to me, and I supposed I would have to contest the nomination, but there were no other candidates and I was nominated at the Democratic primaries, February 19, 1901.

Some support doubtless came to me from partisan politicians who hoped that I would put a lot of money into the campaign. I had spent money very freely in my congressional campaigns, but now the Garfield Corrupt Practices Act was on the statute books. This law provided that no candidate should spend more than one-tenth of the yearly salary attached to the office for which he was running and further stipulated that he must make a public statement of his campaign expenses. I determined to observe this law in spirit as well as in letter and so made no indirect expenditures either. I never bought a lottery ticket, a ticket to any church or social gathering, I refused to subscribe to benefit funds, I didn't even give to beggars while I was running for office. Entering into this practice because I wanted to observe the limitations imposed by law, I found it worked so well that I made it a cast iron rule and adhered to it in all my subsequent campaigns, even after the Garfield law had been repealed.

This was high moral ground, adopted as I have shown, partly because it was necessary, partly because it was expedient. It was a bitter disappointment to those who had hoped that I would " open a barrel," as it was vulgarly styled by the newspapers. It was not until later, after my public work had developed in me a stronger sense of appreciation of political morality that I myself realized the importance of such standards in politics.

I am frequently asked by my friends, " Why did so and so change towards you?" mentioning someone who was with me in the early days of my political career and who later withdrew his support. To such I frequently reply that I think the change has been not so much in these others as in me. I did not feel so keenly about the spoils system at first, for example, though in the very beginning when a party of City Hall employés called upon me and asked me to promise, in exchange for their support, that I would continue them in their jobs if I were elected I declined to do so. When they asked me to pledge myself to dismiss all Republicans holding jobs, I answered that that was one thing I would make a promise about; I'd promise to agree to do nothing of the kind.

My platform declared against granting extensions of franchises to the street railroads at any fare higher than three cents, for public improvements and for equal taxation. Of course, what I wanted to convey to the people in my platform was what I have been trying to make them understand ever since, that the city with its privileges and its responsibilities is *their city,* that it is as much their home in the collective sense as the houses in which they live are their individual homes. As I had done when running for Congress, I proclaimed that it was my belief in Henry George's philosophy that had drawn me into politics.

Most of my time in the campaign was spent in the discussion of the street car question and the unjust appraisal of real property made in the summer of the year before and which, under the state law, was to stand for ten years. I promised the people that in the event of my election I would do everything in my power to right this great wrong.

Between grafting contractors and an unequal appraisal of property the evils of the unjust appraisal are much the greater. The graft of the contractor is practically insignificant. It includes a few conniving officials outside of the law; but an unequal appraisal of property for the purposes of taxation takes dollars out of the pocket of one citizen and puts them into the pocket of another and is larceny of the State for private graft.

There was some discussion also over the controversy

the city was having with the steam railroads over the possession of certain land on the lake front. As a citizen I had brought suit to prevent the then mayor, John Farley, from signing an ordinance passed by a crooked council settling the controversy and conveying the land in question to the railroads without compensation.

The founders of the city, wise in their day and generation, had set apart land on the lake front to be used as a public wharf and landing place for the commerce of the great lakes. In the 'forties the city had sold to the Pennsylvania and other steam railroads a strip of this ground then one hundred and fifty feet wide. The litigation which had been going on for years was over several hundred feet of " made land," the accretions to the strip the railroads had purchased, and on which the union depot and yards are located. The land was estimated to be worth from fifteen to twenty million dollars at the time I brought my suit to enjoin the city from settling and it has increased enormously in value since.

The people were deeply interested in this controversy and the fact that the Chamber of Commerce supported the settlement proposed by the Farley administration added to the existing feeling of outrage. The Chamber of Commerce, made up of fifteen hundred business men, has its policy determined by Big Business which controls this and similar institutions. In contests between the people and Privilege the Chamber of Commerce was with Privilege and against the people on every question which came up while I was mayor.

After I was nominated the *Plain Dealer,* an independent newspaper, supported me, dropping the cartoons which had so persistently pictured me as leaving the duties of the

mayor's office to someone else, and ceased calling me Tom
Johnson of New York. The *Press,* also independent,
gave fair news reports of my meetings and a lukewarm
editorial support, while the *Leader,* the regular Republican organ, opposed me bitterly.

I pursued the same methods I had employed in my
congressional campaigns, holding meetings in tents and
halls and always inviting questions from my auditors. I
challenged my Republican opponent, W. J. Akers, to debate with me or appoint someone to represent him in debate, but no attention was ever paid to this. Congressman Theodore Burton, true to his promise to devote some
time to the Republican committee, in case I should be the
Democratic nominee for mayor, came home from Washington to make speeches against me.

Cleveland was nominally a Republican city, but in municipal elections, party lines were usually shattered in the
interests of Privilege. There were Hanna Democrats as
well as Hanna Republicans — not that Hanna was the
enthroned boss in the same sense that Cox is the boss of
Cincinnati or Murphy of New York. Cleveland wasn't
bossed by any one man. The city government belonged
to the business interests generally, but as the public utility
companies had more use for it than the other kinds of
business enterprise had, they paid the most attention to it.
They nominated and elected the councilmen and of course
the councilmen represented them instead of the community.
The campaign funds came largely from business men who
believed in a " business man's government," and who
couldn't or wouldn't see that there was anything radically
wrong with the system. They were quite contented to

let a few agents of special privilege attend to the details of the city government. Nothing very shocking happened and the community was quiescent. And in that fact lay the danger. Nothing is so deadly as inertia. The greatest obstacle to overcome in any fight in which fundamental moral issues are involved is not opposition, but indifference. To be sure there were a few agitators who had raised the voice of protest upon occasion — there was Peter Witt, and before Peter, Dr. Tuckerman, who was responsible for Peter. When Cleveland shall ultimately have become a free city she will trace the beginnings of her struggle against Privilege back to the days when that kindly country doctor began to wage war on the established order.

The campaign grew more interesting and exciting daily, but Privilege wasn't especially aroused and made no particular fight. Indeed Big Business was rather friendly than otherwise. Some of its beneficiaries who had been associated with me in business were reported as giving their reason for favoring my candidacy " that here was a chance to get good government and a one hundred thousand dollar man for mayor at six thousand dollars a year." They looked upon it as a good bargain. Senator Hanna did not share this view. I have previously stated that I understood his language. He likewise understood mine, and though he sometimes applied to me such terms as " socialist, nihilist and anarchist," he was never one of those who professed to believe that I did not mean to do what I said I would do. From the beginning he regarded my election as dangerous and warned his friends against me. He was making a pretty fair guess at what good government in this instance would cost special privilege in general and his street railroad in particular, and he wasn't taking any chances.

In the last days of the campaign his street railway company attempted to rush a twenty-five year franchise through council. The city was up in arms against this and, though the Little Consolidated had the votes and the mayor was ready to sign, council didn't dare to pass the ordinance. So corrupt was the council and so great the storm occasioned by the proposal that even the Chamber of Commerce was forced to oppose it.

One night when I was so hoarse from continued speaking that I could not use my voice it occurred to me that here was my opportunity to attend a Republican meeting and hear for myself just what the opposition was saying. I arrived at the first meeting while Mr. Burton was speaking and the doorkeeper, recognizing me, refused to admit me, saying that he was acting under official orders, so I went to a second, where it happened there was no doorkeeper. I was accompanied by five friends and we walked in and took seats without being observed. Presently the chairman of the meeting saw me, stopped the speaker in the midst of his speech and requested me to leave the hall. I replied that I had supposed this was a public meeting, but if he wished me to go I would do so, having no desire to intrude. He answered that it was a *Republican* meeting and that he *did* wish me to leave. The instinct of the crowd is always for fair play under such circumstances and of course a great hubbub ensued. As I made my way to the door fully two-thirds of the audience, cheering and shouting, followed me into the street.

I was elected mayor of Cleveland April 1, 1901, receiving upwards of six thousand more votes than the Republican nominee. It should be remembered that Mr. Akers also stood on a three-cent-fare platform and that Cleveland has had no candidate for mayor on any ticket from that day to this who has not advocated three-cent fare or approximately that. A few Democratic ward councilmen were returned, but I was the only Democrat elected on the general ticket.

For some reason none of my enemies — not even the bitterest — ever charged that I would be inefficient. It seemed to be universally conceded that " I could if I would," but that " I wouldn't," was so insistently preached that it was curious that it didn't make more impression. Just as soon as I was elected all suggestion that I would go off to New York or anywhere else and leave the duties of my office to others was absolutely dropped by the Cleveland newspapers.

The law provided that the mayor-elect could take office as soon as he had qualified and it was customary to do so within two or three weeks after election. My injunction which prevented the city from executing the ordinance in the lake front case was to expire at eleven a. m., April 4, and I didn't propose to let precedent stand in the way of the best method of dealing with that matter. I therefore requested the members of the board of elections to work day and night in order that the vote might be canvassed before the expiration of the injunction. As soon as the official count of the votes was announced, therefore, at 10:23 a. m., April 4, *just thirty-seven minutes before the injunction expired,* I took the official oath in the office of the city clerk on the third floor of the City Hall, filed my bond at 10:30 and went directly to the mayor's office

on the floor below.   Mr. Farley looked up as I came in
and mumbled ungraciously:

"Well, Tom, when are you going to take hold?"

I replied that I hoped he would take his time about
moving his belongings, but that I had been mayor for several minutes.

One of the very early acts of my administration was
to cause the introduction of an ordinance in the council
repealing the ordinance of the Farley administration in
the lake front matter.   That case has been in the courts
practically ever since, but has recently been decided in the
city's favor by the court of common pleas and by the circuit court.   The supreme court of the State can hardly
fail to uphold the decision of the lower courts that the
city had no right to dispose of this land.   Eventually the
lake front will be used for the purposes to which it was
dedicated by the founders of the city, and this without
Privilege being able to exact tribute for its use.

When I was elected mayor Cleveland was operating
under what was known as the "federal plan" of city government.   For fifty years or more the cities of Ohio had
what amounted to special charters.   Though applicable in
terms to all the cities of the State (to comply with a requirement of the State constitution), each charter was,
nevertheless, so drawn as to affect only the city for which
it was intended.   To illustrate, cities of not less than
25,000 inhabitants, nor more than 25,250, might be put
in a specified class, and provisions then be made for the
government of all cities of that class.   Only one city, of
course, would come within the class.   It was a trans-
parent evasion of the constitutional prohibition of special

legislation, but for fifty years the courts had winked at or approved it.

Under this practice a charter for Cleveland was granted some ten years before which did away with all the antiquated and corrupting systems of board rule, and established the federal plan. The essential feature of this plan was its concentration of responsibility. Legislative functions were left to the city council, but the mayor was invested with all the executive functions, coupled with a legislative veto.

The mayor and the city councilmen were elected. The heads of the following named departments were appointed by the mayor: Law, public works, fire, police, accounts, charities, and they were known as directors of their respective departments. These directors, with the mayor, formed the board of control, commonly known as the mayor's cabinet. The system was an admirable one since it made the mayor responsible for the administrative government of the city. The power of appointment and removal of the directors was in his hands. It was a better system than any other city in the United States had at that time. If it had embodied the initiative and referendum and the recall it would have been superior to any system of city government now in operation in this country, in my opinion. The city council consisted of twenty-two members elected by districts and sitting in one body and responsible, as has been said, for the legislative part of the government.

On that first morning in the mayor's office I requested the directors of the various departments to continue in office until further notice. The director of public works said, " I ordered the May Company to tear down a storm-door on Ontario street and gave them until ten o'clock this morning to do it. They have ignored the order. What shall I do? "

" Take some policemen and tear it down yourself," I answered. That was my first informal order. I like to remember that my first formal official act was to sign a pardon for a man serving a workhouse sentence.

FREDERIC C. HOWE   WILLIAM J. SPRINGBORN

Two Republican councilmen who early identified themselves with the administration

XIII

THE CITY GOVERNMENT AND THE TAX SCHOOL

I FOUND a city council of eleven holdovers and eleven newly-elected members, twelve of whom were Republicans and ten Democrats. My first move was to organize those of both parties who regarded the public interest as of more importance than party, against the crooked Democrats and the crooked Republicans. Frederic C. Howe and William J. Springborn were two Republican members who at once identified themselves with the administration. Mr Howe soon joined us politically, but Mr. Springborn continued as a Republican for some time. I worked for his election as a Republican member of council the next year and later (after the State gave us a new municipal code which made the directors elective) for his nomination and election as a Republican on the Democratic ticket to the office of director of public works. I commenced at once to take advantage of weakened party lines and to do what I could to weaken them still further.

One of the first things which engaged my attention was the selection of my cabinet, and I made a good many mistakes in my earliest appointments. It was about a year before I really succeeded in getting an efficient set of directors.

There were innumerable matters calling for immediate consideration and I acted as quickly as possible in as many directions as I could. The secret of a good executive is this — one who always acts quickly and is sometimes right.

In less than a week after taking office I ordered uniformed policemen stationed at the doors of gambling houses and houses of prostitution having saloons in connection, and instructed them to take the names and addresses of all persons who entered. It makes a man mighty uncomfortable to go on record in this way, even if he gives a fictitious name and address. This method proved so successful as to the gambling houses that in a short time public gambling in Cleveland was practically abolished. I knew that we couldn't rid the city of the social evil any more than we could rid it of private gambling, but I was determined to permit no saloons in connection with houses of prostitution and to destroy the pernicious practice of the police of levying fines upon unfortunate women. It had long been the custom in Cleveland, as in other large cities, for the police to raid these houses and collect a lot of fines whenever the funds of the police court got low. This simply amounted to blackmail and hadn't the slightest effect in checking the evil, but rather stimulated it and gave rise to a horrible system of favoritism and extortion. I called my policemen together and told them that not a cent was to come into the city's hands by this method, that if the police court had to depend for revenue upon fines imposed in this manner, it would have to go without pay. Street soliciting by either sex was strictly prohibited.

You can't legislate men or women into being good, but you can remove artificial stimulants to make them bad. Cleveland's way of dealing with this problem during my administration compares very favorably, I believe, with the methods employed by any other American city. It became an established part of the policy of Chief Kohler — of whom more later — but the idea of placing a uniformed officer at the entrance to places of questionable repute did not originate with the chief or with me. It was a plan my father used while he was chief of police of Louisville, and he got it from Yankee Bly, a detective famous in Kentucky in the sixties and seventies.

I ordered a strict inspection of theatres and other public buildings, made immediate war on bill-boards and ordered old frame structures torn down, put a force of " white wings " to work cleaning up the down town streets, inaugurated steps looking towards a better lighting system, set the law department to hunting up expiring street railway franchises, moved to reduce water rents, had a contest with the Pennsylvania Railroad over the ownership of twenty-nine streets, looked after some city cases pending in the federal court, established a department examiner to keep an eye on all departments of the city government, took down the " Keep Off the Grass " signs in the parks, commenced to institute people's amusements in the parks and pardoned eleven out of fifteen applicants for pardon in the city workhouse.

I instituted a lot of changes at the City Hall, moving the health department from the third to the first floor, for one thing, so that a contagious disease patient wouldn't have a chance to infect others by his presence in the elevator or in the corridors.

I refused to sign city ordinances unless they were properly engrossed. I insisted that everybody who had anything to do should do it the best that it could be done, and altogether we were a pretty busy lot of workers. So many things seemed to demand attention at onçe that I had my hand on every department of the city government before I had been in office a month. Of course all these activities cost money and as there wasn't sufficient available money in sight, the usual howl of " extravagance " was raised. But I knew these things had to be done if we were to keep our promise to give good government and I went ahead and did them, trusting to devise a way to get the funds afterwards.

Under what is called economy in city government there is much foolish holding back of necessary public improvements. If fraud and graft are kept out there is not apt to be much unwisdom in public expenditures; and from the business man's standpoint the return for the original outlay is very large — even where debt is created within reasonable limits.

With anything like an equitable system of collecting the just revenues of a city, the cost of these improvements, if paid in the first instance by tax levy, would be wise. Good sanitary conditions, public parks, pure water, playgrounds for children and well paved streets are the best kind of investments, while the absence of them entails not only heavy pecuniary loss, but operates to the moral and physical deterioration of the city's inhabitants.

Limitation on taxes for public works is as foolish as limitation on increase in capital and plant of manufacturing enterprises. The question is not " how much do you spend? " but " how wisely do you spend it? " To economize on needed public improvements is worse than wasteful.

The generally accepted standard of values in this connection is all wrong. So obsessed have we become with the idea of property rights that we are constantly forgetting that in the last analysis we are dealing with men and women and children and not with things.

But to give " good government " in the ordinarily accepted sense of the term, wasn't the thing I was in public life for. It was a part of our policy from the beginning of our work in Cleveland, it is true, but as a side issue, merely. While we tried to give the people clean and well lighted streets, pure water, free access to their parks, public baths and comfort stations, a good police department, careful market inspection, a rigid system of weights and measures, and to make the charitable and correctional institutions aid rather than punish wrongdoers, and to do the hundred and one other things that a municipality ought to do for its inhabitants — while we tried to do all these things, and even to outstrip other cities in the doing of them, we never lost sight of the fact that they were not fundamental. However desirable good government, or government by good men may be, nothing worth while will be accomplished unless we have sufficient wisdom to search for the causes that really corrupt government. I agree with those who say that it is big business and the kind of big business that deals in and profits from public service grants and taxation injustices that is the real evil in our cities and the country to-day. This big business furnishes the sinews of war to corrupt bosses regardless of party affiliations. This big business which profits by *bad government* must stand against all movements that seek to abolish its scheme of advantage.

It was these fundamental wrongs that I wished to attack and one of my first acts as mayor was to establish a Tax School designed to show the inequalities in taxation.

Peter Witt was put in charge with Newton D. Baker (who afterwards became city solicitor) as legal adviser and with numerous assistants.

The constitution of Ohio says that all property shall be appraised at its true value in money and the statute carrying this provision into effect uses the same words.

Land and buildings were appraised once in ten years by appraisers elected in the wards of cities and the townships of counties. These appraisers were expected to complete their work in a ninety-day period of time. New buildings as they were erected were added to the tax duplicate by the city annual board of equalization appointed by the mayor, which board also took care of the personal property returns, and was clothed with power to change gross inequalities in appraisals of land made by the decennial appraisers.

Steam railroad property, both realty and personal, was appraised annually by the county auditors in the counties through which the railroads ran. These auditors sat as a board and convened in the largest city of the various counties which the railroads traversed. Auditors were elected by popular vote.

Outside of cities there were assessors appointed by the county auditors whose duty it was to appraise personal property annually.

This, briefly, was the system of taxation in operation when we started our Tax School.

The local taxing board, or board of equalization, appointed by previous mayors, was in the control of tax-dodgers. While it was really vested with great power this board had exercised that power principally in correcting clerical errors or in adding to the tax duplicate the value of additions to small property like painting houses or putting in bathtubs.

The steam railroads, as has been stated, were assessed by boards of county auditors in the counties traversed by the railroads.

Small taxpayers generally were paying full rates, while the public service corporations, steam railroads and large land-owning interests were paying between ten and twenty per cent. only of the amount required by law. More than half the personal property and nearly all the valuable privileges were escaping taxation.

At first our Tax School was maintained by private funds and had no legal connection with the city government, but those in charge of it were granted the use of city maps and were permitted to call upon employés of the civil en-gineer's department for help in connection with the maps. Witt was the first man I appointed and he objected to taking the position, but I would not take " no " for an answer.

The clerks employed first copied the records in the county auditor's office showing the assessed value of all lots and buildings in the city. From these records, on a map sixteen feet square and comprising one whole ward, we showed the inequalities in assessed values. Citizens in general and tax-payers in particular were invited to a large room in the City Hall, at one end of which this map was suspended. Pursuing this method by multiplying the number of maps the assessment of real estate block by block and ward by ward was shown. Discussion was invited, criticisms and suggestions asked for, and by means of this discussion, together with a searching investigation of the records of real estate transfers and leases, we ascertained the real value of one foot front of land by one hundred feet in depth, which method is known as the Somers unit system of taxation and without which no fair and accurate appraisal of land can be made.

When the unit values were finally agreed to they were written into the center of each block on the various maps. The members of the city board of equalization then signed the map making it thereby a public record showing the date on which the values had been agreed upon. Then a photographer made a picture of the map and negatives of this photograph were furnished the clerks who were at work in another room, and they, having the small maps before them showing the individual ownerships and the photographic record of the unit values, worked out and wrote into each space provided on these small maps, the actual cash value of each particular piece of land and the assessed value as well. The total number of sub-divisions of land in Cleveland was one hundred and one thousand and the assessed values varied from two per cent. of to sixty-eight per cent. above the actual or market value.

We were not satisfied with getting this information to the persons who visited the Tax School. We wanted to reach every tax-payer in the city with it. So the Tax School issued a circular letter to the people of each ward, which letter set forth the cash value of all land in Cleveland, the appraised value of all land in Cleveland, the cash value of all land in that particular ward, likewise its appraised value, then the number of parcels assessed at *less* than the average value in the ward, citing the best known pieces as a concrete illustration; then the number of parcels assessed at *more* than the average value and again using the best known piece as the illustration of this point.

The city board of equalization, already referred to, was a municipal institution of long standing. Its members were appointed by the mayor. It was these members who signed the map in the Tax School and it was this board which would have corrected the inequalities in taxation *had not the State legislature wiped it out by legislative enactment,* and provided in its stead a board of review appointed by State officials.

This board of review was paid from county funds for a purely municipal service. To this board we sent the names of all owners and the description of their property which was under assessed. To the people we sent the letter already mentioned and requested all those whose property was over assessed to seek their remedy from the board of review.

So far as I know this was the first intelligent and concerted effort to relieve the people of Ohio of the injustice of the privilege in taxation which had been a decennial bone of contention in the State for eighty years.

By this time the Tax School was operating as a part of the city machinery, council having made an appropriation for its maintenance. The greatest of all privileges is the privilege of having another man pay your taxes and the beneficiaries of this unjust taxation could not stand our agitation, so on October 8, 1902, W. J. Crawford, the Republican boss, and a large property owner, brought suit to enjoin the expenditure of city money in this manner.

The case was carried through the courts, the temporary injunction was made permanent and the Tax School was eventually forced to suspend. However, it had now been in operation twenty months and its work could not be undone. Not only was it instrumental in making public service corporations pay sixty thousand dollars a year more in taxes, but, fearing the result of a tax fight, these same corporations made a secret settlement of back taxes at the end of his term with county auditor Craig who was their friend, by paying into the county treasury more than one hundred thousand dollars of back taxes.

The following year in my campaign for Governor of Ohio we dug out the inequalities in taxation in every city in which my tent was pitched and by the use of a stereopticon we showed not only the inequalities existing in Cleveland but gave many local illustrations as well.

Important changes in the State tax laws may be traced to the work of the Tax School. Land and buildings are now appraised separately for taxation and the old decennial appraisement has been replaced by a quadrennial appraisement and these quadrennial boards of appraisement, consisting of five members, are elected locally and at large without party designation.

Results thus far obtained more than justify the publicity methods which we employed to direct the attention of an indifferent public to this all important question of taxation.

The question of taxation was no less a State question than a local one. Indeed our whole Cleveland movement was more than local, more than a one city movement from the very beginning. The big lesson we started out to teach through the Tax School and in other ways was that taxation in all its forms, however designated, is merely the rule by which burdens are distributed among

individuals and corporations. Farms, buildings, personal
property, land, pay no taxes, yet so persistently have these
inanimate objects been spoken of as being taxed that the
public has all but lost sight of the fact that it is men
and women who are taxed and not things. So long and
so universally has taxation been regarded as a fiscal system
only that comparatively few people recognize it for what
it is, viz.: a human question.

XIV

HOW RAILROADS RULE

AN early opportunity to take aggressive measures on the subject of railroad taxation presented itself. The county auditors' board met in Cleveland in May, 1901, for the purpose of making a valuation of steam railroads whose roads ran through Cleveland and Cuyahoga county. I invited Professor E. W. Bemis, an expert on the valuation of public service corporations and the only such expert on the people's side, to come on from New York where he was then located, and assist us in arriving at the true valuation of these properties. I attended the meeting of the auditors and insisted on being heard.

We had to get at the real tax valuation of the railroads running through Cleveland. Time and again I took Professor Bemis before the auditors. Our desire was to get them to place at least a sixty per cent. valuation upon these properties. As a rule they placed their assessment of railroad properties in exact accordance with the return given them by the auditors and land tax agents of the various railroads who made the returns on their respective properties at fifteen to twenty per cent. of their market value.

I attended a great many of these auditors' meetings, trying to force them to put up the valuation to something like that which had been placed upon the property of

EDWARD W. BEMIS

"An expert on the valuation of public service corporations, and the only such
expert on the people's side."

small householders and other people. I frequently asked them to give me just a few minutes of their time, while my experts showed them how inadequately they were adjudging these valuations, and on one occasion went before the court in mandamus proceedings to compel them to give me a hearing.

I remember saying at one time in the discussion over the Cleveland Terminal & Valley Railroad, "I charge this fact, that railroad companies by distributing favors and passes are getting off with paying from about six or seven per cent., to about fifteen per cent. on their properties, while other property owners are taxed on the basis of a sixty per cent. valuation or higher."

The railroads always had a claim agent or lawyer present at auditors' meetings to swear in their "valuation." I often asked the auditors and the representatives of the railroads: "Is there any reason why railroads should be assessed differently from farm and home property?" but I never got an answer. On one occasion I said, "How do you auditors arrive at a valuation of five thousand five hundred dollars a mile for this railroad property? I claim that instead of being appraised at five thousand five hundred dollars a mile it should be appraised at one hundred and six thousand dollars a mile."

Auditor William Craig said: "Mr. Johnson, our members were not prepared for this. I think we had better postpone the hearing until to-morrow."

Then the claim agent for the "Valley Railroad," remarked: "Yes, we should have twenty-four hours, at least."

"You have had twenty-four years," I retorted, but they took their twenty-four hours.

In the case of the Cleveland Belt & Terminal Railroad, Colonel Myron T. Herrick, afterward Governor of Ohio, then chairman of the railroad's board and its receiver, was present when the auditors were about to pass upon the valuation of the road. The road's written return placed the property at nineteen thousand six hundred and fifty-five dollars. J. E. Taussig, the assistant general manager of the Wheeling & Lake Erie, which owns the Belt Line, in handing over the report, said, " That's all we have to say."

Then I spoke up and told the auditors that this road was sold for four hundred thousand dollars. " You will remember, Myron," I said, turning to Colonel Herrick, " how you and I tried to buy it about five years ago for five hundred thousand dollars, and we thought that was dirt cheap. And it hasn't depreciated any since then, has it? "

" It isn't earning anything," answered Colonel Herrick.

" Well," I said, " the law says that property shall be assessed for what it is worth, not for what it is earning, and it is worth just what it will sell for."

I then called upon one of my assistants who said that he had walked over the entire length of the road, measured the width of the right of way, and ascertained the value of the adjoining property. I then called upon another assistant, an engineer, who testified that he had measured the earth-work of the embankment of the road, and had estimated the worth of trestles, bridges, rails, etc.

" Now then," I said to the auditors, " we demand of you that you assess this road at sixty per cent. of its actual value. If you assess it at nineteen thousand dollars, as this railroad asks you to do, and as it has been assessed in the past, you are taking money out of the pockets of the people and putting it into the pocket of the railroad, just as much as though you went out on the street with a club and robbed a man."

At this point Assistant Manager Taussig interrupted to say that my assistant's figure as to the number of acres was nearly twenty acres too high.

" All right," I said, " if you acknowledge fifty acres, we'll stand on that. Honestly, now, do you think nineteen thousand dollars is what this road ought to be returned for? "

" Based on its earnings, yes. You wouldn't buy anything that wasn't earning anything, would you? "

" My dear sir, that is the way I have made all my money — buying things that other people didn't know how to handle."

" You wouldn't buy this for what you claim it was sold for, four hundred thousand dollars — ? "

" Yes, I will."

" That's a bluff."

" Is it a bluff? I will make a big cash deposit right here and take this road for four hundred thousand dollars."

" You know this road is in such shape legally that it can't be sold," interrupted Colonel Herrick.

" And you wouldn't sell it for anything like four hundred thousand dollars if that were not the case."

At this point the railroad's attorney spoke up:

" All this is nonsense and politics."

" Politics? " I answered. " Of course it is politics. It is the kind of politics with which all the people of Cleveland — Democrats and Republicans — are in sympathy. They want to see these railroads pay their just share of the taxes, and they look to me, as the mayor of all the people, to do my utmost to see that it is done. That's what we are here for, sir; we present figures and facts, and we challenge you to review them. You don't try. You can't. You run away. You say you only ask that you be assessed as other railroads are assessed; that you have precedent in your favor. Yes, you have precedent and you have the votes; you have the county auditors; you have the auditor of this county."

It was also at this meeting that I called upon Auditor Craig for some definite information about the bonds of this road, and he replied, " That was before my time."

" I expected that answer," I said. " That is what they all say. I have been here often, and I have seen roads assessed at fifteen to twenty per cent. of their value. I understand that the auditor of this county believes that railways should be assessed the same as farm lands, which is at sixty per cent. of their value. I want to know what the auditor will do, and what his method of assessment will be."

The auditor answered: " I don't know that I can tell that, or that I would care to."

" Your answer is satisfactory. I am going to prove that you auditors simply guess. You don't know whether or not you are buying a gold brick."

In regard to the hearing before the auditors about the Nickel Plate road, I protested every inch of the way. When their attorney, who was present as the representative of the road, returned the value upon which the Nickel Plate road was to be taxed, I took their return and showed where the report was dishonest. It listed twenty-six first-class passenger locomotives in fair condition at one thousand five hundred and fifty-five dollars apiece; sixty-six first-class freight locomotives in fair condition at two thousand five hundred and nine dollars apiece. I charged that that was not fifteen per cent. of their real value.

" Here," I said, " are six thousand box cars at one hundred and forty dollars apiece. We all know one hundred and forty dollars would not pay for half a truck under one end of one of these cars. Now I ask you again to call on this company to appear before you and explain."

" Now, gentlemen," I went on, " the market value of the bonds and stocks of the Nickel Plate company is about forty million dollars. As about forty-six per cent. of the road is in Ohio, it has over seventeen million dollars worth of property in this State. The law says you shall assess property at its full value in money and that includes railroads, but as you have adopted a rule to assess property at only sixty per cent. of its value, I ask you to apply that rule in this case. If you apply this rule of sixty per cent., the Nickel Plate road will pay on about ten million dollars instead of three million dollars in Ohio as it has been doing and wants to continue to do."

Then Auditor Craig called the other auditors into executive session and the attorney, who seemed to know how the vote would go, said: " Now we will see."

I answered, " Oh, you've got the votes of this board of auditors all right, but you haven't got the last say. We will put this matter up to the State board of railroad equalization at Columbus, and if it does not do the right thing we will put it up to the courts. And if we don't get a square deal there, we will put it up to the voters of Ohio. The people will take this matter up finally and then the railroads will be brought to time."

So thoroughly under the control of the railroads was this board of auditors that the railroad's return was accepted. The result of all this demonstration was that the auditors raised the valuation of the road over what it was the year before less than one per cent.!

I put detectives on the trail of the auditors to find out exactly what relations they held with the railroad companies, but knowing they were watched, they did nothing more criminal than dine with the railroad's representatives and ride on passes. Frequently I tried to get them to let me address them, but they always voted me down. I got out a mandamus to force them to put railroad officials on the stand and make them swear under oath to the actual valuation which they returned in their tax lists.

When I asked for information, half a dozen auditors remarked, "Oh, pay no attention to him!"

I began to laugh and just then the sheriff arrived with the writ of mandamus and served it on the auditor.

"Get on to the grandstand play of this accidental mayor," shouted an auditor named Sissler. "Let's see what he's got."

After he saw what I had, he announced, "I guess we've got to stop."

"That's the first chance I've had," I said.

"Yes, and it's all you will get," said Sissler. "We're sick and tired of this ——— nonsense."

"So am I. Why don't you stop it?" I answered.

After this long session with these men I said to them:

"Gentlemen, you have succeeded in keeping the railroad taxes just where they were. You have but dammed up the courses that will eventually sweep over you. The time will come when you will be sorry."

I carried this question to the people in two very aggressive State campaigns and always into the State conventions of the Democratic party. I showed the methods by which the railroads controlled county auditors. Railroad land agents were very active in nominating conventions before elections; and after election, in addition to giving auditors and their friends passes it was no uncommon thing for them to take auditors and their families to the seashore for the summer. These abuses were so evident and met with such universal condemnation when I called attention to them that a great many auditors fell into line, promised to be "good" and stood on our platform. It was noticeable, however, that we rarely found a majority of our friends on any auditors' board.

We appealed for a public hearing to the State board of equalization, composed of the Governor and several other State officers, which board had power to equalize the returns of the county auditors.

I took Professor Bemis and Attorney Newton D. Baker with me to Columbus to participate in this hearing.

This board tried to hide behind the statute. It claimed that it could do nothing in the way of raising the assessment on the railroads, saying that the county auditors levied the assessment and that all that the State board was for was to handle matters of "equalization."

"Well," said Mr. Baker, "suppose that the county auditors for some reason failed to return a road at all. What then?"

"We couldn't do a thing," answered the chairman.

"Suppose that they return a road for a valuation so low as to be ridiculous, and on its face not one hundredth part of what it should be taxed. What then?"

"We would not be able to do anything," protested the chairman. "The statute says we shall equalize the values as returned by the county auditors."

The total taxes to be paid by a railroad are divided among the several counties according to the railroad mileage therein. This often gives an agricultural county more taxes than a county in which there is a city where the railroad's valuable terminals are located.

"Whether the plan of assessing railroad property by the mile is constitutional," I said, "is a matter that the lawyers will have to decide. Certainly no man will say that it is just. It's true that it benefits the rural counties in that it gives them money they are not entitled to — money that rightfully belongs to the counties in which are located the large cities. It was by that species of argument and powerful lobbies that the railroads secured the enactment of the law establishing this system. I am not here to attack that statute because it benefits the rural counties, but to complain because the boards of county auditors have failed in the performance of their sworn duties, and thereby robbed not only the counties in which are located the large cities but those in which our rural brethren live as well."

"Perhaps the auditors did not know any better," suggested Attorney General Sheets.

"Perhaps they didn't," I replied, "but those who met at Cleveland could not offer such an excuse. We told them better, and we didn't ask them to take our word for it, either.   We asked them to call in the railroad officials and demand their books and see for themselves, and we ask this board to do the same.   We do not ask you to accept our statements alone.   We have pointed out the facts and have told you how you can find them for your-selves.   I think the boards of county auditors combined are very much like other public bodies.   Some of the men are honest, some are fools and some are rascals.   I do not know of a public body that is constituted otherwise, from the Senate of the United States down.

"Now suppose this board," I said, turning to Mr. Sheets, "refuses to equalize these appraisements by assess-ing all the roads at sixty per cent. of their true value in money, what remedy have the people?   None.   If you do not do your duty there is no higher body to which the people can appeal.   But that is not true of the railroads. If you exceed your powers by the fraction of an inch, the railroads will at once appeal to the courts and have it corrected.   The supreme court will undo any illegal act that you may do, but it will not do any legal act which you should have done.   I do not know what you will do, but I do know that there will come a time when the people will find a way of making the great steam rail-roads and other corporations carry their just share of the burden of taxation.

"The big corporations get all the benefits of the pres-ent method of assessment.   How?   By influencing audi-tors, by influencing legislators, by influencing courts and by influencing elections.   Let us take off the mask and be frank with each other.   I say that no auditor or other official who has a railroad pass in his pocket or who accepts other favors from these corporations is a fit man to say how much of the tax they shall pay. Some men may be above these influences, but among those who compose the boards that have to do with the question of taxation in Ohio, I doubt if there are many. Why, gentlemen, this business of extending favors to public officials has even gone so far as to reach your august body. Two of you accepted the invitation of a certain railroad official to take a long trip in a private car to California. I hope it did not influence you."

The board turned a deaf ear to our pleadings. Our next appeal was to the supreme court whither we were followed by the excited attorneys for the railroads. We petitioned the court for a writ of mandamus compelling the board of railroad equalization to review the entire case and appraise the railroads at a fair valuation. If the supreme court had decided in our favor the State board would have had to reassemble and add about two hundred and seventy million dollars to the valuation of steam railway property in Ohio. Such an addition would have increased the tax receipts in Ohio from steam railway property alone about four million dollars.

Our petition was denied. The supreme court referred us to the legislature. The railroad lawyers followed us and here again, with the assistance of the railroad lobby, they blocked our every move.

The increase in the tax rate which resulted from all this effort was so slight that if we had accomplished nothing but that, we might well have felt that it had not been worth while to try. The agitation then started, however, has been going on ever since and will continue, I am confident, until the things we started out to do have been fully consummated.

Some definite progress has been made for the county auditors' tax boards have been abolished and in their stead there is a State tax board which fixes the valuation of steam railroad property *including franchise values*. Two cents a mile is now the legal rate of fare on Ohio railroads, and it is significant that the railroads did not even attempt to have the law declared unconstitutional. The pass is prohibited by law and State and local officials no longer ride free — at least not openly.

I have gone into detail about this matter of railroad taxation simply because it shows clearly how farcical, how unjust the whole scheme of taxation is as applied in this country to-day. The very officers you elect — the auditors, attorneys-general, and so on — refuse to obey even the letter of the law, refuse to do their duty by you, with the consequence that these men you put in office simply put that much more burden on your pocketbook. If, for instance, these railroads had not been able to corrupt these officials of the State and had been compelled to pay their just and due taxes to the State and Cleveland had received her share of this tax money lawfully due her it would have lightened the indebtedness of every citizen in Cleveland: public work of all kinds could have gone forward without any financial setbacks, city and citizen alike would have felt the benefits. But no. The railroads lied, the auditors winked, the people were cheated and the money stayed where it could do the least good and the most harm — in the pockets of Privilege. And this sort of thing is going on every day of your life in your own cities, out through the counties of your own States, in the shadow of your State houses and under the dome of the national capitol.

XV

THE WAY OUT

WHILE our State fight against the railroads was in progress the Cleveland local tax-board or board of equalization as it was generally called, composed of my appointees, was enjoined by the court of common pleas, July 22, 1901, from increasing the returns of the personal property of public service corporations in Cleveland. We fought the injunction and it was dissolved July 30. On the same day the board added nearly twenty million dollars to the tax duplicates of the street railway, the gas and electric lighting companies!

These corporations appealed to the board of revision to prohibit the increased valuation. The appeal was made in November, 1901, and on January 4, 1902, the board of revision sustained the increase.

Three days later the case was appealed to the Republican State board of tax remission, the petition claiming among other things lack of power on the part of local boards to impose the additional assessment in question. This power had never been questioned when it was exerted in extorting additional taxes from the uninformed and helpless — but here was a different case.

On February 1, the State board of tax remission composed of the State treasurer, the State auditor and the attorney general remitted the entire increase.

" I suppose you will want to know why we did this,"

said Attorney-General Sheets to the newspaper men. " We based our decision on the fact that the Cleveland board applied the principles of the Nichols law to determining the value of the property of these corporations. (This law was enacted to apply to the property of express, telegraph, and telephone companies in Ohio. It provided that for tax purposes their value shall be determined by the selling value of their stocks and bonds.) If the board had simply made an error in judgment as to the value of the property we would have had no jurisdiction."

" In other words," said the Cleveland *Plain Dealer,* commenting on it, " if the Cleveland board had gone out and looked at the physical property of the corporations concerned and then guessed at its value, this board could not have remitted a cent, though the guess had been that a total of twenty million dollars should be added. It was because the board based its action, according to the Nichols law, on the market value of the stocks and bonds of these concerns that the State board overruled it."

Continuing, the *Plain Dealer* said: " The fact that the value of the stocks and bonds was confirmed by the Cleveland board by a careful appraisement of the physical property and the cost of reproduction in each case was not sufficient departure from the fixed rule laid down in the Nichols law to suit said board. That law was enacted to apply to the property of express, telegraph, and telephone companies in Ohio. It provided that for tax purposes their value shall be determined by the selling value of their stocks and bonds."

Of course, a decision against the public service corporations would have meant a shutting off of campaign contributions — and that was the real reason why the tax was found illegal.

Privilege was beginning to take notice.

On May 12, 1902, the Republican legislature destroyed the board of equalization, creating in its stead a board of review with unquestioned power to do just what our tax board had attempted.

This board of review is appointed by the State treasurer, State auditor, secretary of State and the attorney general. Although the work is entirely local, and the expenses of the board and the compensation of its members are paid from local funds, the members are not in the remotest way responsible to the city for their actions.

The agitation against State appointment of these boards has been so persistent and the sentiment in favor of home rule is now so pronounced that it is a matter of a short time only until the legislature will be forced to provide for their local appointment or election.

This is, of course, as it should be. A municipality should have right under its eyes the men who are doing this important work. They should be available at all times so that they can be quickly called to account. In fact the mayor, through deputies, might well be the taxing official and the paramount question in each election should be, not " Mr. Mayor, did you see that our money was properly expended? " or " Mr. Candidate-for-Mayor, will you see that our money is properly expended? " but " Have you seen to it, or will you see to it that the money is properly paid in? " With the recall as part of every municipal charter there would be no danger in placing

all this power in the hands of one man for on his shoulders
would rest all the responsibility, and he could be easily
removed if he abused the one or shirked the other.

The most pressing of all civic problems is that of municipal home rule by the people themselves, and it is more
pressing in the United States than elsewhere. Our old
questions of State sovereignty were set at rest by the logic
of the Civil War. In national affairs the central government is now supreme. The only power States can any
longer hope to preserve is power over their internal affairs — the exclusive right of home rule in matters of
State concern. The readjustment of the relations of the
nation with the State is suggestive and prophetic of a similar readjustment of the relations of States with their cities.
Along with the decline in the political power once asserted
by the States has arisen a necessity, if popular liberty is to
be preserved, for an extension to municipalities of the
same principle of home rule to which the States themselves
may still lay claim.

Municipalities must cease to be answerable to their
States, except in matters of State concern, and become answerable in matter of home concern only to their own
people. Every city should make its own laws, design
its own organization, govern itself by the ballots of its
own people, absolutely untrammeled by outside dictation
or interference, except with reference to matters of outside concern. More and more as the years go by are our
cities going to reach out and demand such control of their
own affairs from their States.

In that way the city will rapidly rise; she will learn
more about self-government. And the voice of her people will be heard, direct, demanding of her officers the

THE JOHNSON MANSION ON EUCLID AVENUE

things the people want; and the officers will hear, and do — or lose their jobs.

I have shown that in our people's fight in Cleveland and Ohio we did not waste time on superficial issues, but made our attacks directly on Privilege's most valued power — its control of taxing machinery. I have shown how Privilege used local, county and State officers, city councils, the State legislature and the courts to frustrate our efforts. Is it not strange that witnessing the power of Privilege through the control of these agencies the people do not awake to the fact that with these agencies in their hands *they* would be supreme?

Since we have dealt so largely with the question of steam railroads let us consider the source of their power and the remedy for the abuse of that power.

The original idea behind the railroad was entirely different from the idea which attaches to it in common thought to-day, and to the departure from this original idea we may trace the evils now complained of. It was at first simply the idea of providing a roadway or passageway — a highway for vehicles moved by steam, just as there were then roads or highways for vehicles moved by horses. It did not provide for exclusive use, but for general use, subject to a charge or toll, just as charges were made on some horse roads. But, seeing the advantage of exclusive use, the companies building these steam highways, by means of heavy or discriminating tolls or other methods, prevented general use, stopped competition and made themselves the sole users. The rail or steam roads in the United States, instead of becoming what they were intended to be as the term applied to them, " public highways," indicates, became private highways.

And what has been the tendency of these private highways? When railroad building began in the United States some seventy years ago, each road was separately organized with its own officers and distinct interests. But separate interests melted into common interests, and many small companies formed into single large companies, and one set of officers effected economies that grew out of concentration of management and combination of effort. This centralizing movement has proceeded so fast that we can anticipate the end of this perfectly natural tendency if indeed we have not already reached it. We must see the appearance of the one directing mind, the kingpin, the dictator, the supreme monarch in the railroad world. Compare the powers of such a man with the powers of the President of the United States. Who would command more men? Who receive the larger revenues? Who have the larger pay-roll? Who have greater control of the pockets of the people. In short, whose favors would be the more courted? One might distribute honors by the appointment of foreign ministers, judges, etc., at small pay, but which would appoint the most men at fifty-thousand-dollar salaries? Which would have the dominant power — the man representing the people, or the man representing privilege? the one voted for by men? or the one voted for by shares of stock? Can interstate commerce commissions prevent it? Why, railroad owners themselves cannot prevent it, for it is in the natural order under present conditions. If government control failed before railroads were consolidated, what can it do after consolidation is perfected? If discriminating rates have worked evils on trade in the past, what must be their effect in the future? If railroads have hitherto con-

trolled legislation, what will they do when all their power
is vested in one man?

We see the evils of this form of special privilege.
Now what about the remedy? Socialism would seek the
cure in government ownership. The philosophy of the
natural order, which would promote competition and
place as little power as possible in the hands of the government would seek the remedy in throwing the steam
highway open to general use. No wonder the Socialists
point to railroad centralization under present conditions
as the greatest standing indictment of competition, a co-
lossal example of its utter failure and say that competition having broken down the only alternative is government ownership and operation. The Socialist, regarding
competition as the source of the evil, demands its destruction. We who hold that the evils arise from a de-
nial of competition demand the abolition of law-made
advantage, of governmental favor.

Is not the simple, easy, practicable remedy to be found
in going back to the original conception underlying the
railway to make a really " public " highway for private
transportation companies or individuals to use? In making the highway public property, should we not destroy
the essence of monopoly power in the railroad? With
the States owning the roadbeds and the cities owning the
terminals, and no favor shown to any transportation company, but free play being given to competition, would not
the public get the maximum of service at the minimum
of cost? What harm could come from discriminating
rates to shippers where any number of transportation
companies were competing for traffic over the same highway? Would not this establishment of the condition of

freedom to individual enterprise do more than the most severe State or interstate regulations in fixing rates? Indeed, this is the only plan which will establish competition from all points to all points. It would mean just plain freedom, and what could be better for all men and for all legitimate and normal businesses than freedom?

This proposal is in perfect harmony with the natural order and in absolute accord with the rule of public practice on almost every other kind of public highway that we have had or now have. The underlying principle is to make the pathway a publicly owned and controlled way, open to all on equal terms, whether absolutely free or subject to toll. And the end to strive for in the railroad problem is to open such roadways to equal use by all who desire to use them as exists on public country roads or streets, on rivers, canals, lakes and the very ocean. And just as there are police regulations for the use of streets, sheriff regulations for the use of the country roads, and other regulations pertaining to the navigation and condition of vessels on the rivers, canals, or other bodies of water open to public use, so on steam highways there would be necessary regulations, as for instance, in the dispatching and signaling of trains. But the fixing of rates could be safely left to individual competition as on the other highways.

In making the change from private to public ownership of railroads the tax power should be used rigorously so as to put railroad property on a level with other taxable property. The power to fix rates should be used so as to reduce profits to a fair return on the actual investment of capital, excluding fictitious capitalization based on franchise or special privilege value. This would leave all the value that does and of right ought to belong to the railroad companies. Then attempts should be made to buy all their property, exclusive of rolling stock, which latter they would however be free to use in a competitive business with others over the then public highway, which they had hitherto treated as their exclusive and private highway. An alternative would be for the government to build steam highways and open them to general competition.

This but returns to the original conception of the railway, and indeed to almost every other form of highway, such as country roads, streets, turnpikes, canals, rivers, lakes and the ocean, in which the public owns the way and on which the business of transportation is left to private enterprise, subject of course to control and direction of public officials.

And just as toll-bridges are giving way to free bridges, and toll-gates disappearing from turnpikes and canals, so, in pursuit of economy, the minimizing of the numbers of government officials and the removal of temptations to fraud, should the steam highways be open to use without charge, the expense of maintenance being made a public burden, as is the tendency to treat all other public highways.

But if I were ambitious to rule a country absolutely, I should not try to get control of its railroads even under the present system when, as we have seen, one-man power can be carried to such great lengths. I should devote myself with singleness and tenacity of purpose to becoming its landlord. The ownership of railroads gives power as, and only as, it is really ownership of land; the power of street car companies is based on the same thing, privileges

in the ownership of streets which is land; the power of
the Standard Oil Company rests upon the right of way
for its pipe lines, and that right of way is land. A man
who controlled all the land of a country would be the ruler
of that country no matter who made its laws or wrote its
songs.

If this is true why does it not indicate to the people their own source of power? If a tyrant can rule
them by gaining control of the land of their country, why
cannot they destroy tyranny by themselves resuming and
retaining control of their land?

But we must have a method whereby this can be accomplished and the method, I believe, is in the single tax as
Henry George's philosophy is commonly called in this
country. The single tax proposes the abolition of all
forms of taxation except a tax upon land values. It would
eliminate taxes upon industry, personal property, buildings
and all improvements. It would tax land values, including the value of all franchises and public utilities operated
for private profit. It is the community which creates land
values and franchise values, therefore these values belong
to the community and the community should take them in
taxation.

To abolish taxes on industry would be to reduce friction in making things and trading things. It would stimulate business and be a blow to tyranny, both economic
and political. The effect of a tax upon land values would
be to force all needed land into immediate use, and circumstances would be created under which anybody could get
profitable work who wanted it. This would be because
the demand for labor would always exceed the supply.
Any man competent to do business could find profitable

business to do because the effective demand for goods would always exceed the output. There could be no oppressive organization of capital, because capital would have no privileges. There could be no coercive labor unions because every worker would be his own all-sufficient union. And there would be no tyrannical government because all the people would be economically free, a condition that makes tyranny, either economic or political, impossible.

These are the principles which must be put into practice if our cities and our States are to be freed from the domination of Privilege.

XVI

GOVERNMENT BY INJUNCTION

OUR movement early commenced to have an influence outside of Cleveland, and it was in the midst of my first mayoralty campaign that I received a call from Columbus, the State capital, to help in a contest then going on between that city and its street railroad company. I had my hands pretty full in Cleveland, but I went down to Columbus to give such assistance as I could, taking Professor Bemis with me.

Some of the grants to the Columbus Street Railway Company had been made before the State legislature passed a law which limited the life of all street railway franchises to twenty-five years. Some of them had already expired, some had been granted without date of expiration. A citizens' committee of twenty-five and sixteen out of the nineteen members of the city council invited me to address the council committee of the whole on the street car question. I made a number of speeches which, combined with the articles which appeared daily in the Columbus *Press Post* from Professor Bemis's pen, did something to enlighten the citizens on the real status of the street railway controversy.

I offered to take the grants on favorable terms, fair to the old company, agreeing to buy the physical property, the valuation to be reached by negotiation or arbitration, and to operate at three-cent fare. The council refused to

consider my proposition and the grant was made to the old
company, but so amended as to provide for seven tickets
for a quarter until the receipts of the company should
amount to $1,750,000 annually, and then the fare was to
be reduced to eight tickets for a quarter.   The courts up-
held the validity of this grant, but the condition of eight
tickets for a quarter has never been complied with.
Whether the street railroad company has actually swindled
the public or whether they have shuffled the bookkeeping
in such a way as never to reach the limit I never have been
able to find out.   At a five-cent fare Cleveland was taking
in $6,000,000 a year, so it is perfectly clear, after allow-
ing for the difference in population in the two cities, that
Columbus couldn't fail to reach the mark of one million
and three-quarters.

The judge who rendered the decision in favor of the
street railway company, holding that some of their grants
were perpetual unless the legislature repealed them, was
Judge A. N. Summers.   Several months before his decision was made public a number of us learned what it
would be.   My knowledge of it came to me in a confidential way so I could not make it public.   Stock advanced from a very low price to a very high figure while
this case was pending.   It was long drawn out and between the time that the decision was known and the time
that it was made public the Republican State Convention
of 1903 was held and nominated Judge Summers for the
supreme bench.   In the State campaign that year I publicly
made charges against Judge Summers and offered to divide my time with him or any representative he might
select to come to any of our meetings and explain this remarkable transaction.   The judge never answered me on

the stump.   His friends said the knowledge of the decision
leaked out through a stenographer.   My charge was that
stock gamblers were profiting by this knowledge on the
one hand and the judge on the other since he was receiving the support of the public service corporations in his
campaign.   I insisted that whether his position was due
to carelessness or to viciousness the people ought not to
elect him to the high office of supreme court judge.   He
was elected.   This is a way public service corporations
have of rewarding faithful servants.   When all is said
and done, I think he was not much worse than the rest of
the court and a rather better lawyer than most of them.
The people had not been sufficiently aroused to hold judges
accountable for their actions.   Ohio elects her supreme
court judges for six years and by reason of changing from
annual to biennial State elections Judge Summers's term
held over an additional year.   It was not until the last
State election (November, 1910) therefore that he was a
candidate for re-election and then he was defeated.   The
people are beginning to wake up and Privilege is finding
it somewhat more difficult to bestow rewards of this kind
now than ten years ago.

While the activities described in previous chapters in
behalf of the equalization of taxes and the promotion of
public improvements and good government were going
forward the other promise of our platform — to try to
give three-cent fare on the street railroads — was not
neglected.   The people looked upon this as *the* important question, but in the beginning comparatively few of
them realized the intimate relation between it and all the
other problems we were trying to solve and they did not
in the least comprehend the difficulties in the way.   There

were many who clamored for the immediate redemption of the three-cent fare pledge without taking into consideration the legal obstacles which blocked our path or the almost insurmountable barrier which the coalition between the public service corporations and the courts presented.

It will be remembered that Cleveland's street railways were at this time controlled by two companies, popularly known as the Big Con and the Little Con. The last named was Mr. Hanna's company and the Big Con was the result of the consolidation of the Andrews-Stanley interests with my lines. As has already been stated I had sold all my Cleveland street railway interests in 1894–95. The contest to secure three-cent fare was between the city and these two companies which had a common interest in opposing anything which threatened their monopoly of the city's streets. They acted as a unit and in 1903 they consolidated. The reader will be less apt to be confused if these interests are referred to from the beginning as one company and this I shall do.

The State laws had been carefully framed and as carefully guarded to protect existing street railroads in their privileges and to prevent competing lines, and it was only through competition that we could hope to secure a reduction in fare.

There were three ways in which grants could be made and we shall consider them in the order of their respective advantages to Privilege.

The first and easiest provided for the most valuable form of street railway franchise, namely, the renewal of an expiring grant. This could be made only to the company in possession of the grant and was not hampered by restrictions of any kind.

The second provided for extensions to existing lines and required consent of property owners along the proposed route.

The third, for making grants for new lines, was so complicated as to make it next to impossible to build a competing railroad.

These were the legal conditions which faced us, and it must be remembered that they were prescribed by State statutes and that the municipality had no recourse but the courts, and the courts, as has already been shown, were operating in the interests of the public service corporations. We were undecided as to which was the wiser course for us to pursue,— to have council make a grant covering a number of streets, or one for a small branch from which future extensions could be made. As the question of grants for new lines had never been tested in the courts we felt pretty sure that we should be defeated no matter which horn of the dilemma we took. We had not only to decide upon the policy of the administration, but to find someone to whom the grants could be made who would not only be able to finance the enterprise but whom we knew to be absolutely trustworthy.

On December 6, 1901, there was introduced into the city council the first legislation for the establishment of new street railroad routes upon which the rate of fare should not exceed three cents. On February 10, 1902, one bid was received, accompanied by a deposit of fifty thousand dollars. This bid came from J. B. Hoefgen, a man who got his first street railroad experience with me in Indianapolis years before, and now an independent operator located in New York. He was declared the low bidder and the grant was made to him March 17,

1902. We knew he wouldn't sell out to the old company or fail to keep faith with the city in any other way. The making of this grant, which covered a large number of streets, had been preceded by a property owners' consent war extending over several months. Representatives of the street railways followed closely on the heels of the men who were getting consents for Hoefgen and brought every possible pressure to bear to have these consents revoked. It was like a game of battledore and shuttlecock with an organized force playing it for each side. The courts held that property owners had a right to change their minds up to the time the ordinance was passed. Some of them did so seven or eight times or as often as they were paid to. The Hoefgen Company finally secured a lot of consents at the eleventh hour and turned them in just before the ordinance was passed when it was too late for the railroad companies to secure revocations.

Council could not make a valid grant unless a majority of the property owners representing the feet front along each street of the proposed routes consented in writing to the construction of a street railroad, and then only to the company offering to carry passengers at the lowest rate of fare. If the street railroad company, through property owners' consents, could get control of just one street in a group of streets to be covered by proposed new lines council was rendered helpless, and though a majority of the citizens of the entire city favored the new grant they had no way of giving expression to their will in the matter.

To overcome this difficulty we early found it necessary to change the names of streets. The three-cent line in question was to run upon Hanover, Fulton, Willett streets and Rhodes avenue, a continuous thoroughfare with four different names. The low fare people had a majority of consents on Fulton street and Rhodes avenue, but lacked a majority on Hanover and Willett. Council changed the name of the entire thoroughfare to Rhodes avenue and in this way wiped out the minority on Hanover and Willett with the majority on Fulton and Rhodes. This method of attack or defense was persisted in pretty thoroughly by the administration.

When the courts declared the Hoefgen grant invalid, as of course they did, we asked to have this order made final. We wanted to clear the way for immediate action in another direction. This done, we now proceeded to try the alternative previously alluded to. We picked out eleven routes and required a bond in the form of a cash deposit of $10,000 to be made with each bid. This made it necessary for the old company, as a matter of self-defense, to be the lowest bidder on all ten routes, and to put up a deposit of $110,000. The new company had only to succeed on one and to put up a deposit of $10,000. Having secured a grant on one route they could secure further grants as extensions to their original line. No deposits were necessary on extensions though property owners' consents were required. *I was using, in the interests of the city, exactly the same methods to secure grants for the low fare people which the Hanna-Simms Company had used to prevent grants to me when I was seeking them as a street railway operator back in* 1879. This plan was persisted in and was the one which eventually won the victory for the city and vindicated our campaign promises. And by a curious coincidence too the first three-cent grants were for routes over part of the same territory that was involved in that 1879 contest.

Surveying at Franklin Circle for three-cent fare line

Photos by L. Van Oeyen

Laying the first rails for the three-cent line

But before we were successful many extraordinary things happened, not the least of which was the practical destruction of the city government of Cleveland.

Privilege was thoroughly aroused now, and had evidently arrived at the conclusion that safety from our agitation was to be secured only by killing it and everybody connected with it. Two days after the first three-cent fare ordinances were introduced in the city council a press dispatch reading as follows was sent out from Columbus:

"December 8, 1901.

" A suit to test the constitutionality of the Cleveland law under which the city is now being governed was filed in the supreme court this afternoon.

"It is a quo warranto suit styled the State of Ohio, ex rel Attorney General vs. M. W. Beacom and the other members of the board of control, otherwise known as Mayor Johnson's cabinet. It is based upon the contention that the act of May 16, 1891, applies only to the city of Cleveland and is therefore special legislation."

The suit was brought by an obscure lawyer, but it was not at all difficult to trace it to the real perpetrators — the public service corporations of Cleveland. In the latter part of June, 1902, the supreme court declared unconstitutional the charter under which Cleveland had been operating for about twelve years, though its legality had never before been questioned. Ten days before our three-cent-fare franchises were to be bid for, the supreme court, upon application of Attorney-General Sheets, enjoined the city of Cleveland from making any public service grants of any kind. Other cities of the State were operating under charters just as " unconstitutional " as Cleveland's, but not one was enjoined. All other cities were left free to carry on their own affairs. By these rulings of the supreme court our hands were literally tied in our street railway fight and they were kept tied for eleven long months.

During the summer of 1902, a special session of the State legislature, inspired by Senator Hanna, was called to adopt a new municipal code — one which should apply to all cities of the State, and remove from Cleveland the obloquy of " special legislation."

Though the legislature was importuned and beseeched to give to all the cities of Ohio the Cleveland form of government, known as the federal plan, and thus provide a uniform system in accordance with the constitutional requirement, and at the same time give an excellent plan of municipal government, they refused to do so. Instead, they went to Cincinnati, a city governed by a self-confessed boss who issued his orders by telephone, for the model of that code. The new code provided for board governed cities and is very advantageous to government in the interests of Privilege. Its divided power and no responsibility prevent the people from locating the sources of corruption.

Aimed directly at Cleveland and clearly intended to reduce the mayor to a figure-head, the blow went wide of the mark, as later history will prove.

When my first term as mayor was drawing to its close in the early spring of 1903 and we took an inventory — not of the things we had accomplished — but of the things we had been prevented from doing we found that we had kept the courts pretty fairly busy as the following record of injunctions indicates:

No. 1.

July 22, 1901.— City board of equalization enjoined from increasing the valuation of the Cleveland Electric Railway Company.

No. 2.

Nov. 9, 1901.— Enjoined from entering into contracts for cheaper street lighting.

No. 3.

Nov. 9, 1901.— Enjoined from entering into a contract for cheaper vapor lighting.

No. 4.

April 6, 1902.— Enjoined by common pleas court from carrying out three-cent railroad franchise.

No. 5.

April 7, 1902.— Enjoined from permitting construction of three-cent-fare railroad.

No. 6.

May 11, 1902.— Enjoined from carrying out three-cent franchise by circuit court.

No. 7.

June 30, 1902.— Injunction against three-cent franchise made perpetual.

No. 8.

July 19, 1902.— Enjoined from considering the granting of any franchises. Circuit court.

No. 9.

Aug. 9, 1902.— Temporary injunction by supreme court against considering the granting of any franchises.

No. 10.

Aug. 15, 1902.— Permanent injunction from considering the granting of any franchise.

No. 11.

Nov. 19, 1902.— Injunction by the supreme court removing the police department from the control of the administration.

No. 12.

Dec. 20, 1902.— Enjoined from making any investigation into inequalities in taxation.

No. 13.

March 6, 1903.— Enjoined from making contracts for paving of streets.

These injunctions were the first of the more than fifty which hampered the progress of the people's movement in Cleveland. Injunctions got to be so common during my administration and were made to serve on such a variety of occasions that the practice gave rise to the witticism that "if a man doesn't like the way Tom Johnson wears his hat he goes off and gets out an injunction restraining him from wearing it that way." Everything we attempted was made the object of misrepresentation, vilification and attack. My part in our various activities and my aggressiveness naturally drew the fiercest wrath and the bitterest abuse to me personally.

XVII

MAKING MEN

THE chief value of any social movement lies perhaps in the influence it exerts upon the minds and hearts of the men and women who engage in it. In selecting my cabinet and in making other appointments I looked about for men who would be efficient and when I found one in whom efficiency and a belief in the fundamental principles of democracy were combined I knew that here was the highest type of public officer possible to get. I have stated that I made a good many mistakes in my first appointments, but it must be remembered that innumerable problems faced us. It was like organizing a new government, but more difficult, for we had the old established order with all its imperfections, its false standards and the results of years of wrong-doing to deal with. We really did not have a fair field in spite of the excellent plan of city government which Cleveland had when I was first elected. Men had become contaminated with the spirit of laxity at best, of exploitation at worst, but I soon learned that at bottom men are all right. They would rather be decent than otherwise, and if they have a chance to do really useful work they want to do it. The greatest thing our Cleveland movement did was to make men. It couldn't be enjoined from doing that. The questions we raised not only attracted better men — men who couldn't be interested in politics when it dealt chiefly with spoils,— but it also brought out the very best in men of less exalted ideals.

Many of my appointments gave offense to those within my own party and excited criticism outside. In order to avoid criticism one must follow precedent even when precedent is bad. According to established custom valuable jobs belong by all that is holy in politics to true and tried party workers. They are rewards for the workers. Instead of awarding these jobs as prizes I looked about for men best fitted for specialized public service. The minister of my church, a man of rare spirit and humanitarian impulses, was placed at the head of the charities and corrections, while I chose for city auditor a genial and popular Irishman who had been a liquor dealer. This appointment was offensive to the Puritanical element, while those who insisted on a " business man's government " disapproved of the appointment of the minister. A college professor whose radicalism had resulted in enforced resignation from several colleges was given charge of the city water works with its hundreds of employés, much to the indignation of the Democratic organization. A delegation from the Buckeye Club, an influential Democratic society, called upon me to protest and ended by saying:

" You've got to discharge the professor or we'll fight the administration."

When they were all through I asked pleasantly:

" Is that your ultimatum, gentlemen ? "

They answered with emphasis that it was. I smiled and said:

" Very well; I think I ought to tell you now that I am not going to discharge the professor."

A brilliant young college graduate just working his way

into practice was made city solicitor, to the amused scorn of some of the wiseacres in the profession. An aggressive Populist, regarded by practically the whole community as a wild-eyed anarchist, was entrusted with the important office of city clerk, a young Republican councilman was selected to take charge of the department of public works and a Republican policeman was raised from the ranks and made chief.

There were plenty of predictions of the disasters sure to follow this unheard-of manner of making appointments, but time justified them so completely that, though I was criticized for many things, even my bitterest enemies didn't charge me with making weak appointments.

As time went on our organization gathered to itself a group of young fellows of a type rarely found in politics — college men with no personal ambitions to serve, students of social problems known to the whole community as disinterested, high-minded, clean-lived individuals. Over and over again the short-sighted majority which cannot recognize a great moral movement when it appears as a political movement, and which knows nothing of the contagion of a great idea attributed the interest and activity of these young fellows to some baneful influence on my part. " Johnson has them hypnotized," was the usual explanation of their devotion to our common cause.

In selecting its servants Privilege has never cared a straw to which party men belong. It is quite as ready to use those of one political faith as those of another. The people have been slow to profit by the lessons they might have learned from the methods of their exploiters.

Though our work had been hampered by injunctions at every turn and on every possible occasion our political strength was growing and the personnel of the administration improving in every way. More and more the men connected with us were coming to comprehend the economic questions underlying our agitation.

When the time for another mayoralty election came round we had carried four successive elections, had a Democratic administration, a Democratic council, a majority of the county offices, Democrats in the school council and a Democratic school director in the person of Starr Cadwallader, and for the first time in many years there were Cuyahoga county Democrats in the State legislature. Not injunctions, not court decisions, not acts of the State legislature nor all of these agencies combined had been able to prevent the people from expressing their will through their ballots. I was more eager to succeed myself as mayor than I could possibly have been had our plans been permitted to work out without encountering the opposition of Privilege.

If Big Business was somewhat passive in the campaign of 1901, quite the reverse was true in 1903.

I had by this time incurred the enmity of the tax-escaping public service corporations and big landlords and of the low dive-keepers and gamblers, all of whose privileges had suffered under my administration. The opposition of these interests was augmented by various other groups allied with them in greater or less degree. Many of the church and temperance people opposed me because the town was wide open, while some of the saloons opposed me because the night and Sunday closing laws were too rigidly enforced. The civil service reformers and the party spoilsmen had their grievances, the former because we had not practiced the merit system with regard to city

Photo by L. Van Oyen

Getting ready to pitch the tent in the Public Square, Cleveland, 1902

employés, the latter because we had. The Municipal
Association, an organization supposed to be distinctly non-
partisan and above the influences of Privilege, having for
its object the consideration and recommendation of candidates to voters, issued an eleventh hour manifesto showing
that the city administration had been very lax in enforcing
some of the laws most necessary to the well-being of the
municipality.

Let me repeat what I have previously said, that it isn't
necessary for Privilege to bribe men with money, with
promises, or even with the hope of personal reward, if it
can succeed in fooling them. It is this insidious power,
this intangible thing which is hard to detect and harder to
prove, this indirect influence which is the most dangerous
factor in politics to-day.

The Republicans nominated Harvey D. Goulder, a
leading lawyer, president of the Chamber of Commerce
and a prominent member of the Union Club. I conducted
my campaign on the lines of my earlier contests and when
Mr. Goulder refused to debate the issues — three-cent
fare, municipal ownership of street car lines, and just taxation — with me I conceived the idea of sending a
stenographer to his meetings to take verbatim reports of
his speeches in order that I might reply to them in my
own meetings. The nearest we ever came to a personal
meeting was at a political gathering to which we had both
been invited. When I arrived Mr. Goulder's haste to get
away and his evident ill-nature at being caught in the same
room with me caused him to say some unpleasant things
about the Jewish club whose guests we were, from which
it was inferred that he was accusing someone in the hall
of having stolen his overcoat. The coat had simply been

mislaid and was soon found.   I felt sorry for Mr. Goulder.   I didn't think he really intended to insinuate that the coat had been stolen, but the incident made him a lot of trouble.

In order to curry favor with union labor the Republicans conceived the brilliant idea of nominating for vice mayor Solomon Sontheimer, president of the Central Labor Union.   In their speeches some of the Republicans referred to the widely separated interests represented on the ticket by Mr. Goulder and Mr. Sontheimer as a " marriage between capital and labor."   This marriage was doomed to quick divorce, for on election day, when I was elected over Mr. Goulder by about six thousand votes, Charles W. Lapp, the Democratic candidate for vice mayor, won over the Republican, Mr. Sontheimer, by upwards of ten thousand.   It had been a bitter campaign and nothing was left undone by the Interests through the Republican organization, aided by a goodly number of Democrats, to beat us.   The enemy had an unlimited purse, but how extensively it was used could only be guessed at.   In 1901, it will be remembered, I was the only Democrat elected on the general ticket; in 1903 we carried every office on that ticket.   Newton D. Baker was elected city solicitor, Henry D. Coffinberry, city treasurer, J. P. Madigan, city auditor, and for directors of public service, Harris R. Cooley, William J. Springborn and Daniel E. Leslie.   With few exceptions these officers were already serving the city as appointees of the mayor under the old plan of city government, and we worked together now as we had then like one harmonious family. Most of these officers coöperated as heartily with me as if they were still subject to appointment and removal by the chief executive.

Mr. Baker, though the youngest of us, was really head of the cabinet and principal adviser to us all. He has been an invaluable public servant and is still city solicitor, having been returned to office in each successive election, even in 1909, when I was defeated with the majority of our ticket. Newton Baker as a lawyer was pitted against the biggest lawyers in the State. No other city solicitor has ever had the same number of cases crowded into his office in the same length of time, nor so large a crop of injunctions to respond to, and in my judgment there isn't another man in the State who could have done the work so well. He ranks with the best, highest-paid, corporation lawyers in ability and has held his public office at a constant personal sacrifice. This low-paid city official has seen every day in the courtroom lawyers getting often five times the fee for bringing a suit that he got for defending it. He did for the people for love what other lawyers did for the corporations for money.

Mr. Cooley, who had been at the head of the city's charitable and correctional institutions from the very beginning of my administration, continued in this department, the duties of the new public service board being divided upon lines which assigned to him this field for which he was so admirably adapted. If service of a higher order on humanitarian lines has ever been rendered to any municipality than that rendered by Mr. Cooley to Cleveland, I have yet to hear of it. His convictions as to the causes of poverty and crime coincided with my own. Believing as we did that society was responsible for poverty and that poverty was the cause of much of the crime in the world, we had no enthusiasm for punishing individuals. We were agreed that the root of the evil must be destroyed, and that in the meantime delinquent men, women and children were to be cared for by the society which had wronged them — not as objects of charity, but as fellow-beings who had been deprived of the opportunity to get on in the world. With this broad basis on which to build, the structure of this department of Cleveland's city government has attracted the attention of the whole civilized world. How small the work of philanthropists with their gifts of dollars appears, compared to the work of this man who gave men *hope* — a man who while doing charitable things never lost sight of the fact that *justice* and *not charity* would have to solve the problems with which he was coping.

In the very beginning Mr. Cooley came to me and said, " The immediate problem that is facing me is these men in the workhouse, some three hundred of them. I've been preaching the Golden Rule for many years; now I'm literally challenged to put it into practice. I know very well that we shall be misunderstood, criticized and probably severely opposed if we do to these prisoners as we would be done by."

" Well, if it's right, go ahead and do it anyhow," I answered, and that was the beginning of a parole system that pardoned eleven hundred and sixty men and women in the first two years of our administration. To show what an innovation this was it is well to state that in the same length of time the previous administration had pardoned eighty-four. The correctness of the principle on which the parole system is based and the good results of

its practice are now so generally accepted that it could
not again encounter the opposition it met when Mr. Cooley
instituted it in Cleveland. The newspapers and the
churches — those two mighty makers of public opinion —
were against it, yet it was successful from the very start.

In his first annual report Mr. Cooley recommended that
a farm colony be established in the country within ten or
twelve miles of the city, where all the city's charges, the
old, the sick, the young and the delinquent might be cared
for. To quote his own words:

"Underneath this movement back to the land are simple fundamental principles. The first is that normal environment has a
strong tendency to restore men to normal mental and physical
condition. The second is that the land furnishes the largest opportunities for the aged and defective to use whatever power and
talents they possess. In shop and factory the man who cannot
do his full work is crowded out. Upon the land the men past
their prime, the crippled, the weak can always find some useful
work."

Before the end of his nine years' service Mr. Cooley's
hope was in part at least realized. From time to time the
city purchased land upon his recommendation until twenty-
five farms — nearly two thousand acres in all — had been
acquired. The city council voted to name this great acre-
age the Cooley Farms, and so it is known. It is divided
into the Colony Farm, which has taken the place of the
old infirmary or city almshouse, the Overlook Farm for
tuberculosis patients, the Correction Farm for workhouse
prisoners, the Highland Park Farm, the municipal cemetery. Then there is the farm of two hundred and eighty-
five acres at Hudson, twenty-three miles from the city,

which is the Boys' Home. This farm was the first of the city's purchases and the land was bought at less than forty-four dollars an acre. Here in eight cottages, each in charge of a master and matron, the boys from the juvenile court find a temporary home. There is no discipline suggesting a reformatory. There are schools with some manual training in addition to the regular school curriculum, and the care of the stock and other farm work to occupy the boys. The principle is the same as that of the George Junior Republic, but adapted to municipal needs. The boys respond wonderfully to the normal environment provided here. The juvenile court, though a state institution, always had the hearty support of the city administration and the court and the Boys' Home have coöperated most successfully.

The city's purchase of the first eight hundred and fifty acres of the Cooley Farms, on which the whole magnificent project hinged, was almost prevented by special privilege. Everything the administration attempted had come to be the object of its attack and at that time we no longer had a majority in the council. One Monday afternoon Mr. Cooley took one of our friendly councilmen out to the farm to show it to him. As something of the greatness of the proposed work dawned upon the man he grew enthusiastic and expressed himself most feelingly in favor of it. That night at the council meeting, when the purchase of the land was under consideration, this man got up and denounced the whole plan in a speech so bitterly sarcastic that it was with extreme difficulty that we saved the day. His speech all but defeated the appropriation. Mr. Cooley was so surprised that he could hardly credit the evidence of his own senses. It was perfectly clear that the councilman had "been seen," between the time he had visited the farm site with Mr. Cooley in the afternoon and the hour of the council meeting at night. Mr. Cooley felt, as I did, that the enemy might at least have spared this project. The appropriation was made, the farm was purchased, but the incident had sad consequences.

The councilman — a young fellow — had undoubtedly gone into his office with the thought of doing good work and making it a stepping-stone to bigger and better service. When he talked with Mr. Cooley in the afternoon it was himself, the real man in him, that spoke. He believed in Mr. Cooley's work. What happened between that time and the hour of the council meeting we do not know, but that man was never quite the same afterwards. Somehow he had been undone. He has since died. He wasn't bad, but Privilege came along and laid hands upon him and spoiled his chance. Its path is strewn with tragedies like this.

All of the departments under Mr. Cooley were placed on a new basis, each as radical and as rational as the parole system or the method of conducting the Boys' Home. Over the entrance to the Old Couples' Cottage is inscribed, "To lose money is better than to lose love," and the old men and women, instead of being separated as formerly and simply herded until death takes them away, live together now, and useful employment is provided for all who are able to work, for idleness is the great destroyer of happiness. Especial care has been taken to better the surroundings of the crippled and the sick. The buildings on Colony Farm are of marble dust plaster finish with red tile roofs and the Spanish mission style of architecture. Beautifully located on a ridge

six hundred feet above the city, they look out onto Lake
Erie ten miles away.   A complete picture of the buildings,
even to the olive trees which are one day to grow in the
court and the fountain which is to splash in the center, to
the canary birds singing in gilt cages in the windows of
the cottages, to the old ladies sitting at their spinning
wheels in the sun and to the old men cobbling shoes or
working in wood in the shops, existed in Mr. Cooley's
mind when the city bought the first of the land and long
before a spadeful of earth had been turned in excavating.

The tuberculosis sanitarium is half a mile from the
colony group, protected by a forest of seventy acres on the
north and northwest and looking out over open country
on the other sides.   Here is waged an unequal contest
with a disease which science can never eliminate until the
social and industrial conditions which are responsible for
it are changed.

A mile and a half from Colony Farm is the Correction
Farm for the workhouse prisoners.   The men come and
go as they like from their work on the farm, at excavating for new buildings or quarrying stone.   Refractory
prisoners, instead of being dealt with by the old brutaliz-
ing methods, are bathed and given clean clothes and then
sent off by themselves to reflect — not to solitary confine-
ment in dark cells, but to one of the " sun dungeons "
originated by Mr. Cooley.   These rooms — three of
them — in one of the towers of the building are painted
white, and flooded with light, sunshine and fresh air.   It
is part of Mr. Cooley's theory that men need just such surroundings to put them in a normal state of mind when they
are feeling ill used or ugly.—" Sending them to the
Thinking Tower," he calls it.— A volume would be in-

adequate to give even a partial conception of this branch
of our administration's activities.

All of the land in the city farms has increased greatly
in value since it was purchased. Purely as a business venture it has been a good investment. Its value as a social
investment cannot be estimated.

William J. Springborn, who had been so valuable a
member of the city council, proved equal to the duties of
his new office. He had charge of all the business departments, the engineering contracts, the building of bridges,
the paving of streets, etc. He had had experience enough
in both business and politics to keep out corruption and
prevent grafting. His biggest work was in connection
with contractors where the highest degree of watchfulness
and efficiency is required. The conduct of Mr. Springborn's department was always a matter of pride with the
administration, and great was the consternation of his
friends and exceeding great the jubilation of his enemies
when the newspapers, in sensational headlines, told a story
one morning of how Mr. Springborn had been buncoed.
He had been swindled in a most artistic manner, the
principal mover in the game being a man whom he had
known for many years. A few days before this story
came out he had told me he was going out of town on
a business errand, and though he explained very little
of the contemplated transaction to me it aroused my
suspicions. I begged him to take a lawyer with him.
He refused. I then threatened to send a detective to
watch him, but I saw I was hurting his feelings, so I
gave it up. I knew I'd have to abandon my plan
of helping him and let him go and buy his experience.
When he got home from South Bend, Ind., where

the swindle was perpetrated, I sent for him. He came to me at once, explained everything fully, freely, and said that he realized that he was deeply disgraced, that he should have to withdraw at once from his church in which he had been a worker for a long time, and from the public service, so that no odium might attach to church or city because of his demoralization. I remember that I asked him just one question — "Will, did you rob anybody?" "No, I was robbed," was his answer. "Then," I said, "I won't hear to your resigning or in any way showing the white feather. It is no crime to be robbed, the crime is in the robbing. You'll stay and I'll stay with you." His answer to my own question made me understand all I needed to know about the case. His church friends and many of his old admirers were less lenient, but they later saw their error, for Mr. Springborn continued his city work and his efficiency was in no way impaired — if anything, he was better equipped after the unfortunate occurrence than before. Politicians — enemies — made a great deal of the matter and tried to ruin his reputation, but without success. The principal in the bunco game was sent to the penitentiary.

Mr. Leslie had charge of the parks and the market houses. He made the children feel that the parks really belonged to them and continued our policy of summer and winter sports.

The waterworks had long since been placed in charge of Professor Bemis, who kept politics out and business in, in the conduct of this department, better than it had ever been done before. Formerly the waterworks department had provided places for lots of good party workers. Professor Bemis did away with all that. He was invaluable also in our State taxation fights, and our local street railway contests, for he was the expert on valuations of public service corporations.

Peter Witt was elected city clerk in May, 1903, and held that office as long as I was mayor, though a hostile council once elected in his place someone who never succeeded in getting possession of the office, the supreme court holding that the other man had not been legally chosen.

Not the least notable of the men associated with my administration was Fred Kohler, whom I appointed chief of police at the beginning of my second term. Kohler had been on the police force since 1889. He was a patrolman at first, later a sergeant, then a lieutenant, and for the first five months of my administration a captain in charge of the first police district with headquarters at the central station. Kohler seems to have shown unusual ability almost from the beginning of his connection with the police department and for that reason he was more or less unpopular, arousing the jealousy of the less efficient. Only strong men make enemies and if Kohler's strength is to be measured by the enemies he has made he deserves to rank with the strongest. Some of our partisan party workers brought tales about Kohler to me. I had no reason to suspect these persons of ulterior motives, and thinking I was acting in the best interests of the city I caused him to be removed from the down town district and stationed in an outlying section of the city. Being " sent to the woods," as this was called, was very inconvenient for Kohler as it made his headquarters some six miles from his home. But he went without protest and continued to do good work. After a while I began to sus-

pect that I had been fooled about Kohler and one day I
sent for him to come to my house to see me.   He came.
I liked his looks and I liked his manner.   He inspired me
with confidence at once.   I was sure now that he had been
maligned and I told him so.

"I have done you an injustice," I said, "and I've just
found it out.   How would you like to be chief?"

"I haven't asked for it," he answered.   "I'm a Republican."

"I don't care anything about your politics and I know
you haven't asked for anything."

As soon as the way was clear, then, that is, May 1,
1903, Fred Kohler was appointed chief of police of the
city of Cleveland and he is still serving in that capacity.
While I was mayor I had more complaints on account of
him than on account of any other city official, but I found
that the chief was almost invariably in the right.

I couldn't hold men responsible for their work unless
I backed them in what they did, and a man I wasn't willing
to back I felt ought not to hold the office.   I demanded
and expected the best.   My fellow-workers knew this and
it was not often that they failed to come up to my ex-
pectations.

Nobody connected with the administration originated
more improvements in his department than Kohler did.
I was frequently given personal credit for innovations
which properly belonged to the chief.   After we got to
working together he never worried me with details.   He
had that judgment so rare in executive officers which made
him rely on himself.   He discouraged indiscriminate arrests; he gave orders that men merely drunk should be

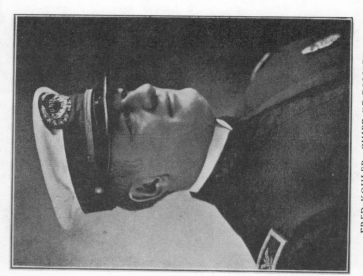

FRED KOHLER, CHIEF OF POLICE

"He got results and on these results he built what has come to be
known as the Golden Rule policy."

HARRIS R. COOLEY

"If service of a higher order on humanitarian lines has ever been
rendered to any city than that rendered by Mr. Cooley
to Cleveland I have yet to hear of it."

taken home instead of dragged into police court and made
to suffer the humiliation of a fine and branded with a
police court record.   The greatest efficiency was no longer
measured by the number of arrests an officer made.

Kohler's practices coincided well with the policy of our
charities and corrections department.   But he arrived at
his conclusions from an entirely different line of reasoning
than Mr. Cooley had arrived at his.   Cooley was an ideal-
ist, the gentlest of men, the son of a minister, himself a
minister who believed in applied Christianity.   To him
the teachings of the Sermon on the Mount were personal
commands.   He never asked whether a thing was expedient, but always whether it was right.   Now Kohler had
been brought up in a different school.   Police service isn't
especially calculated to develop the softer virtues.
Kohler is German, with the masterful race characteristics
strong in him.   He is a martinet with his men,— his discipline almost military.   He arrived at his conclusions
after the most thorough tests of his various methods.   He
got results and on these results he built what has come to
be known as the Golden Rule policy — a name Kohler
never applied to it.   He called it common sense and so it
was, but then so is the Golden Rule for that matter.

Kohler always had enemies.   Whether he kept the
same ones or raised a new lot annually does not matter.
They were always there.   These enemies had their best
chance after I left the City Hall and their terrific attack
on his personal character and his official record culminated,
in the summer of 1910, in his suspension as chief and in
his trial before what was considered an inimical tribunal
— the civil service commission — with the result that

though all the years of his record were searched in the hope of finding something which would reflect unfavorably upon him, he was completely exonerated and immediately restored to office.

XVIII

THE new city government went into operation May 4, 1903. That the administrative department was not to be impaired by the abolition of the federal plan which had placed the chief responsibility upon the mayor has been shown; but what about the legislative department? Here the code contained provisions so ridiculously absurd that one would be disposed to laugh at them if he could forget for a moment the menace to democratic institutions exhibited in this joint action of Senator Hanna and " Boss " Cox in framing a code expressly intended to strike at a person — in this instance the person happening to be myself.

The code was so fixed that the mayor could not appoint the board of public safety without the assent of two-thirds of the council. In case the mayor and the council should not agree the governor of the State was empowered to make the appointment. The code abolished the excellent feature of the federal plan which permitted the mayor to participate in all debates in council and department heads to participate in debates relating to their respective departments. There is not a shadow of doubt that the whole thing had been carefully planned to minimize my power. Out of a councilmanic body numbering thirty-two we now had twenty-three members who were committed to our civic programme and one of

the first things the majority did was to restore the pre-
rogative of the mayor and the department heads to participate in discussions in the council.   This they were able
to do for by some curious oversight the code-makers had
empowered council to invite non-members to address
them.   Our friends defeated this piece of petty politics
by making a standing rule of council extending an invitation to the mayor and to the heads of the various departments to address the meetings of council whenever they
desired to do so.

   If the reflections I have here indulged in on the matter
of the arbitrary rulings of the new code seem bitter my
address to the council on the occasion of inaugurating the
new city government did not in the slightest degree question the wisdom or the integrity of the legislative body
which had imposed this code upon us.   Instead I said it
was not for us to quarrel with the tools that had been
placed in our hands, that what was required of us and what
we must render was the best workmanship in all respects
that the circumstances permitted.   I ventured the prediction that the officials of Cleveland would prove equal
to the delicate and difficult task before them.   " Working
harmoniously together," I said, " without regard to party,
with malice toward no man and injustice to no interest,
but in response to a lively spirit of fair play to all,
whether rich or poor, I believe that the members of this
new city government will overcome every obstacle, those
that are designedly thrown in our way as well as those
that naturally arise, and so triumphantly achieve the beneficent results they have been elected to secure.   .   .   .
What greater honor could any of us desire?   What object could there be more worthy of any man's ambition

than to succeed in giving strength and tone and exalted character to the municipality of which he is a citizen? to succeed in effectively coöperating in the work of establishing in his own city municipal self-government upon the basis of equal justice, and thereby setting an example of practical democracy to the civilized world? "

That was what I wanted to do for Cleveland — just that. It seemed the natural thing, the right thing for any mayor, for any citizen to desire for his city. But I was accused of wanting to do almost everything but the one thing that I did want to do, and from every motive, except the one that really prompted me.

Of course all this outside interference, this " guardian angel business," as one of the newspapers styled it, strengthened us in our fight for home rule. If a movement is really based upon a principle of right, upon a fundamental truth, nothing injures it. Its progress may be checked but it cannot be permanently stayed. Its enemies aid it in the long run.

As soon as our new form of government was in operation and the supreme court injunction against us raised we went ahead with our street railroad plans. The second step towards low fare was taken May 4, 1903, the day on which the new municipal form of government went into effect, when eleven low fare ordinances were introduced in council. On July 18 bids were opened, only two being received, one for a cross-town line on Denison avenue, an isolated route on the west side and having no connection with the down town district, from Albert Green, representing J. B. Hoefgen's successors; the other for a line on Seneca street from J. B. Zmunt. On September 9 the grant for the Denison avenue line was made to Green. It will be remembered that a cash deposit of ten thousand dollars was now required with each bid. A few minutes after council had made the grant to Green a councilman rushed in with an armful of revocations, but it was too late. The ordinance had been passed. The Cleveland Electric Railway Company claimed a majority of consents and was asking for an extension to their lines through Denison avenue. They said they had the consents, but weren't ready to file them. They never did file them and on September 4 the board of public service denied their application and granted that of the three-cent-fare bidder. Council confirmed this unanimously and on September 9, the requisite number of consents having been filed, made the grant to Green as already stated. Commenting on this the Cleveland *Plain Dealer* said, "Unless blocked by the courts there can now be no obstacle to the immediate fulfillment of at least a part of the original issue with which Mr. Johnson went before the people in his campaign." I was not quite so sanguine and when interviewed merely said that the three-cent line would be in operation long before those who were opposed to it were ready for it. I knew we needn't expect Privilege to lie down until it was whipped to a finish and that hadn't been accomplished yet, by a good deal.

Ground was broken for the Denison avenue line September 23 and then the enemy got busier than ever. Every one of the property owners' signatures on the consents was scrutinized by the courts and fought over like the signature to a contested will. Every fly speck that might possibly offer an excuse for a law suit was examined. A mile of the road was completed and the work was going on when it was stopped by an injunction, a few days after the fall election, that is on November 12. The hearing on the injunction was first set for November 16, then postponed to the 30th and so it dragged along. The company had expended thirty thousand dollars on the construction of the line and was under bond for twenty-five thousand to complete the work. Injunctions multiplied so rapidly and checked the progress of construction so effectually that the enterprise was often referred to as the three-cent-fare railroad buried in the mud. It took time and more patience than in my earlier life I would have supposed existed in the whole world to put that venture through.

At last the supreme court decided the case in favor of Green on the ground that the plaintiffs had permitted him to spend so much money before having him enjoined. This fact created an estoppel. But for Senator Hanna's political activity, he being a candidate to succeed himself in the fall of 1903 when this was going on, and the unquestioned fact that an injunction would hurt him he certainly would have moved before election day and prevented an estoppel. The city's real success at last in creating a line from which extensions could be made was due to the fact that Senator Hanna sacrificed his street railroad interests to political necessity. He had been quoted as saying, " When I can't combine business and politics, I will give up politics," but public sentiment in Cleveland was making it increasingly hard to combine business and politics and even Senator Hanna had to defer to public opinion.

When at last those three miles of track on Denison avenue were completed they furnished the long desired base line from which other lines could be extended. It was the only bit of railroad in the city not under the control of the Concon, for by this time the merger of the Big Con and the Little Con had been effected. This merger was commonly attributed to my activity in the city's interests. On July 6, 1903, the Concon commenced to sell six tickets for a quarter and to give universal transfers — clearly a measure of self-defense.

From this little line on Denison evenue extensions could be made and one after another was made. Property owners' consent wars were raging on the streets all this time and the council chamber and the courts were the scenes of constant battles. The city was powerful in the council, the Concon powerful in the courts. First one side would move, then the other. As the franchises of the old company expired renewals instead of being granted to them were granted as extensions to the three-cent line and so inch by inch the three-cent line grew longer and became more and more threatening daily. The administration policy already referred to of changing the names of streets was often necessary. This was the most intense period of the street railroad struggle so far, and for this reason detailed information as to dates and specific activities has been given. It was the fear that all grants as they expired would go to the three-cent-fare company which finally gave the city its most striking victory in the year 1907. That year the valuation of the street railroads of the city was made by F. H. Goff and myself after four months of public hearings, at the end of which time the property was leased to a holding company to be operated for the public good. I shall tell more of this later.

Simultaneously with the street railway war other matters of moment claimed my attention as mayor. I had become convinced that a combination existed among local contractors for running up the price of paving. It had been the custom to call for a few bids at one time. I decided to break up the combine by calling for bids on the entire paving for the year 1903. I called before me a representative of the Barber Asphalt Company and told him that his company could never hope to do any asphalt paving for our administration since we did not believe in that kind of paving but that they might secure the brick paving for the city if he could assure me that they would do it at a great saving to the municipality. When the bidding took place this company underbid the local contractors by one hundred and ten thousand dollars. The defeated contractors immediately got a restraining order from the supreme court enjoining us from entering into a contract on account of the illegal character of the charter under which the city was operating. Upon final hearing the injunction was dissolved. Luck was on our side in this case. Senator Hanna was not interested in street paving and he had no objection to supreme court decisions which did not affect him.

The editorial comment of one of the local newspapers was significant: " The municipal administration was treated to a genuine surprise in the action of the supreme court dissolving the injunction in the paving contract. So accustomed has the administration become to supreme court injunctions every time it attempts to do anything that the action   .   .   .   was quite unexpected."

Believing in the municipal ownership of all public service utilities, I was eager to take advantage of everything

the laws made possible in this direction. For many years
Cleveland had owned its waterworks, and though the
municipal ownership of street railways was not nor is
yet permitted, there was no legal obstacle to a municipal
lighting plant and our administration took steps to establish one. On the night of May 4, 1903, when the new
city government went into effect, an ordinance was introduced into council providing for a bond issue of two
hundred thousand dollars. This passed by unanimous
vote May 11. When the ordinance was published it was
discovered that it was so worded as to provide for an
" electric light and power plant." It developed that
there was nothing in the statutes to cover a power plant.
In order that prospective buyers of bonds might raise no
question on this point it was thought best to pass the ordinance again with the words " and power " eliminated.
At once the Cleveland Electric Illuminating Company got
very busy. It didn't want to be obliged to compete in the
lighting business with its own best customer — the city.
It went to council. That body was composed of nine
Republicans and twenty-three Democrats: twenty-two
votes were required for the necessary majority of two-
thirds on all legislation of this character. The Illuminating Company succeeded in winning over three Democratic members. These men voting with the nine Republicans defeated the ordinance when it was again introduced. Another instance of what outside influence does
to councils!

We decided then to call a special election on the bond
issue and named September 8 as the date. On September 1 Attorney-General Sheets, at the instance of Thomas
Hogsett, acting in the interests of the Cleveland Electric

Illuminating Company, brought suit to prevent the special election, and a restraining order was granted on the ground that the Cleveland board of elections was an unconstitutional body and that the Longworth act providing for special bond issue elections was likewise unconstitutional. The hearing was set for September 22, nearly two weeks after the date fixed for the election. It happened that on that very same day the city was also enjoined from entering into a contract with the Municipal Signal Company of Chicago for the installation of a police signal system.

Our campaign for the bond issue election had been planned and the first meeting was scheduled for that night, September 1, so a few hours after the restraining order had been served, Mr. Baker, Mr. Cooley, Mr. Springborn and I presented ourselves at the tent and found our audience waiting for us. In its news report of that meeting the *Plain Dealer* said, " The old siren song of the injunction has not lost its charm. It was the injunction that neighbor talked of to neighbor, it was the injunction they came to hear discussed, it was the injunction that caused men to wonder that Mayor Johnson had the temerity to open the campaign at all." Naming the speakers the report continued, " All explained the municipal lighting plant proposition with as great seriousness as if the matter were really to be disposed of next week."

We had another meeting the next night and another the next, and the board of elections was providing for registrations to be on the safe side. In the meantime City Solicitor Baker hastened to Columbus and managed to have the hearing set for Saturday, September 5, three days before the proposed election. The hearing was held,

Mr. Baker arguing for the dissolving of the injunction, Mr. Hogsett who by the way had been director of law under the administration preceding mine, and Senator Hanna's ever faithful Sheets, presenting the arguments against it. The supreme court refused to dissolve the injunction, our special election couldn't be held and our municipal lighting proposition was retired to temporary oblivion.

How many times in our tent meetings, both in Cleveland and out in the State, when I was asked, " Why do you believe in municipal ownership? " such instances as this one came to mind when I answered:

" I believe in municipal ownership of all public service monopolies for the same reason that I believe in the municipal ownership of waterworks, of parks, of schools. I believe in the municipal ownership of these monopolies because if you do not own them they will in time own you. They will rule your politics, corrupt your institutions and finally destroy your liberties."

"My enemies called my tent a circus menagerie."

A poster in the campaign of 1902

XIX

STATE CAMPAIGNS

SIMULTANEOUSLY with these activities in Cleveland I was conducting a State wide campaign — the inevitable and logical result of earlier canvasses in behalf of the central principle round which all our agitation revolved, viz., just taxation. The greatest privilege monopolists own is the privilege of making other people pay their taxes for them. It is no small job to hammer that truth into the consciousness of a people whose favorite maxim seems to be, "Let well enough alone," and who apparently regard whatever *is,* as " well enough."

Our attempt to make some impression on the county auditors' tax boards, after showing up the low assessment of railroad property, has already been described. Occasionally we got an auditor to vote with us but we really made no headway. Then I started over the State, attacking county auditors and showing up their methods, and those of the railroads.

Of course, this kind of campaigning was making me as obnoxious to the machine Democrats of the State as I was to the public service corporations in Cleveland. In 1901 there was little difference between the methods or the aims of the Republican and Democratic parties in Ohio. Friends of the Standard Oil Company contributed to the campaign funds of both. In Cincinnati, Columbus and Toledo, Privilege depended upon the local bosses of the two leading political parties to join forces whenever such alliance was necessary to its service. In lesser degree this coalition of Democrats with Republicans for the benefit of Big Business existed in smaller places too, but in these larger cities it was quite open and shameless. It was very plain to me that the first thing we had to do was to clean house. There was no hope in the Democratic party so long as it could be manipulated by political crooks. In 1902 we were able to write the State platform and it contained demands for home rule, just taxation and a two-cent-a-mile steam railroad fare. Herbert S. Bigelow of Cincinnati, a student of sociological problems and an able advocate of the single tax was nominated for Secretary of State. This was before the introduction of biennial elections and before all the state officers were elected at one time. It was not a gubernatorial year. I traveled over the State in an automobile speaking from it, in halls or from the steps of public buildings in the day time and usually in a tent at night, having the tents sent from place to place by wagon train. Mr. Bigelow accompanied me and proved to be a good campaigner. Home rule and the railroad questions were our principal issues.

At a tent meeting, in Crawford county I think it was, word came to me that eight Democrats in the State legislature (then sitting in Senator Hanna's extra session, the one which enacted the municipal code), notwithstanding their platform pledges had voted for a curative law which had for its object the saving of a franchise granted to a street railroad in Cincinnati operated by the Widener-Elkins Syndicate under the Rogers law of 1896. Grants made under this fifty-year law were beginning to be questioned in the courts, so the legislature in an attempt to save the public service corporations passed this curative act. I at once announced that I should go into the counties of the eight Democratic legislators who had voted for this measure (I was speaking in the home county of one of them that night), and denounce them to their constituents as unworthy of trust, and that if any of them ever dared to run for office again I should defeat them if it was in my power to do so.

This pledge I made good. My bitterest fight was against W. H. Earhart of Richland county. When he became a candidate for renomination in the spring of 1903 I made a quick automobile tour of his county speaking in every town, village and hamlet and scattering literature broadcast. I was charged with violating my own principle of home rule. I answered, " I stand for home rule. If I advocated the election of a county official whose jurisdiction was confined to party lines I might be open to criticism, but I am here to give reasons why a legislative candidate should not be elected. The legislature is a State office in which the legislators pass laws for Cuyahoga county as well as for Richland. The situation is not so secret or so sacred that it should not. be open to the public to hear about it."

My opening meeting was at Mansfield, the county seat, where I had been warned that I would be egged when I appeared on the Opera House stage. Though I inquired for the eggs as soon as I got up to speak none came at that meeting or any other. Earhart was beaten at the primaries.

In one of the other counties, the home of Representative Wells, another of the faithless eight, I was approached by the local managers in the fall campaign of 1903 and importuned not to mention Wells's name on the plea that he was *for* the State ticket and nothing was to be gained by raking up old scores. As I was the candidate for governor, they no doubt felt sure their persuasions would prevail. But I kept my word and devoted part of my speech to Wells's record.

So far as I know not one of these eight men, "black sheep" we called them, has ever dared to show his head in politics since and Wells alone of the whole number came to one of my meetings though I visited the home counties of all of them and invited them to come.

We didn't elect our State ticket in 1902, but we made big gains in the counties where our campaign was waged hardest and we carried Cuyahoga county.

Our fight to elect honest and intelligent members of the State legislature may be said to have been continuous. In the summer of 1903, and before the State convention, I participated in the legislative campaigns of a number of counties. The election of a United States Senator was the important question to come before the next legislature and Mr. Hanna was a candidate for reëlection.

The Democratic State Convention met at Columbus August 25 and 26. I was a candidate for the gubernatorial nomination, not because I thought it likely that the Democrats could elect a governor but because I believed I could make a more effective campaign as a candidate than as a free lance, and because I had been persuaded that my name might lend some strength to the legislative ticket. The boss-ridden element from Cincinnati didn't want me and sent a contesting delegation; so too a group in Cleveland — discharged city employés for the most part — were gathered into an eleventh hour rump convention managed by an attorney for the gas company, and elected delegates to Columbus. By noon of the second day, however, all open opposition had disappeared and I was nominated by acclamation, August 26.

Our platform declared for Home Rule and Just Taxation, the Initiative and Referendum, the City's Right to Own and Operate Public Utilities if the people desired, Franchises to be submitted to Vote, Two-Cent-a-Mile Steam Railroad Fare, and against Government by Injunction, Waiver of Injury Claims by Employés, Acceptance of Passes by Public Officials, Fee System in County Offices. The platform was denounced as " communistic " by members of our own convention in a minority report.

Immediately following my nomination I called upon all who did not believe in the principles we were advocating not to vote for me. I invited all the crooks and thieves within the party to get out of it. If ever a campaign was fought on platform issues and not on the personality of any of the candidates that campaign was so far as our side was concerned. We carried our educational propaganda into nearly every county of the State, following the same line of campaigning that I had instituted the year before traveling by automobile and shipping the tents from town to town by rail. The great questions were, home rule, equitable taxation and the unholy alliance between the Republican party and the owners of Privilege in the State of Ohio.

It is quite unnecessary to state that the public service corporations contributed nothing to the Democratic campaign fund *that year*. From the Columbus convention I went to Noble county, the home of State Auditor Guilbert who had ordered our Cuyahoga county auditor, Mr. Wright, to cease probing the tax records of five public service corporations in Cleveland, and spoke August 27 to several thousand people at the county fair. I got home August 28 — that was the day we announced the election on the bond issue for the municipal lighting plant which we expected to hold September 8, and I announced also that the State Democratic campaign would be opened the day after our special election.

On August 29 I addressed a very large crowd at Silver Lake — a picnic resort a few miles from Akron,— the home of the manager of the State Republican campaign, Senator Charles S. Dick. Colonel Myron T. Herrick, the Republican nominee for governor, a Cleveland banker, mentioned in the early chapters of my story, had been invited to attend the meeting also but did not put in an appearance. The next day I filled two dates for Mr. Bryan at Oak Harbor and Toledo, respectively, he being unable to make these places.

September 1, 2 and 3, we held meetings in Cleveland in the interests of the municipal lighting project, as has already been stated. On September 6 I served for the second time in my life as a police court judge, being called upon because practically all the qualified officers were away on their vacations. I tried forty-seven individual cases. The next day was Labor Day, and after reviewing the industrial parade with twenty-two thousand marchers in line, I left by automobile for Sandusky where I had an engagement for the next day. On the next, September 9, we opened the State campaign at Akron where Honorable John H. Clarke, the Democratic candidate for the United States Senate and I spoke to a crowd estimated by the newspapers at seven thousand. From that time until the night before election I spoke every day with the exception of Mondays (Monday being my day off so that I might always be in Cleveland for the meetings of the city council), and about four days in mid-October when my voice gave out and I was obliged to cut a few meetings. The campaign was a most aggressive one. It opened in the hottest of summer weather. Before it closed there were cold rains and a blizzard or two. We traveled through mud and wet, sometimes speaking while drenched to the skin. I spoke from four to seven times daily, and once seventeen times in one day, always winding up with a tent meeting at night and traveling by automobile except when the roads were so bad that we had to resort to horses and a surrey for short trips.

I addressed all kinds of meetings — family reunions, farmers' picnics, small groups of people hastily gathered together at country cross roads and to thousands and thousands in the tents,— the number at one meeting alone reaching eighteen thousand, and crowds of one thousand to five thousand being not uncommon.

I made that whole campaign without once mentioning in my speeches the name of my opponent, Colonel Herrick. Our fight was not against Herrick but against Mark Hanna. When the Republicans opened their campaign a little while after we had been going the interest grew more intense. At that meeting Senator Hanna picturesquely denounced me as a " carpetbagger followed by a train of all the howling vagrants of Ohio with a crazy quilt ticket and pretending to stand upon a Populistic, Socialistic and Anarchistic platform." The campaign slogan of " Stand pat " was worked into many doggerel rhymes set to popular airs and at first no effort was made to meet the real issues. Personalities, campaign songs, red fire and brass bands were the weapons of the enemy.

Both in city and State campaigns I always discouraged brass bands, red fire and the usual artificial paraphernalia of political contests. We relied entirely on the merits of the questions we were presenting. The cost of tent and other meetings and of literature represented our outlay. The absence of funds for other expenditures offended the old-fashioned Democratic politicians. They believed campaigns couldn't be won without money, and the other side certainly demonstrated that they could be won *with* money. But we were not fighting for the day, nor for that year only. We were really breaking ground for the clean campaigns of the future.

Mr. Clarke and I were eager to debate with Senator Hanna but neither he nor any of his associates would accept our challenges. As the campaign progressed the Republican speakers were compelled to discuss the issues to some extent and then it was that Senator Hanna set up the time-honored scarecrow of " Socialism." Said he, " The moral features of this campaign are paramount. This is because the Socialist party strikes at the home. And here I want to cry out the warning that the Socialist party of the United States has for the first time a national leader. Yes, I charge that Tom L. Johnson is the national leader of the Socialist party. I beg of you to rise and kill the attempt to float the flag of Socialism over Ohio. We invite to this country people from foreign shores who are ambitious and industrious, but we do not invite from foreign shores men imbued with the desire to get something for nothing. Socialism is only a short step from anarchy and you should rise up and suppress it if for no other reason than that our late lamented president, the honored McKinley, was a victim of that damnable heresy. . . . A vote for Johnson is a vote for chaos in this country. . . . Socialists like thieves steal up behind to stab."

These sentiments no doubt had their influence in the campaign, but I think they did not scare the common people as much as Peter Witt's " picture talk," scared the privileged crowd. They had the newspapers of the state with them and made the most of this advantage. We had just three newspapers of any consequence on our side. We had no money, we had alienated a lot of professed Democrats, we were fighting the most successful organizer and the biggest money-getter for political purposes then in public life in America. And yet it was not Hanna, the man, that we were fighting, but Hanna the representative and defender of Privilege. In those days there could be but one result in such a contest. When the election returns came in we were beaten, if one counts defeats by votes which I didn't, for when I was asked on election night when the next campaign would begin, I answered, " to-morrow."

In large headlines the newspapers proclaimed the death of Democracy in Ohio and of the non-partisan movement in Toledo, Mayor Jones having supported us and his forces having suffered serious rout. But the non-partisan movement wasn't killed, nor was the Democratic party, as future history was speedily to prove. The prin-

MY STORY

ciples we advocated in that campaign were just as true at
its close as they had been at the start, and some of them
have since been splendidly vindicated. In spite of the
big Republican majority we made gains in many Republican counties and later events prove that these gains had
a very wholesome significance.

Looking back on that campaign now we can almost say
that we weren't beaten for since then Ohio has enacted into
law many of the things we fought for.

The changes in the tax laws as they affect steam railroads, the abolition of the pass, the two-cent-a-mile steam
railroad fare, as also the substitution of a local quadrennial board of appraisement for the old decennial appraisers have already been mentioned. In addition to these,
municipalities now have the referendum on street railway
franchises so a corrupt city council can no longer make a
street railway grant worth the paper on which it is written
for the voters have the power to veto it; some of the powers of mayors taken away by the Cincinnati code have
been restored; the fee system in county offices has been
abolished.

It is true that most of these measures have been enacted into law by Republican legislatures, but they have
come largely as a result of our agitation. Some of the
most important were introduced by Democrats from Cuyahoga county and lost, only to be introduced and carried
later by Republicans; as for instance the measure for the
taxation of public service corporations which Frederic C.
Howe worked so hard to carry while he was a member of
the senate.

The success of these activities is not here put forward
as a boast of personal achievements in any sense. It is

Pitching the tent in a cornfield

Photos by L. Van Oeyen

"The tents were sent from town to town by wagon train."

used simply as a practical illustration of the claim made in the opening paragraphs of this story that Truth once set in motion along any line is foredoomed to victory. This cannot be reiterated too often.*

* Appendix.

XX

HOW PRIVILEGE FIGHTS

THE effort to " get Cleveland " by means of the new municipal code was a dismal failure. The next move of our political foes was to abolish spring elections. For a long time there had been a growing tendency in Ohio towards something akin to independent voting in the municipal elections which were held in the spring. Privilege seemed to have its best hold on the State elections, which occurred in the fall. Early in Governor Herrick's administration this question came up. The governor asked me what I thought of it. I told him I thought it was a good thing, that one regular election a year was enough. He looked a bit surprised and I said, " You didn't expect me to say that, did you, Myron? " I did not discuss the motives for the proposed legislation with him or any of the other advocates of it, but it seemed passing strange that any of them should think us so stupid as not to see just why they were throwing the municipal elections in with the state elections. They reasoned that on a long ticket headed by the candidates for governor and other state offices they could surely count upon the head of the ticket carrying with it the names at the bottom — the candidates for municipal offices. Ohio, staunchly Republican in State and national elections, would finally rid itself of those two pestilential creatures, Jones and Johnson, who somehow kept getting elected as mayors of Toledo and

Cleveland, one as a non-partisan and the other as a Democrat.

Early in 1904 the State legislature abolished the spring election and because of this the terms of the principal municipal officers in Ohio cities instead of expiring in the spring of 1905 held over until January 1, 1906, the officers for that year being elected in November, 1905. This first biennial state election resulted in a practically clean sweep, but for the Democrats instead of the Republicans. The verdict of the last State election was reversed. For the first time in many years and for one of the few times in the whole history of the State, Ohio elected a Democratic governor. Mayor Jones had died but the non-partisan movement in Toledo was stronger than ever and not only was Brand Whitlock elected to succeed Jones but he carried with him into office the other municipal candidates on the non-partisan ticket — a result never achieved in Mayor Jones's lifetime. In Cleveland we elected our whole ticket including our legislative candidates, a fine body of democratic Democrats.

Shortly thereafter it was provided by constitutional amendment that State officers should be elected at one election and municipal officers at another, so this election of 1905 was the only one which combined a State with a municipal election.

My own plurality was the largest I had ever received, being double that of either of my previous elections. In that campaign my opponent was William H. Boyd, the only Republican candidate who ever consented to debate with me, and the one who put up the most manly fight of any who ever ran against me. For some reason Mr. Boyd did not have the undivided support of the business and privileged interests, a rather significant fact in the face of his willingness to debate campaign issues. When I suggested the debates I asked Mr. Boyd to join with me in arranging for them without the formality of a challenge from either side. He agreed and it was part of the arrangement that he should make the rules for one meeting, I for the next and so on. When the plans were completed I said to him,

"You are a trained speaker in daily practice before courts and juries and have an immense advantage over me, but I am going to beat you in these debates." This nettled him a little and he asked me why. I said,

"Because I know this case better than it is possible for you to equip yourself to understand it between now and election day."

We had six enormous meetings in halls, the last four in Central Armory, the largest auditorium in the city. We preserved good order in spite of bad blood on both sides and the tremendous interest of our respective partisans. I had taken the precaution to have the floor covered with sawdust, for I had often seen meetings practically broken up by someone who could not hear, perhaps, rising to go out and making such a noise on the floor that immediately everyone else who had difficulty in hearing felt encouraged to do the same thing. So the sawdust prevented a lot of noise and ensured most of the people staying through the meetings. Large-faced clocks were placed in full view of the audience and by these our time was divided. It was one of the rules that any eruption or disturbance on the part of the audience was to be deducted from the time of the party supposed to benefit by it, and I have frequently seen wild demonstrations almost instantly quelled by a mere gesture of the time-keeper toward the clock.   As I got to know Mr. Boyd better I appreciated that his motives were more sincere and much nearer the public good than they were credited with being by his enemies.   There is no doubt that the debates helped our side.

There had been fifteen injunctions against the low fare movement by this time but we were patiently hammering away on our original proposition.   The Cleveland Street Railway Company had made various experiments in the matter of fares.   After abandoning the six tickets for a quarter and universal transfers they tried three-cent fares, then four-cent fares for stated short periods, none of the trials being made in really good faith, and yet all showing the weakness of the company's case.   The city was consistently pursuing its policy of granting no renewals of franchises and the question of expiring franchises was constantly coming up.

The best street railway grant from the standpoint of the public interest is one that has already expired.   The public has no interest in a franchise being for any specific length of time.   The time limit serves private interests and affords an excuse for tying the public's hands.   For three or four years short lines and parts of other lines were permitted by the city to operate without specific grants.   I recall one case where it was absolutely necessary to connect up a big public park with a new line.   The street railway and the city couldn't agree on a grant, so I said to the company, " Go ahead and build the line. The city won't bother you.   Some taxpayer may, but if you are quick enough I don't believe you will meet any opposition in that direction."

That line, one-half mile long, was built and put into operation very quickly. A great hue and cry was raised in council because the line had been built without a grant. Councilmen not friendly to our movement raised the objection. I explained the danger of making a grant as compared to the safety of what had been done but they were not satisfied. I then suggested that if council would pass an order to tear up the tracks I would see that it was done. No one was willing to make such a move and the mere suggestion of it cooled the ardor of the critics. They said they were in the minority and hadn't votes enough for such action. Finally I said to them,

" If you will offer a resolution protesting against this and argue it in council, I'll see that the line is taken up even if the resolution doesn't pass."

This took away their last argument as I knew it would. No one was willing to interfere with so obviously necessary an improvement. I was criticized for this and accused of disregarding the law, but the only sensible thing to do was to build. It is a great pity that more street railroad grants are not made on such terms, for this avoids the necessity of giving away a lot of public rights or tying them up for a definite period, for any grant however safe-guarded might be interpreted by the courts as giving some rights and prolonged litigation would certainly follow in which the company would gain time if nothing more. It got to be one of the features of our controversy that the street railroad could build lines, but couldn't get grants.

Here is a specific case in point which illustrates the wisdom of such a course: A street railway line was needed around the new postoffice building. Everybody wanted it, but in this instance the street railway company didn't want to build it.   Nothing short of an act of Congress could bestow the property owners' consents necessary to a valid grant, for the federal government owned a majority of the feet front on each of the four sides of the building. The city therefore, without power from council or any other legal authority, and even without funds for this specific purpose, did construct this piece of railroad and owned it.   Any property owner in the city, any taxpayer could have prevented it by applying to the courts, but in all this big city of Cleveland there wasn't one person with sufficient hardihood to interfere.   It only shows what can be done when everybody is willing and what obstacles can be thrown in the way when some private interest is trying to balk a public enterprise.   There is hardly a city in the country where there are not a lot of unused grants which street railway companies preserve very carefully, running cars over them once a month or at some other regular interval.

Municipal ownership would save all this.   Without the private interest street railroads would be built with the same care and operated with the same considerations of public utility that obtain in fire lines and police stations. A careful study of all we did in the long street railroad war in Cleveland furnishes the best arguments I know in favor of public ownership and operation of this kind of property.

Grant for the sake of argument that a municipally owned street railroad will not be as economically managed in some directions as one privately owned, but there are a great many credits to this account.   There wouldn't be the foolish and expensive litigation that private companies indulge in. There wouldn't be the laying down of routes to prevent competition. To be sure, cars might be kept extravagantly neat and clean, and passengers might receive wasteful consideration, the pay of the men might not be put down to the lowest possible notch and strikes to enable the payment of dividends wouldn't exist at all.

The opponents of municipal ownership would bring all these objections which you now hear against street railroads as readily against the municipal operation of the fire department if they had any idea they could make them pay. But arguments for fire departments in private hands have almost passed away. Fire departments operated by private interests and protected by public franchises are said to exist in China now, and as a matter of history did exist in the time of the Cæsars. The franchise for putting out fires was considered a very valuable right by the plutocratic public service corporations of ancient Rome.

Our fights were not always with Privilege from the outside. When councilmen could be reached and made to oppose measures for the public good, the representatives of Privilege were probably happiest. They knew what happens to a house divided against itself and some of the hardest contests we had was to keep the council in line for the city. I think I never lost sight of the fact that we were working for the city. Accustomed to think in business terms, I regarded Cleveland as a great corporation — the biggest in the State of Ohio — its inhabitants as the stockholders and the city officers as the directors.

Roughly speaking, there are three kinds of councilmen,

just as there are three kinds of congressmen and three kinds of State legislators. There is the earnest, intelligent man working for better things, there is the crook working for better pay, there is the painstaking good fellow working for he doesn't know what. He wants to be right, tries to be right, thinks he is right, but is conscientiously wrong on almost every subject. A combination of any two of these classes in any legislative body always wins. The least hopeful, the hardest to move because of his imaginary virtues is the one who belongs to the third class. I always got the best results from combinations of the first and second classes, for the second, whatever his other shortcomings may be, is usually wise — too wise to be fooled — and between right things and wrong things, unless the price is high enough, he will be for the right. He won't go wrong just for the fun of it. Left to his natural bent and usual good judgment he will go right. My experience in this direction has impressed two things very strongly upon me — one, that the intelligent crook may be relied upon many times when the perfectly good, well-intentioned man will fail; two, that legislative bodies left to themselves will go as nearly right as the native honesty and intelligence of the members make possible, for the corruption of such bodies comes from without, not from within.

We had some experience in this direction when the East Ohio Gas Company was negotiating with the city for a franchise. The application for a franchise was made in a tentative sort of way. The whole thing had an air of mystery about it at first and I didn't understand what the hesitation was about until I met a friend who asked me whether the fact that the Standard Oil people owned the natural gas wells would handicap a company seeking the franchise. I answered that it would have the other effect. It would inspire me with confidence that they wanted to build a gas plant and not get a franchise to sell out. I learned then that this idea that I would be antagonistic because of the connection of Standard Oil Company people was what held them back. John O'Day, head of that branch of investment, came to Cleveland to see me then and asked frankly whether the East Ohio could get a franchise. I told him I would use my influence to that end if they didn't attempt to tamper with the council. I told him that whatever trade was made must be for the benefit of gas users and when we had agreed on the price he must take his people away, leaving everything else to the council and to me.

Matters progressed smoothly at first, but it wasn't long before opposition to the proposition sprang up among the coal dealers and the artificial gas people. After a long fight, in which I made some offensive charges against members of council in connection with these last named interests, we got to a place where the measure was to be finally passed or defeated on a certain night. On the afternoon of that day Councilman Kohl came to me and said that a man named Dr. Daykin had offered him five thousand dollars in cash for his vote and asked me what he should do about it.

" If you were really a game man I would suggest a line of action," I answered, " but I don't think you would carry it out, so there's no use in my advising you."

This appealed to his vanity and he begged me to advise him. He said he would do anything I suggested except go to jail, and he'd even do that if I would promise

MR. JOHNSON IN 1905

to protect him.   I therefore advised him to keep his appointment with Dr. Daykin and take whatever money was offered to him.   In less than two hours he came back with two thousand dollars.

That night a dramatic scene occurred in the council chamber.   I was speaking, Dr. Daykin was among the spectators sitting outside the railing.   I charged that attempts had been made to bribe some of the councilmen in order to prevent the passage of the ordinance.   The charge created a sensation, for bribery wasn't taken lightly in that body, or in that community.   The councilmen and the lobby were giving the closest attention to what I was saying.   The interest was intense.   At a certain point in my speech and by pre-arrangement with Kohl he threw the two thousand dollars on the table before me, and no other proof of my charges was necessary. In the excitement Dr. Daykin hurried for the door, but I was watching him and called out, " You won't get very far, Doctor.   Some of my friends are waiting for you outside."   The ordinance passed without a dissenting vote.   Whether it would have been possible to carry it without this incident I do not know.

Dr. Daykin was arrested and after a long trial in which many persons testified he was acquitted.   We thought he was acting for a combination of coal dealers and the artificial gas people, but did not know positively, and weren't able to prove it.

The reason I wanted the franchise passed to the Standard Oil people was that I was eager to get for the people of Cleveland cleaner and cheaper fuel and light than the coal companies or the artificial gas people could furnish them.   I believed the Standard Oil people had a monopoly of the natural gas field — there was no one else from whom to buy — the city could not compete with them.

Whatever the fault of the Standard monopoly it wasn't due to Cleveland or to Ohio; neither the city nor the State was responsible for it. At bottom it was a land monopoly. Our friends the Socialists hold that such monopolies should be taken over by the government and operated for the benefit of the people. I contend that they can be taxed out of existence. It really doesn't make a great deal of difference, so far as I can see, however, whether the community owns and operates a monopoly, or whether it takes in taxes the value to which it is rightfully entitled. That the people should get the benefit is the important thing — the method is secondary.

One of our liveliest fights — the one on which the final success of our municipal lighting plant was based — has already been alluded to along with the activity of the Cleveland Electric Illuminating Company and its success in preventing the repassage of the ordinance by council and the special bond issue election. In the fall of 1903 we lost the bond issues which were submitted, along with everything else, so our municipal lighting project was still a thing of the future. In the 1904 election the citizens of Cleveland voted eight to one and those of the village of South Brooklyn three to one in favor of annexing South Brooklyn to the city. The city council appointed City Solicitor Newton D. Baker, Frederic C. Howe and James P. Madigan, annexation commissioners. Now South Brooklyn owned a small electric lighting plant and for this reason Privilege was opposed to annexation. To have Cleveland acquire a municipal lighting plant in this way was as obnoxious to the Cleveland Electric Illuminating Company as the city's other plan had been, and its fight was now directed against annexation. The first move was to have council reconsider its action on the appointment of the annexation commission and appoint another friendly to the lighting company. I refused to confirm the appointment of this second commission and publicly charged fifteen Republican councilmen with misfeasance and two Democrats with bribery. A councilmanic investigation was started. The city solicitor ordered the Cleveland Electric Illuminating Company to open its books for examination by council. The company got out a temporary injunction restraining the city from enforcing this demand, which order was made permanent a few days later by Judge Beacom, whom I had appointed director of law at the beginning of my first administration. The city carried the case to the circuit court, which sustained the decision of the lower court, and so the investigation was effectually blocked. I made the unfriendly councilmen very angry by maintaining that the Cleveland Electric Illuminating Company seemed to have more power than forty thousand voters, but it was true that the expressed will of the people in the 1904 election had to wait more than a year before it could be put into effect. Before the next election I went into the wards of the two Democratic councilmen, above referred to, and defeated their re-nomination.

After the pronounced victory in the 1905 election, when we carried twenty-five of the twenty-six wards of the city, the councilmen got together and voted to accept the report of the annexation commissioners, which provided for the immediate annexation of South Brooklyn. The councils of both city and village passed the necessary ordinances, December 11, 1905.

Under the law, annexation would not be complete until a record was filed with the county recorder and a copy forwarded to the Secretary of State. The work involved in preparing these papers prevented the completion of the annexation until the Thursday following the Monday night council meeting, but in the meantime, on Tuesday morning, the mayor and the solicitor of the village of South Brooklyn called at the City Hall, and told Peter Witt, the city clerk, that an ordinance granting a renewal of street car rights on certain streets to the Cleveland Electric Street Railway Company had had two readings and that they feared it might be given a third reading and passed, thereby further entangling the street car situation. Without consulting anybody Witt called up Chief Kohler and asked for an officer. His request was at once complied with and he hustled one of his deputies and the policeman off in a municipal automobile with instructions to bring back the town clerk and all the records of the village of South Brooklyn. The automobile got back to the City Hall about noon with the cargo it had gone after. The village clerk turned over all the records, but Witt was taking no chances and at his request three policemen were detailed to watch the town hall in South Brooklyn, the village policemen (three in number) were also given instructions to keep a sharp lookout and to break up any attempt to hold a council meeting. No such attempt was made and by Thursday annexation was finally accomplished, and Cleveland was in possession of a small municipal lighting plant.

The city later acquired another such plant in the annexation of Collinwood.

When Newburg was in process of being annexed to Cleveland a twenty-five-year franchise to the Cleveland Electric Street Railway Company was hurried through the village council, the signature of the mayor only being required to complete the ordinance. The newspapers all said that the mayor had announced that he would sign it, and that was the general expectation. The last meeting of the village council was held the last night that the village had legal existence as such, and it certainly looked as if our problems were to be complicated by a village grant to the street railway company. But at the last moment the mayor vetoed the ordinance. The newspapers said that the first intimation anybody had that he was not going to sign was when he called up his wife that night and told her he had changed his mind. Our whole movement seemed to be constantly beset with incidents fraught with the greatest possibilities of defeat or success. There was something doing all the time.

It was early in my third term that Chief Kohler found it necessary to take drastic steps to stamp out an effort to revive public gambling. In a rapidly growing city with a numerically inadequate police force, it is almost impossible to keep this vice within bounds. Kohler did it, though, but he did not hesitate to employ heroic measures on occasion. He seized the gambling paraphernalia from a hotel and smashed it with an ax, destroying two mahogany tables, cards, markers and chips. After his third raid on this hotel the chief appealed to John D. Rockefeller as owner of the property to coöperate with him in his efforts to stop gambling there. Kohler has a way of holding the owners of property responsible for the uses to which it is put instead of placing all the blame upon the tenants, which is sometimes very disconcerting to big landlords.

At the very time when gamblers were inveighing against the administration on one hand, the ministerial association of the city was complaining about it on the other. Personal representatives of both called upon me. The gamblers admitted that I had " played no favorites," but had treated them all alike, and the ministers gave me credit for not making promises and then breaking them. I really took some pains to explain to these last named gentlemen that I was quite as much interested in the welfare of society as they were, but that I was trying to reach the root cause of the conditions of which they complained, whereas they seemed to be concerned with symptoms only.

But whatever the other matters that engaged our attention they were small compared to the street railroad question which was always up. It was this that engaged most of our time, used up our energy and taxed our ingenuity. The chief reason why this was such a big question was that it involved the largest financial problem, for the receipts from the street railroad were about equal to the receipts of the city government from all sources.

XXI

PERSONAL LIABILITY SUIT AND THE "PRESS" GUARANTEE

THE summer of 1906 found the street railway fight raging fiercely. It was constantly growing in intensity and bitterness and in personal animosity towards me. This animosity culminated in the fall of 1906 in an effort to connect me personally with the three-cent-fare street railroad grants. The old company contended in one breath that these grants had no value, and in the next that my relationship to them was so close that it constituted a personal pecuniary interest. This personal liability question grew out of an injunction to prevent the low-fare people from operating cars on Concon tracks for about six hundred feet on Detroit avenue,— which tracks had been for years considered free to joint occupancy of any company with the consent of the city.

The Concon proposed to show personal financial interest in the low-fare company on my part, thereby proving invalid the grant signed by me as mayor. A summary of the low-fare movement from its inception to this time will help the reader to understand the absurdity of this foolish charge.

The aim of the low-fare propaganda was municipal ownership which the laws of Ohio did not permit, but we were getting ready for it in making the fight for better service and lower fares, thus teaching the people that they had some jurisdiction in the regulation of public service utilities. Our entire Cleveland fight in one sense was a struggle to have recognized the sacredness of public property by private interests as the sacredness of private property is recognized by public interests. We never attacked private property. We were always engaged in the struggle to force the recognition of the rights of public property, whether in public hands or private hands. We never advocated the breaking of a contract, no matter how unfair that contract was to the people, but constantly resisted the claims and quibbles of ingenious lawyers to extend over public property private rights that did not exist.

In spite of the tremendous pressure brought against it by the public service corporations, through unfair newspapers, constant litigation, and political tricks of various kinds, the low-fare movement made its way. The organization of a new traction company known as the Forest City Railway Company was secured and grants were made to this company with the provision that they could be acquired by the city at not more than ten per cent. above cost, as soon as a municipal ownership law could be obtained. The Forest City line was obstructed every time it made a move, as has already been repeatedly shown. It costs money to build and equip railroads, but the expense is enormous when you add to it the cost of litigation growing out of a new injunction suit nearly every day. It was not easy to capitalize an enterprise which was so badly handicapped, and to find a person too honest to be bought, willing to take the risk of losing money without any possibility of making more than an ordinary six or seven per cent. investment was one of the most difficult tasks I had to face during the whole of the low-fare fight. But the man for just this emergency came to us in the person of my friend, ex-Congressman Ben T Cable of Rock Island, Illinois. Mr. Cable put one hundred thousand dollars into the company and later an additional two or three hundred thousand. At any time when the fight was warm he could have sold out to the old company at an immense profit, and not only defeated the low-fare movement but brought discredit upon all connected with it. He fulfilled every obligation and his service to our cause cannot be over-estimated. I didn't see then and I don't see now how we could have prevented a disastrous defeat without Mr. Cable's timely assistance.

The opposition newspapers meanly insinuated that he must have some ulterior motive and delighted in calling him my " cousin," as if to prove thereby that he could not aid the low-fare fight in a disinterested way. When the final history of that struggle shall be written Mr. Cable's service will surely be given the high place that it deserves.

In 1905 the city proposed to the old company a settlement of the whole vexed problem by means of the organization of a holding company. It was my idea that this holding company should take over all the street railway interests of the city as lessee. A fair rental should be paid and the property operated in the interests of the public and not for profit. As security to the old company a twenty year franchise should be granted to the holding company with the agreement that it should revert to the private interests if the holding company failed to make good under the terms of the lease. The city offered to place a valuation of eighty-five dollars a share on the Concon stock, which figure was much too high, for the price offered would have given the old company about three times as much for their property and unexpired franchises as it would have cost to rebuild the whole system in first class condition. The advantages that would accrue to the city it is impossible to measure in money, as it would remove the biggest incentive for bad government by Big Business. This offer they rejected and in 1908 they were forced to accept a settlement based on a price of fifty-five dollars a share.

The Municipal Traction Company was then organized as the holding company and completed in the summer of 1906 with A. B. du Pont as president and director, Charles W. Stage, Frederic C. Howe, Edward Wiebenson and William Greif as the other directors, and W. B. Colver as secretary. The directors were salaried and self-perpetuating, but neither they nor the company were to profit in any other way. Their books were open to the public and all their transactions were public. The holding company owned no railroad, but became the lessee of the Forest City Company. The capital for construction was raised by the sale of Forest City stock at ninety cents on the dollar and deposited in trust for use in construction by the holding company. The holding company agreed to construct and operate the low-fare lines, to pay six per cent. on the capital, to pay off the capital at ten per cent. above par and to devote the entire surplus to extensions and improvements. Everything had been done openly. There had been no secret negotiations with the old company nor in other directions.

Both the Cleveland Electric and the Forest City were seeking franchises. As the Cleveland Electric was known as the Concon, so the Forest City and the other low-fare

Asking the Mayor's permission to play ball on streets

companies organized later were called the Threefer. Here is a parallel comparison of their offers to the city for such franchises:

CONCON.	THREEFER.

CASH FARES.

Five cents.	Three cents.

TICKET FARES.

Seven for twenty-five cents; $3\frac{4}{7}$ or 3.57.	Three cents.

TRANSFERS.

Limited as at present to lines to be built.	Universal under constant council regulation.

FRANCHISES.

Irrevocable grants. Bargain to be made now for twenty-five years.	Revocable grants. Franchise to be terminated at any time.

SERVICE.

Promises with no reserved right to council to enforce.	Full power left to council to regulate at any time under penalty of revoking franchises.

EXTENSIONS.

Promised, but at discretion of the company; profit on unlimited capitalization.	Promised and discretion left in the city; profit on actual cost only.

SUBWAYS AND ELEVATEDS.

Subways or elevateds some time, if a rate of fare can be agreed upon.	Subways and elevateds whenever council directs, and at a 3-cent fare.

CONCON.	THREEFER

CAPITALIZATION.

$150,000 per mile.	$50,000 per mile.

DIVIDENDS AND PROFITS.

All that can be gotten on $150,000 per mile.	Only six per cent. on actual money investment within $50,000 per mile.

CITY OWNERSHIP.

Prevented for at least twenty-five years.	Always possible if desired by the people and permitted by the Legislature.

TITLE TO THE STREETS.

Passes absolutely for twenty-five years.	Remains absolutely in the city for all time.

PUBLICITY.

Books closed to the council, city and public.	Books kept open to all who may care to look.

POPULAR VOTE.

One vote to be binding for twenty-five years.	Submission to the people at any time.

FINALITY OF SETTLEMENT.

Makes a repetition of the present struggle continuous and inevitable.	Ends the struggle for eliminating private interests from this public service.

GROWTH IN NET EARNINGS.

All benefits reserved to the stockholders of the company.	All benefits reserved to the people of the city of Cleveland.

Early in the summer council ordered the Concon to move its tracks on Fulton road from the center of the street to one side to make room for the tracks of the Forest City, which company had a franchise to lay tracks on the west side of the street. Having had so much previous experience with the old company's disregard of orders from council the city was authorized to remove the tracks at the Concon's expense, provided the latter had not complied with the order at the end of the thirty-day period stipulated therein. No attention whatever was paid to the city's order; it wasn't even acknowledged. The thirty days elapsed, then two weeks more; then, early on the morning of July 25 a big force of workmen under the direction of the mayor and Server Springborn proceeded to rip up the tracks. Every preparation for getting the work done quickly and in the best possible way, and with the least damage to the pavement, had been made in advance. The ends of the track were torn up first so that the cars of the Concon could not block the work. This move on the part of the city was a complete surprise and found the old company quite unprepared. It was about eleven o'clock a. m. (and the work had been going on since seven) before the injunctions were served on the mayor and Mr. Springborn. These injunctions were so ambiguously worded, due no doubt to haste and to the court's lack of information regarding the real facts in the matter that it was anything but clear what they proposed to restrain. It was too late anyway to restrain us from removing the tracks that were already up. Our " lawlessness " occasioned a great howl among the real law-breakers and Mr. Springborn and I were charged with contempt of court. The contempt proceedings occupied about a week and at the end of that time, on August 3, I was exonerated, but Mr. Springborn — certainly the least culpable of any person connected with the transaction from first to last — was found guilty. He was fined one hundred dollars, which, I am happy to say, he never paid.

The Forest City Company, which had proceeded with the laying of its tracks on the west side of the street, was enjoined July 26 and the work had to stop while the matter was fought out in the courts. Eventually it was able to proceed once more. In the city's case we were also successful, the court holding that the city had acted within its rights and was under no obligation to replace the old company's tracks.

The track which the city tore up was, by a curious coincidence, on the very street the bidding on which had been the occasion of my coming to Cleveland twenty-seven years before. It was on this street in 1879 that I had been beaten by Simms and Hanna, and it was over this street too that a three-cent car was to run a few months later.

When stock of the Forest City Company to the amount of $400,000 was offered for sale, the Cleveland *Press* editorially recommended it as a safe investment for persons of small means and more profitable than savings bank deposits, describing the plan July 1, 1906, as follows:

"The Forest City Railway Company has sold $350,000 worth of stock at 90. It has offered for sale and is now soliciting subscriptions for $400,000 more of the stock. All of this stock is to be put out at 90. The Municipal Traction Company under the terms of its lease of the Forest City Railway Company has guaranteed 6 per cent. cumulative dividends on the par value of this stock. The entire amount received for the sale of this $750,000 worth of stock at 90 is to be invested in about 13½ miles of street railway construction and equipment. This means a capitalization of about $50,000 a mile; no bonds; no water. The Cleveland Electric Railway Company (the old monopoly company) is bonded and capitalized at about $150,000 a mile. The difference in these two propositions must be apparent to the merest tyro in finance."

The stock sales as a result of this stand on the part of the *Press* and from advertisements in various magazines were very satisfactory. The Forest City railroad was fast nearing completion, twenty-four injunctions had expired one by one, there were fewer obstacles in the way of success than at any time before, and a three-cent-fare railroad in actual operation in a city where such a thing had for five years been declared impossible, and where no stone had been left unturned to render it impossible, was hourly becoming more and more certain of accomplishment. This was the status of affairs when the personal liability question was raised. For five days I was kept on the witness stand in a notary's court testifying to facts which were matters of common knowledge. The opposition newspapers of Cleveland referred to these as testimony " wormed " out of me, " dragged " from me, etc., and through the Associated Press the newspapers of the whole country were furnished with a great talking power against our movement. One of the mooted questions was whether I had guaranteed the Cleveland *Press* against loss when that newspaper had invited and guaran-

teed stock subscriptions. The *Press's* own statement on
the matter is so clear and comprehensive that I quote it in
full. On October 24, 1906, it had the following:

"Here's a Nice Little Scoop on the Concon Lawyers."

The Only Authentic Record of the Deep, Dark Mystery of That
" Press " Guarantee.

At the examination of Mayor Tom by the Concon attorneys
Wednesday morning, the question was asked as to whether Mayor
Tom had guaranteed *The Cleveland Press* against loss when *The
Press* guaranteed the stock of the Threefer.

Mayor Tom said that whatever there was in the way of such
a guarantee was in writing and that he would decide at the afternoon hearing whether or not he would produce the writing.

It makes little difference whether Mayor Tom decides to produce the writing or not, as *The Press* happens to have a copy and
by publishing it herewith scores a scoop on the Concon lawyers:

Here's the writing:

Whereas, The Forest City Railway Company is inviting subscriptions to its six per cent. (6%) cumulative dividend stock,
and the undersigned desire to aid in the establishment of a 3-cent-
fare street railway in the city of Cleveland, with the ultimate
municipal ownership thereof, and to that end desire to induce
popular subscriptions in small sums from the people of Cleveland; and

Whereas, *The Cleveland Press* proposes to invite subscriptions
to such stock and to recommend its readers to make such subscriptions, and to offer to them the guarantee hereinafter set out:

Now, therefore, the undersigned hereby agree, each with the
other, and with the Scripps Publishing Company, publishers of *The
Cleveland Press,* and with each subscriber to such stock through
the columns of *The Press* as follows, to wit:

To each original subscriber or his personal representative whose subscription has been made through *The Cleveland Press,* and who subscribes for an amount not exceeding two thousand dollars ($2,000) of the par value of said stock, we agree to purchase the stock so subscribed on sixty days' notice, given within ten (10) days after any dividend or interest period, and to pay therefor the amount paid by each subscriber with six per cent. (6%) interest thereon from the date of his payment, less any interest or dividend which he has received; this offer to purchase to be open for two (2) years from the date thereof.

They also severally agree with The Scripps Publishing Co., its successors and assigns, that they will each on demand repay to it any sums which it may pay out under the following guarantee:

[Here appears a copy of the guarantee which was attached to the stock of each subscriber, who subscribed for stock through this newspaper.]

In making the above agreement and guarantees, each of the undersigned agrees to bear and discharge one-half of the same, it not being intended that this shall constitute a joint obligation of each for the whole.

It is mutually understood and agreed that the amount of stock to be sold under the above guarantee shall not exceed the sum of four hundred thousand dollars ($400,000) of par value.

In testimony whereof we have hereunto set our hands and affixed our seals this 29th day of June, A. D., 1906.

E. W. Scripps.

Tom L. Johnson.

The circumstances under which this contract was drawn up are interesting.

E. W. Scripps, the founder and controlling stockholder of *The Press* was in Cleveland last June and expressed a desire to see Mayor Tom.

Mayor Tom called on him and among other things discussed was the progress of the fight for lower street car fares.

Mayor Tom outlined what had been and what was proposed to be done, and Scripps said: " If you are so sure of the success of your plans why don't you personally guarantee the stock of the low-fare company?"

"I am perfectly willing to do so to the extent of my fortune," was the mayor's answer.

"Well, I'll go halves with you to the extent of $400,000 worth of stock which is now for sale WITH THE DISTINCT UNDERSTANDING THAT NEITHER OF US IS TO PROFIT TO THE EXTENT OF A DOLLAR," said Scripps.

Up to this point the matter of guaranteeing the stock was a personal matter between Scripps and Johnson.

How to get this guarantee before the people in the best possible way was then taken up by Scripps with H. N. Rickey, editor-in-chief of *The Press.*

After some discussion the whole matter was turned over to Rickey, to handle in any way he saw fit, or not to handle at all so far as *The Press* was concerned.

Rickey consented to guarantee the stock through *The Press,* provided neither Johnson nor Scripps would consider any step taken or any contract drawn up as confidential and that Rickey would be under no obligation, either stated or implied, to keep any of the facts here set forth from the readers of *The Press,* whenever in his judgment they would make a good news article.

This seems to be the psychological — not to say dramatic — moment.

In passing it might not be out of place to suggest that there probably will not be any doubt, if there ever has been any, that *The Press* guarantee is worth 100 cents on the dollar.

The next day the *Press* said editorially:

THAT HELPS SOME.

The horrible accusation is made by the Concon and its newspapers against E. W. Scripps, *The Cleveland Press* and Mayor Tom, that to the extent of guaranteeing investors against loss, they have lent their credit to a three-cent street railway company in Cleveland.

For E. W. Scripps and itself, *The Cleveland Press* pleads guilty to this accusation.

As Mayor Tom has admitted the accusation at least fifty times during the past year, no further proof seems to be necessary.

The net result to the people of this city of the efforts which Mayor Tom and *The Cleveland Press* have made for lower street car fares in Cleveland is this:

A three-cent line has been built and equipped and will be ready to carry passengers over its fourteen miles of track just the minute that the Concon injunction department will permit. This three-cent line is prepared to take over every Concon franchise as fast as it expires.

As for the Concon, that company is, figuratively speaking, on its knees, begging the people to extend its franchises for twenty years at seven tickets for a quarter.

Not a bad situation FOR THE PEOPLE OF THIS CITY to be in, is it?

Were it not for the well-known innate modesty of *The Press,* we might be inclined to crow a little over the part we have played in bringing about this most delightful situation.

If either the Concon or its newspapers will show us how it is possible for the people to lose when two street railway companies are fighting like the very devil for the privilege of carrying passengers at a rate of fare which will mean the saving of millions to street car riders in the next decade, we shall never again say one word in favor of lower street car fares in this city.

No matter how hard *The Press* tries to please the other newspapers of this city, it doesn't seem able to do it.

After twenty-seven years of effort in this direction, it doesn't appear to be any nearer to it than when it started.

Our only consolation is that THE PEOPLE generally seem to approve of us and our methods; and after all THAT HELPS SOME.

My own position in the matter had been publicly set forth in a formal statement made at the time of the " *Press* guarantee," in which I said:

" Inasmuch as I am associated, in the public mind, with the enterprises herein set forth, I deem it fitting that I make a full statement of my position. I am not now and never have been financially interested in the Forest City Railway Company. I have, however, in the discharge of my pledges to the people of Cleveland, aided in every way in my power the efforts to construct and operate a system of low-fare railroads in this city. I have in the past a number of times when requested become liable as surety in bonds and guaranteed the payment of obligations of the Forest City Railway Company, but the net result is that while I have in the past stood to lose if the enterprise failed, I never have and never will reap any financial benefit from its success. I believe that it will succeed and that the people who ride on street cars will benefit from reduced fares and that those who invest money in the low-fare road will reap fair dividends and profits from the venture. To my mind this is not a philanthropic enterprise, but rather a plain and sound business proposition. I believe that publicity and the high personal integrity of the directors of the Municipal Traction Company will guarantee the carrying out of the plans set forth in absolute fairness to the public and to the stockholders of the Forest City Railway Company. Secrecy and over-capitalization are two cardinal vices of the modern public service corporation. Neither of these can have any place in this plan. With the utmost regard for all the rights of existing companies, I shall do all in my power to further the success of the Forest City Railway Company and the Municipal Traction Company, but my interest shall not be of a pecuniary nature. In lending such aid and encouragement I feel that I shall be doing no more than I have promised the people of Cleveland. For five years a struggle has been waged in Cleveland to secure reasonable fares. In all that time I have, as mayor, and as a citizen, waged no unfair war on any private interest. This enterprise shall have my hearty support and I confidently invite the support of the public, both as citizens and as investors. The grants to the Forest City Railway Company will establish street railroad facilities where they are very much needed, and will, on a capitalization of fifty thousand dollars a mile, in my judgment, produce a net revenue of more than fourteen per cent. on the actual capital invested. The Cleveland Electric is earning eight per cent. net on a capitalization of about one hundred and fifty thousand a mile. This would mean, if capitalized at actual cost, between twenty and twenty-four per cent., so that the estimate of fourteen per cent. net earnings is conservative. The city of Cleveland has made the greatest growth in its history in the last six or eight years, and during all that time the building of street railroad tracks has been almost at a standstill. Extensions equaling one-third of the present system are now greatly needed. The lowering of the fare will greatly stimulate traffic, and make more tracks and equipment necessary. When asking for grants for extensions, both in new territory, and for grants on streets where franchises have or will expire, the Forest City Railway Company is likely to receive at the hands of the city favorable consideration not only because the fare is lower, but because all earnings above the fixed payment to the investors are to accrue indirectly to the benefit of the city. The city shall provide in all grants to that company proper safeguards, but can afford to be much more liberal in making grants under these circumstances than where there is no limitation of future profits. This plan really secures to the people of Cleveland better service and lower fare and the benefit of all future growth in franchise values and economies in the operation of street railways."

The evidence showed plainly that if the low-fare project failed, I should lose about four hundred thousand dollars, but that in no event could I profit a penny by the enterprise. When the court asked me why I had made guarantees to creditors and stockholders, I answered:

" I'll tell you why. Some men like to leave monuments behind them; some build hospitals, some libraries. Others build universities. I want to see that there is a street railroad built that will be run in the interests of the people."

XXII

FIRST THREE-CENT FARE CAR

TWELVE or fourteen miles of track on the west side, overhead construction and power-houses had been completed and everything was in readiness for operating the line from Denison avenue to the point of contention already referred to — the six hundred feet on Detroit avenue from the intersection of Fulton road to the viaduct.

Sixteen months before this Judge Robert W. Tayler of the United States Court of the northern district of Ohio had held that the Concon's franchise on Central and Quincy avenues had expired on March 22, 1905. Council had therefore granted the Forest City Company the right to operate on these two routes, and while the city could have stopped the operation of the Concon cars it permitted them to continue without interference. We thought it better to permit the service at the higher fare than to deprive the car-riders of it. Now, however, when the low fare lines got ready to connect with Central avenue, which extends eastward from the Square and which was reached by free territory tracks in the down town portion of the city, more injunctions were forthcoming. Workmen were promptly prevented from tearing up Brownell, now Fourteenth street, preparatory to laying the tracks for the connection, and at about the same time, John W. Warrington of Cincinnati, applied to the supreme court of the United States to prevent the city of

237

Cleveland from interfering with the Cleveland Electric
Street Railway Company's operations on Central and
Quincy avenues and Erie street. Warrington was accredited with being one of the chief influences in having
secured from the supreme court of Ohio a reversal of
that court's decision in the case of the Rogers law. Under this law the Cincinnati Traction Company held a
fifty-year franchise on all the street railways in Cincinnati. The supreme court declared the law unconstitutional. Then Warrington and his associates took it up
and secured a reversal of this decision. He was said
to have been one of the principal movers also in the
framing of the municipal code, so our city's affairs were
not wholly unfamiliar to him.

While all this was transpiring in the last days of October the cars of the Forest City Railway Company were
on their way from the factory in the east to Cleveland,
and on November 1, 1906, the first three-cent-fare car
made its first trip from Denison avenue to Detroit avenue
over the unenjoined part of the road. By common consent I was the motorman. City officials and other friends
of the municipal ownership movement were the passengers on that initial run, but the company rules were enforced and every passenger paid his fare. It was just
five years and six months to a day since I had been elected
mayor the first time, and at last part of our dream had
come true — not that I had ever doubted that it would!
but it was good to feel that we had really gotten somewhere finally.

It was a sunshiny day and the brightness of the day
seemed to be reflected in the faces of the men, women and
children who crowded around us at the car-barns and lined

"By common consent I was the motorman."

Photos by L. Van Oeyen

First three-cent fare car—November 1, 1906

the streets all along the route. They had even decorated
their houses, some of them, with flags and bunting as if it
were a holiday, and here and there women on the streets
threw bunches of fall flowers from their own little gardens
towards the big new yellow car as it passed. A committee of women, I remember, brought a big floral piece
to me at the car-house and said they wanted to thank us
for getting the three-cent fare for them. That was the
best of it — it was a people's victory — a victory for
women and children as well as for men, and they all knew
it. I don't know, of course, but I think I was the happiest person in the whole crowd, and I guess I looked
it, for one of the newspapers said that my smile expanded
and broadened until it eclipsed everything behind it in
the three-cent car.

With the operation of the first three-cent-fare car the
stock of the Cleveland Electric Railway Company went
down to sixty-three.

I confidently believed that the injunction on Detroit
avenue would be dissolved in a few days and that the low-
fare cars would run over into the center of the city without further obstruction, but I was too hopeful. Shortly
after the line was put into operation I went out of town on
business, to Chicago if I remember rightly, as that city
was in the midst of its traction war then and Mayor
Dunne and I exchanged several visits. When I got back
Mr. du Pont, president and operating manager of the
Municipal Traction Company, met me at the station with
the somewhat disheartening news that the injunction still
held, but immediately followed it up with the startling
suggestion to " jump the viaduct." We had been in a
good many tight places together in the course of street

railway operations in other cities and we agreed that
physically this feat could be accomplished, but whether it
could be done legally neither of us knew. After nearly
a whole day's conference with his lawyers they gave their
sanction to Mr. du Pont's plan, I believe because they saw
he was going to do it anyway. The next day, under his
personal direction, in the midst of an interested crowd in
which the Concon attorneys figured conspicuously, a Forest City car was derailed at " injunction point," as Secretary Colver humorously dubbed the place where the low-
fare cars were forced to stop. By the use of horses,
jacks, a gang of men and the municipal's own current (for
du Pont was careful not to use any of the Cleveland Electric's power), the car was pushed, bumped, lifted, carried
along somehow, and at last safely landed on the tracks
on the viaduct and others soon followed.

It will be remembered that I said in the beginning of
this story that it was the city's ownership of those tracks
on the viaduct that gave the community its chief strength
in the struggle to come years later. Low-fare cars were
on those tracks now where they couldn't be enjoined.
That ancient expedient — a free bus — was at hand to
transfer passengers from the terminal of the Forest City's
right of way on Detroit avenue to the waiting cars at the
west end of the viaduct, but it wasn't really needed. The
passengers were more than willing to walk that six hundred feet.

From 2 :30 p. m. until midnight the cars were operated
over the viaduct at intervals of five or six minutes. A
switch had been put in on the west approach of the bridge
where the cars could be stored when not in use. Within
a few days the three-cent cars would have been operating

to the Public Square, but the day after they were gotten onto the viaduct the Threefer was met with the most outrageously unjust injunction which it had so far encountered, and that is putting it pretty strongly. The restraining order affecting the strip on Detroit avenue which had just been jumped was now made to include territory on Superior street between the east end of the viaduct and the Public Square. This portion of Superior street had been free territory since 1850. A free territory clause was contained in the first franchise ever granted by the city, the question had twice been fought out in the supreme court and both times that body had declared the territory free. For any man or set of men to claim the exclusive right to this portion of street was certainly the height of arrogant disregard of the city's right to control its own streets. But be that as it may, the low-fare cars were now stopped at the east terminal of the viaduct. At one of the hearings one of the Concon's eminent attorneys made those present gasp for breath when he gave voice to the remarkable statement that, " if the right which we claim is well founded, it is our contention that no one has the right to interfere with us in the operation of cars even to the extent of running a 'bus line."

The court granted the restraining order on the ground " that the ordinance of the city council fixing the compensation for the joint use of the tracks by the defendants was invalid because of the admitted financial interest of Mayor Johnson in the defendant company." This decision came just at Christmas time in 1906.

The night of December 26 the Forest City Company attempted to lay temporary tracks on top of the pavement on Superior street, N. W. If it had succeeded the three-cent cars would have been running to the Square by seven o'clock the next morning. The low-fare people believed the Concon could not enjoin them from laying these tracks, but at three o'clock in the morning an injunction was served at the instigation of a property owner, who was also a Concon stockholder. There was nothing to do but to stop the work. A day or two later, by permission of the court, the Forest City people removed their wagons, tools and equipment from the street awaiting the action of the court on the temporary restraining order. On January 2, 1907, Judge Beacom ruled that the Forest City Company had no right to construct separate tracks on Superior avenue. The company promised to remove its temporary tracks immediately and at once put that promise into execution. On that same day Judge Ford issued injunction No. 32 against the Low Fare Company stopping the laying of tracks at Sumner avenue, S. E. The Low Fare Company had a franchise from the council for tracks on Sumner avenue and on New Year's day had put a force of one hundred laborers to work at laying tracks on Sumner avenue from East Fourteenth to East Ninth streets. The company already had tracks on these streets which it wished to connect by the Sumner avenue route. Six hundred feet of track had been laid when the work was stopped by Judge Ford's injunction, January 2. This is the way the holiday season was being celebrated by the contending forces in Cleveland.

But the people were getting the benefit of the contest, for on December 31, 1906, the Concon commenced to sell seven tickets for twenty-five cents. It was now fighting desperately to have all the low-fare grants declared void on the ground that I was financially interested in them.

Photo by L. Van Oeyen

"The night of December 26, 1906, the Forest City Company attempted to lay
temporary tracks on top of the pavement on Superior St., N.W."

All of the facts as to this contention have already been related and the utter absurdity of the charge shown. It isn't worth while to follow the legal intricacies of the thing; and it is anything but pleasant to recall the methods employed to poison the minds of the people, but if one purpose of the story of our nine years' war with privilege in Cleveland is to arm other fighters in other fields with courage to resist and to endure, it would be less than fair, perhaps, to say nothing on this subject. Under the heading Street Railway Talks the Cleveland Electric Street Railway Company was running daily double column reading matter in several newspapers purporting to be educational propaganda on the local situation. No. 120 of the " talks " appeared November 24, 1906, under the usual note, reading:

" NOTE — Each day you will hear something new on the street railway situation.   Read it, and if you disagree or care to make any suggestions concerning it, we shall be glad to hear from you."

" THE CLEVELAND ELECTRIC RAILWAY COMPANY,
" By Horace E. Andrews, President."

This is what talk No. 120 said:

STREET RAILWAY TALKS.

No. 120.

THE CHICAGO NEWSPAPERS are giving some attention to the Cleveland branch of the TOM L. JOHNSON STREET RAILWAY TRUST.

THIS IS THE WAY IT LOOKS to the CHICAGO JOURNAL:—

" Mayor Dunne needs to be warned against TOM JOHN-

SON, of Cleveland, whom he seems to regard as an all-wise authority on traction.

" JOHNSON MAKES FREQUENT VISITS TO CHICAGO in the pose of an adviser of Mayor Dunne, and Dunne visits Cleveland to absorb instruction from Johnson.

" The association for which Mayor Dunne is responsible, is scandalous and disgraceful. It should be stopped in the interest of MAYOR DUNNE'S REPUTATION, which IS BOUND TO SUFFER FROM CONTACT WITH A MAYOR WHO DURING HIS TERM OF OFFICE HAS BEEN TRYING TO OBTAIN A TRACTION ORDINANCE FOR HIMSELF AND HIS FRIENDS from the Cleveland City Council.

" We are not familiar with the statutes of Ohio, but on general principles we should say that SUCH CONDUCT AS THAT OF WHICH MAYOR JOHNSON HAS BEEN GUILTY OUGHT TO BE A FELONY. The mayor of any city should be that city's best friend and counselor. He should be on guard to protect the community against franchise grabbers. He should not use the power of his position to gain any benefits from the city for himself. WHEN HE APPEARS AS A BEGGAR FOR A FRANCHISE, HE SHOULD BE INDICTED AND PROSECUTED.

" If found guilty he should go to the penitentiary and stay there long enough to give him time for repentance.

" THAT IS MAYOR JOHNSON'S CONDITION AT THIS MOMENT, according to general report.

" HE IS TRYING TO INDUCE THE CLEVELAND CITY COUNCIL TO GIVE HIM A STREET CAR FRANCHISE with the hope, no doubt, that the existing traction companies will BUY HIM OFF AT A LARGE FIGURE.

" He knows as well as other traction men that A THREE-CENT FARE STREET RAILROAD IS AN IMPOSSIBLE PROPOSITION IN THE UNITED STATES.

" He himself, in Philadelphia and New York, where he was a street railway owner, WOULD HAVE NOTHING TO DO WITH A REDUCTION OF FARES TO THE THREE-CENT BASIS for he knew that with such a reduction his companies would go into bankruptcy.

" He knows that A THREE-CENT FARE ROAD IN CLEVELAND WOULD NOT BE A SUCCESS as an operating concern, however great might be its success as A CLUB FOR BLACKMAIL against existing companies.

" But the rate of fare has nothing to do with the right or the wrong of MAYOR JOHNSON'S ATTEMPT TO EXTORT A FRANCHISE from the Cleveland city council except as the three-cent fare factor in it shows how conscienceless a man may be when he is afflicted with the greed for money.

" THE POINT IS THAT THE MAYOR OF THE CITY IS USING THE INFLUENCE WITH WHICH HE IS TEMPORARILY FURNISHED TO OBTAIN A CONCESSION FOR HIMSELF.

" Such a man is an evil counselor for Mayor Dunne, who should refuse to give ear to his pleadings.

" Mayor Dunne is an honest man, but very ready to listen, and when he heeds an adviser as sharp and keen as MAYOR JOHNSON, WHO CAN MAKE THE WORSE APPEAR THE BETTER REASON, he is in danger of forfeiting the respect in which he is held.

" Mayor Dunne does not think of Johnson as a man guilty of what ought to be felony, but only as mayor of Cleveland and a pleasant person to meet.   Doubtless Johnson, who is master of the arts of persuasion, uses that of flattery and makes Mayor Dunne believe himself to be a great and good man.

" Under these circumstances, Mayor Dunne should be especially careful of himself and hearken not to the voice of THE FAT CASUIST OF CLEVELAND.

" If he listens long to him he is likely to do something that will cost him all his friends and well-wishers in Chicago, and in

exchange for them gain nothing but the SNEERING AP-
PROVAL OF MAYOR JOHNSON, which will be with-
drawn the very moment Johnson has NO FURTHER OCCA-
SION TO MAKE USE OF HIM.

" Mayor Dunne is no match for Tom Johnson in skill and
resources. He should keep away from him, therefore, and preserve his dignity without risking the loss of it at the hands of
THAT ADROIT ADVENTURER."

This is the kind of " educational campaign " the Concon was conducting through paid advertisements in the
newspapers, the *Press* alone declining to print them, when
the " financial interest " suit was on in the courts. They
managed to bring the case before a pliant judge and a
very stupid man withal, and they got from him the desired
decision. Later, after a full hearing before a reasonable
judge, this foolish verdict was set aside, but it had served
its purpose of delaying the extension of the three-cent
fare lines and seriously embarrassing the Forest City Railway.

When the Forest City Company found itself confronted with the probability of having all its grants declared invalid because of the " personal interest " claim
they were forced to decide quickly what move to make
next in order to retain the advantage the city had so far
gained over the old monopoly company. It was at this
juncture that the Low Fare Railway Company came into
being. It was incorporated by W. B. Colver and others
and financed by a man who believed in our movement and
who was not a resident of Cleveland. It started free
from the claim of personal interest.

The Low Fare Company bore the same relation to the

Municipal Traction Company that the Forest City did. The low-fare companies were eager to push ahead and extend their range of operations eastward on Central avenue, but while the question of this franchise was in the United States Supreme Court no move could be made. At the hearing before this court the Concon was represented by Judge Warrington, already mentioned, and by Judge Sanders of Squire, Sanders and Dempsey, the Concon's local attorneys. The interests of the city and of the low-fare line were in the hands of City Solicitor Baker and D. C. Westenhaver, who had lately come to Cleveland from West Virginia and become a partner in the firm of Howe & Westenhaver. He did most of the fighting for the low-fare companies. All the big lawyers, those of established reputation, were employed by the other side or so tied up that they couldn't accept cases for the three-cent-fare crowd — except Mr. Baker, of course, whose public employment kept him on the city's side. Privilege certainly had a powerful influence with some judges and it did its best to monopolize the best legal talent available. The odds against us in the whole long fight were so great that perhaps we couldn't have gone on as we did year after year, hopefully, cheerfuliy — even getting a lot of fun out of it, as we certainly did — if we had been able to look ahead and foresee the obstacles and count the cost. And yet I think we should have gone on just the same.

The Low Fare Company had been granted rights for a through route from east to west on East Fourteenth street, Euclid avenue, the Public Square, Superior avenue, the viaduct, West Twenty-eighth street and Detroit ave-

nue. All the low-fare grants, both of the Low Fare
Company and the Forest City, were made to expire at
about the same time, twenty years from the date of the
original Forest City grant, September 9, 1923.

The New Year found the city nearer three-cent fare
than it had been at any time during the six years of the
fight and on January 7 the low-fare people were made
very happy by the decision of the United States Supreme
Court in the Central avenue case, which confirmed Judge
Tayler's decision that the franchise of the Cleveland Electric Street Railway Company on Central avenue, Quincy
avenue and East Ninth street had expired in 1905. The
news came to us in Judge Babcock's court, where the
Sumner avenue injunction suit was being heard. Mr.
du Pont left the court room and hurried to the offices of
the Cleveland Electric, where he found two or three of
the company's directors who had not yet heard of the decision. Several other directors came in before he left and
he proposed that an agreement be effected whereby the injunction against the Forest City on Detroit avenue be held
in abeyance, the low-fare people on the other hand doing
nothing to interfere with the Cleveland Electric's cars on
Central avenue, which were to be operated at a three-cent
fare. If either side wished to terminate this agreement
twenty-four hours' notice was to be given.

The Sumner avenue grant to the Low Fare Company
was declared legal on January 9, so the people won another important victory.

Cleveland Electric stock went down to sixty after the
United States Supreme Court decision in the Central avenue case, and immediately thereafter the old company
came to the council seeking some kind of a settlement.

Photo by L. Van Oeyen

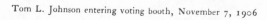

Tom L. Johnson entering voting booth, November 7, 1906

Somehow all the disagreeable litigation didn't seem to prejudice the car-riders, for the low-fare lines were exceedingly popular from the very start — much too popular for the comfort of the old company in spite of everything that had been done to make the project fail.

XXIII

AFTER SIX YEARS OF WAR

THE New Year (1907) found the city in a stronger position than it had been at any time since the beginning of the fight. Immediately after the United States Supreme Court decision in the Central avenue case, the Municipal Traction Company and the Cleveland Electric entered into a thirty-day truce, each side agreeing not to resort to litigation while the truce was operative, the Concon to be permitted to run without interruption on Central and Quincy avenues and the Threefer to be unmolested in operating from its western terminal up to and around the Public Square.

On the twelfth day of January, then, the first three-cent-fare car ran to the Public Square. It had taken two and a half years to get the grant for that car to run to the Square, and nearly four and a half years from the time the grant was made for it to wade its way through injunctions to that point. This shows Privilege's power to delay anything which is against its interest, and illustrates the persistence of our movement to hold on under all difficulties. The agreement permitting the opening of the line to the Square was carried out as soon as it was made, and before the public had a chance to be informed of it. The appearance of three-cent cars on the East side of the viaduct was a signal for enthusiastic demonstrations by pedestrians and car riders. Women waved their

1. A. B. DU PONT. 2. MAYOR JOHNSON. 3. VICE MAYOR LAPP. 4. MAYOR'S SECRETARY, W. B. GONGWER. 5. PETER WITT. 6. FREDERIC C. HOWE.

"It had taken two and a half years to get the grant for that car to run to the Square and nearly four and a half years . . . for it to wade its way through injunctions to that point."

handkerchiefs towards it as if it were a personal friend and ever so many humorous incidents occurred on the cars. Everybody seemed happy and friendly and everything seemed to point to a peaceful settlement and a speedy victory.

Enough has been told in detail to show how the fight was waged. It is not necessary to follow each of the low-fare companies in the matter of the grants made to them, nor into the courts to trace the trail of each injunction. The people of Cleveland had been patient, law-abiding and long-suffering to a remarkable degree, and when the old company and the Municipal Traction Company, pursuant to the request of the former and a resolution of the city council, commenced to negotiate a settlement there was general satisfaction.

Before the truce was six days old it developed that the Concon was violating it by going after property owners' consents and revocations on Rhodes and Denison avenues, but when President du Pont called the attention of President Andrews to this the latter ordered all consent operations stopped. It was hoped that settlement would come by means of the holding company plan — that the Cleveland Electric would lease its lines to the Municipal Traction Company, which was in position to take them over at a just rental value and to continue the operation of all cars in the interest of the community. These negotiations were conducted by Presidents Andrews and du Pont. They continued through January, through February and on until late in March. Every few days the newspapers would announce that a final settlement was about to be reached, and then again that negotiations had been broken off. At last on March 25 each side presented a statement to the city council. They had been unable to agree upon the valuation of the Cleveland Electric property. The figures presented were as follows:

ANDREWS'S VALUATION.

Total physical and franchise values............$30,500,000.00
Added one-ninth, per agreement.............. 3,388,888.88

Grand total $33,888,888.88
Funded and unfunded debt deducted.......... 9,341,000.00

Net valuation........................$24,547,888.88
Stock value, per share, this valuation.......... 105.00

DU PONT'S VALUATION.

Total physical and franchise value............$17,908,314.24
Added one-ninth, per agreement.............. 1,989,812.69

Grand total $19,898,126.93
Outstanding stock, per share................ 45.10
Redeemable on suggested plan............... 49.61

Far apart as these figures were I did not feel that they precluded a settlement. One of the daily newspapers asked me to sum up the situation and this is what I said:

"You ask me to sum up for you the street railway situation as it exists to-day.

To begin with let us eliminate one or two things that may be in the public mind through misapprehension.

Mr. Andrews has not offered to lease his road on a basis of $105 per share.

Mr. du Pont has not offered to lease on a basis of $49.61.

Mr. Andrews has said that he can figure out a value of $105

per share, but we are not informed what are the factors or processes in his calculation.

Mr. du Pont says that he can figure out $49.61 per share, and that that figure is a cold, hard trading figure, containing only about 21 per cent. good will or bonus-for-peace factor. Let du Pont tell how he arrived at his figures.

The situation to-day then is: How far ought Andrews to come down, and how far ought du Pont to come up?

If each man will give his processes as to each disputed item, these disputes ought to be settled singly and without great trouble. That is what the council is now trying to get at. Progress along such lines means progress toward a complete, satisfactory and comprehensive settlement. I believe that the Cleveland Electric Railway Company, as well as others concerned, desire such a settlement.

Now let us proceed carefully, without undue delay, and also without undue haste. The public interest — for the first time in years — is not suffering by reasonable delay. We have lowered fares all over the city, and each of the two companies, one a public one and one a private one, is vying with the other to earn and keep public favor. So there is no public clamor for a settlement to be marred by haste, though we all agree that not a minute of unnecessary delay should be tolerated. The sooner the three-cent rate comes to everybody the better.

There is one danger just now. It will be to the advantage of certain interests to start a hullaballoo over some side issue so that the main point may be obscured. This is the old tactics and we can expect it again. This time the side issue will be as to rates of fare in the suburbs. Let us meet that, settle it and dispose of it so that we can give our undivided attention to the main question.

First, ninety people ride in the city to every ten outside.

Second, the people of Cleveland and their council are not the guardians of the suburbs.

Third, the suburbs, in times past, nearly all of them, against advice and protest, have, through their councils, made long-time grants to the Cleveland Electric railway.

Fourth, each dollar of revenue cut off from a long-time suburban grant must be made up in added generosity in grants by the city of Cleveland.

Now, then, this is what I propose, that three-cent fare in Cleveland for the benefit of the ninety must not be imperiled for the sake of the ten who have bargained and granted away their chances to make contracts for themselves.

If the suburban people made twenty-five year contracts they are bound just as the people and council of Cleveland are bound by existing franchise grants.

But the suburban people must be treated just as generously and fairly as possible. I should not expect to charge five cents if service could be rendered in a given suburb for four cents. I would not charge four if the service could be given at three or three and a half.

Let us have three-cent fare and universal transfers in the city, and, with open books, agree to serve each suburb at exact cost of service. Take this in its broadest sense when I say " at cost." Let all the profit be made in the city at the three-cent fare, and simply charge the fare in the suburbs that will meet actual cost of operation and interest on physical property. Figure it just as closely as possible and have the books open to the people and officials of each suburb, so that they may know they are getting their service at cost — and that is relatively even cheaper than the cost to the people of Cleveland themselves. I think no honest man could ask more. Let us proceed to seek a fair, equitable settlement and let us not be sidetracked on a ten per cent. question, so as to lose sight of the ninety per cent. question.

As to arbitration: I believe that is just what is going on now. The council is now sitting as a board of arbitration, seeking to learn what the exact differences are between Mr. du Pont and Mr. Andrews. If each of these men will be frank and free to explain his figures and processes, their differences will be brought out so plainly that adjustment will not be difficult. I think the arbitration now in progress will meet all needs."

All street railroad conferences had been public for a long time and these were generally well attended. When any new question came up there was always an increased attendance, and the council meetings following the report just referred to were in effect town meetings.

The special street railway committee of council presented a report recommending the holding company plan on a basis of sixty dollars a share for Concon stock, which report was adopted by council, April 2, by a vote of twenty-nine to one. On April 4 the *Plain Dealer* announced in large head lines, " Directors of Cleveland Electric Will Accept Offer of Council if Three-Cent Fare is Assured," and said:

"The directors of the Cleveland Electric Railway Company, at a meeting at the Union Club yesterday afternoon, adopted a resolution covering all the points to be made in the reply of the company to the council offer of sixty dollars per share for Cleveland Electric stock on the holding company basis.

The communication is to be drawn up to-day and submitted to the board for final approval at another meeting. . . . The communication will then be ready for council and it is expected that a special meeting will be called for Friday, when the reply of the company will be formally submitted. President Andrews refused to discuss the nature of the resolution . . . but on authority of a leading interest in the company it is stated that the reply will be an acceptance of the holding plan at the figure offered by the council committee. The acceptance will be in the form of a challenge to the mayor, and in such form that if the city accepts, it must either make good on the proposal to operate for three-cent fare within the city limits, and five-cent fare outside, or the property will revert to the Cleveland Electric shareholders under a seven-for-a-quarter twenty-five year franchise."

Council met on Friday morning to receive the Company's reply. In the meantime, on April 2, Mayor Dunne had been defeated for re-election in Chicago and his municipal ownership programme turned down. How much influence this had on the action of the directors of the Cleveland Electric we do not know, but it is certain that it gave them hope that what had been accomplished in Chicago might be accomplished in Cleveland. The whole community was interested in the negotiations and the lobby of the council chamber was crowded with eager spectators. I was presiding and called the meeting to order. City Solicitor Baker and City Clerk Witt sat back of me. President Andrews and his directors, most of whom were present, sat at my left. Back of these were the councilmen at their desks and back of the rail and crowding the gallery as many citizens as could squeeze in.

The Cleveland Electric's communication was handed to the city clerk to read, Secretary Davies of the Concon holding a copy of the statement and following it closely to see that the clerk read it correctly. A hasty glance over the document showed Witt its character. If, actuated by the bitterest hatred, he had drawn up that statement himself he could scarcely have read it more effectively. It was not only a refusal of the city's proposition and notice that the seven tickets for a quarter were to be immediately withdrawn and the old five-cent fare re-established, but a most insulting attack on the mayor, the city council, and the friends and promoters of the low-fare movement. As Witt read on, page after page of the document, which made more than a page of newspaper copy when in type, he fairly " acted out " the insinuations, the cruel charges, the arrogant assumptions of the signers of that statement. He was getting angrier every minute, but kept himself well in hand, and when he had finished I asked the pleasure of the council. A member moved that the statement be received and time given to consider it. I said that the communication was a flat refusal to accept the proposition, referred to the charges against the mayor and the council, saying that we should be able to take care of these, and concluded by saying, " This question will not be settled by personal attacks, but for the benefit of the people," and asked if others wished to talk. Peter Witt was demanding the floor, as a citizen, but Mr. Baker spoke first. He said in part:

" I am speaking under strong feeling. It is not unusual for public officials to be insulted, yet it is not often .that the board of directors of the greatest corporation in the city lends its presence to sanction the reading of a studied insult. . . . I want to say that the persecution has not been on the part of city officers. This company has bought dozens of houses and lots on streets to prevent the getting of consents by the low-fare company, not to protect Concon rights but to foster monopoly. I challenge anyone to show that this administration ever tried to take away one right of the Concon. All the obstructions, all the injunctions have come from the company. I cite one instance: For two years after the Central avenue franchise expired they enjoyed the use of the streets. For your disgruntled acts I have only toleration. Your charges of persecution I throw back at you. You are the persecutors."

Mr. Baker's restraint, in spite of his emotion, my own calmness — for all through the reading of the Concon's statement I had the feeling that the things it said might be about a man from Kamchatka or some place equally remote, they didn't mean *me* — only added fuel to the flaming wrath of Peter Witt. By unanimous vote he was given the floor and as he rose, he turned to me and said, "Tom, I have deferred to your wish and your judgment on many occasions, but this morning I'm going to have my say. They are all here and I'm going to give it to them. If you don't like it, you can go to hell."

And then — and then — well I suppose it is a safe assertion that no similar body of distinguished gentlemen and leading business men was ever treated to such a scoring as those men got that day. Witt not only denounced the policy and methods of the railway company, charging that in the past it had bribed councilmen, corrupted legislators, used dishonest judges, and for months had the City Hall watched by a private detective, but one by one he called the men present by name and shaking his finger at them declared the responsibility of each for the particular things of which he held that man to be guilty. By this time the lobby was ready to roar its approval of Witt's speech but was restrained by the desire to hear every word he uttered. The incident, dramatic, almost terrible in some of its aspects, was not without its funny side. When Witt assailed the first man, by name for instance, hurling out his, "You, —— ——," and pointing his finger at him, the gentleman thus accosted was so surprised that he slid down in his chair and doubled up as if he had suddenly received a stinging blow on top of his head.

Nobody, either then or afterwards, ever attempted to reply to that speech of Peter Witt. He closed by saying, " To grant your company a renewal of franchises would be to capitalize your past corruption that future generations might pay tribute thereon. You will never get a franchise renewal. Whether Tom Johnson be here as mayor or not, with the present temper of the people you will never be able to obtain another concession at the hands of this council. Public opinion will prevent it."

Directly after the close of the meeting the Concon stopped selling seven tickets for a quarter and went back to the five-cent cash fare or eleven tickets for fifty cents.

These happenings occurred on Friday. Almost immediately the Cleveland *Press* addressed a letter to President Andrews and to me, asking us each to answer a question. The question put to me was whether I would recommend to the council that a guarantee of three-cent fare inside the city be included in the lease of the Cleveland Electric Railway, as proposed by Mr. Andrews. My answer was, " Yes," and it was published on Monday. The question put to Mr. Andrews was whether if the city followed his suggestion and incorporated the three-cent fare guarantee he would lease his company on the holding plan at sixty dollars per share. His answer was, " No," and it was published on Wednesday.

On the fifteenth of April Horace Andrews sent a communication to council saying that unless a purchaser approved by council took over the tracks and equipment of the Central and Quincy avenue lines before midnight on April 23, the company would proceed to tear up the tracks. This was a complete surprise and a week's time

was, of course, very short in which to handle so important
a matter, but a council meeting was immediately called
for ten a. m., April 16, and the Cleveland Railway Company requested to attend by an accredited delegate who
should inform the council what the property it desired
to sell consisted of, and what it considered a fair value
for same. President Andrews's astounding reply to the
council's communication sent *in response* to his own letter
was as follows:

"Replying to your request that we inform you as to what
the property is that we are willing to dispose of in Central and
Quincy avenues and what we consider its fair value, we beg
to say that which we are willing to sell is the investment of this
company in these streets. The question of its fair value we will
take up with a proposed purchaser who makes a bona-fide application and gives reasonable assurance of his ability to purchase.
As the city can, in no event, be a purchaser, we cannot see the
propriety of taking up the negotiation for a sale of this property
with the city council."

Could anything better illustrate the company's total
disregard of the public interest than this communication?
Were the people who daily used the lines in question,
who were dependent upon them for service, not to be
considered at all? Was it no part of the province of a
city government to assist in maintaining car service on
streets which had not been without it for forty years?
Was this then a simple matter of buying and selling between private individuals, or between corporations which
were unmindful of the patrons who made their very existence possible?

Mr. du Pont promptly sought an interview with Mr.
Andrews. How satisfactory it was may be judged by

the following extracts from his (du Pont's), letter to the Cleveland Electric Directors:

" The council at your request approved the Forest City Railway Company, as such purchaser and granted you permission to remove your property as requested in the event of a disagreement.

I, as the representative of the Forest City Railway Company, met Mr. Andrews, your representative, this afternoon to discuss the questions of property and price under the terms of your communication of April 15 to the council. Mr. Andrews, however, at once departed from the terms of that offer, and insisted upon an assurance of the ability of the Forest City Railway Company to pay an unnamed price for an unknown property.

He vaguely expressed the willingness of your company to sell to the Forest City Railway Company property. He declined to negotiate as to price or even roughly to indicate what property was represented by your investment in Central and Quincy avenues until you should be satisfied of the financial ability of the Forest City Railway Company to pay.

I asked what form the assurance should take in order to satisfy you, but he declined to make any suggestion as to the form, amount or character of the assurance. In order that an attempt might be made to comply with this new and exceedingly indefinite condition I asked Mr. Andrews to say, not specifically or in dollars and cents but in a general way what items of property were to be sold, but he declined even roughly to indicate what property he had in mind or whether it included cars, carhouses, tracks, poles, and wires or any of them. I next asked Mr. Andrews to state a sum of money and guarantee of ability to pay which would be satisfactory to your board, but he declined to name any sum.

From the foregoing it appears that while your company has told the council of the city of Cleveland that it is willing to sell its investment in certain streets to a purchaser to be approved by the council, and the council has approved a purchaser, yet you

decline to advise that purchaser either what the investment includes or what it is worth so that he may satisfy the requirement
that you now make as to an assurance that the cash price will be
paid."

Mr. du Pont then offered to buy tracks, poles, trolley,
span and feed wires in place on certain streets for the
sum of $149,993.19 cash, to be paid April 23 at twelve
o'clock at the Citizens Savings & Trust Company, upon
delivery of a good negotiable title and a promise not to
interfere with the operation of the road. The Concon
rejected du Pont's offer, naming $448,473 as its price,
also giving no assurance that it would continue to respect
the peace pact and not stop the operation of the Threefer
to the Public Square. And so the war was on again,
and presently the good old never-failing injunction re-
appeared.

The old company directly served notice on the Forest
City that its operations from Fulton road, N. W., to and
around the Public Square must cease, while the Low
Fare Company was enjoined from operating cars on Euclid avenue between East Fourteenth and East Ninth
streets. The Forest City cars continued their operations
twenty-four hours after notice had been served, the peace
pact having provided for a twenty-four hour notice to
quit. At the end of the twenty-four hours the Forest
City cars stopped running, but the service was not interrupted, the privilege of operating having been transferred
to the Low Fare Company which had not yet been enjoined on this route, and which proceeded to operate its
cars here. At one point the Forest City was ordered to
remove a section of its track. Workmen proceeded to
tear up the rails to the evident satisfaction of the old

company's representatives who were on the spot to see that the order was carried out. A messenger was sent scurrying over to the Cleveland Electric offices to report that it was all right, the tracks were coming up. When the bearer of these glad tidings got back to the scene of action he rubbed his eyes and wondered whether he was asleep or awake, for the tracks instead of coming up were going down. As soon as the Forest City rails were removed the track was replaced by the Low Fare Company with rails of its own. The whole thing was accomplished in about two hours. That was once when the injunction mill didn't grind fast enough.

At midnight on April 23, the Cleveland Electric discontinued its operations on Central and Quincy avenues, and both low-fare companies were enjoined from operating on the abandoned lines. This dog-in-the-manger policy could have but one effect in any enlightened community and I used to marvel at the short-sightedness of Privilege in so flagrantly violating all democratic traditions.

XXIV

THE BURTON-JOHNSON CAMPAIGN

AT about this time I appealed to the people of the community to support the low-fare movement by subscribing to its stock. The banks of the city were far from friendly towards the enterprise and it was becoming increasingly difficult to get any help from them. It was evident that if this people's project was to succeed it must be financed by men and women of moderate means who believed in the movement and wanted it to win. The moneyed people were against it, particularly of course those who owned stock in the old company. Our fight was the more difficult because it was directed against a company owned by resident stockholders. It would probably have lacked some of the bitter personal features if the Cleveland Electric had been owned by outside stockholders. The Concon added two local bankers to its board of directors at this juncture. Public subscriptions were opened for low-fare stock making it more attractive than a savings-bank deposit, the purchaser having the privilege of surrendering his stock at will and getting back his money plus six per cent. for the time it was invested. This bothered the banks a great deal for men and women were purchasing the stock and paying for it with their savings bank deposits. It wasn't an uncommon thing for bankers to try to dissuade their depositors from such a " foolish investment," but in spite of this money came in rap-

Characteristic group receiving election returns in City Hall

Photo by L. Van Oeyen

idly — sometimes as high as one hundred thousand dollars in a single day. This novel plan of raising money had many advantages, but the savings banks were the losers, and they fought desperately to discredit it.

With the beginning of operations on the three-cent line it was suggested that a bank and trust company be established in the interests of the low-fare people and the necessity for this was apparent. In order to give them a trust company in sympathy with our movement the Depositors Savings & Trust Company was organized. The presidency was offered to a good many young bankers all of whom declined it because they feared that connection with it would cut off their careers with larger institutions. Many of them had their pay raised lest the offer of the presidency should tempt them to leave their present jobs. I was then importuned to take the presidency. I accepted it most reluctantly, for I thought it a mistake at the time and I still think my taking it was an unfortunate blunder. It put me in a position which gave my enemies a new point of attack. From first to last this enterprise gave me only care and anxiety. When, largely on account of business transactions outside the city and connected chiefly with my brother's estate, I became financially embarrassed, I called the directors together and advised the giving up of the bank. A great many of the local banks were unfriendly to the Depositors Savings & Trust Company, but a few of them acted very nicely indeed. The bank's affairs were wound up with some loss to all the stockholders, the heaviest loss being mine, because I was the largest stockholder. The depositors never lost a penny nor were they delayed a second in getting their money.

On the first of May (1907) the Concon commenced to tear up its tracks on Central avenue and continued, with more or less interruption, until that work was completed. The Low Fare Company which now had a grant on this street was enjoined from proceeding with the laying of its tracks. And so it went on day after day. Injunction followed injunction. Property owners' consents continued to complicate matters. The courts held that it was not bribery to buy consents, and some property owners signed for and against as many as five times. This decision really amounted to putting up legislation to the highest bidder, for the party who could pay the most to property owners for consents was the only one to whom council could make a valid grant. New lawsuits raising new points of law followed one another so quickly that for a while I spent more time in the Court House than I did in the City Hall. At least in one case a judge who had been nominated by our particular friends was won away by the influence of the Union Club.

During this summer the exposure of the Concon's " yellow dog " fund was made. From the company's own books and vouchers it was shown that hundreds of thousands of dollars which had been spent in fighting three-cent fare had been charged to operating expenses — that is, to the cost of carrying passengers. Real estate purchases made to control consents, exorbitant legal fees, useless newspaper advertisements and other expenditures which would, perhaps, have borne scrutiny even less well were charged to operation.

When public service corporations spend money to defeat the people's interests the cost must eventually come out of the people themselves in added cost of service.

Just as the people's money in savings banks is so frequently used in the perpetuation of Privilege, so too is it used by the public service monopolies. It is the people who use the commodities the public service corporations have to sell who furnish the money for " jack pots," for " yellow dog " funds, for the funds under whatever name, that are used to preserve and safeguard the power of Privilege.

It was a summer of continual and bitter strife. I did not go out of town at all except for an occasional few days at a time. I announced early that I was a candidate for reëlection — in fact that I should continue to be a candidate for mayor at each recurring election until I was defeated. The most determined opposition that I had so far encountered began to crystallize into a great movement to defeat me. The fight was now so intense that many people who had never been active before began to take sides. The banks, the Chamber of Commerce, the leading business men, all the privileged crowd were a unit against me and were exerting themselves to find a Republican candidate who could defeat me.

They selected Theodore Burton, now United States Senator, then member of Congress from the Cleveland district. Mr. Burton was serving his seventh term in Congress and had been twice returned without opposition. His political position was considered as strong as his personal reputation was high. Mr. Burton didn't want to be a candidate. He had no ambition for municipal politics. He didn't like the affiliation between his party and the traction ring. But the pressure was great and the newspapers said that President Roosevelt and cabinet secretaries Taft and Garfield joined with the local Republican leaders in an effort to persuade him that he was called upon to sacrifice his seat in Congress in order to save the fair name of his city. He yielded and in announcing his willingness to accept the nomination, said in a public statement:

" I will accept the nomination for mayor of the city of Cleveland provided assurance is given:

1. That the platform of the party and those who are to be its candidates will clearly show the absence of any alliance or affiliation with any public service corporation, street railway or other, and that the problem of the relations of the municipality to these companies can, under my leadership, be settled by the officials elected with supreme regard to the interests of the people.

2. That the delegates in the convention next Saturday will coöperate with me in nominating a good representative ticket. In this connection I desire to express myself with reference to the caucuses next Thursday. There is an unusual degree of competition in many wards for the selection of councilmen and delegates. I sincerely hope the respective contests will be conducted with decorum and with no semblance anywhere of dishonor or fraud.

It is my understanding that others whose names have been mentioned for the mayoralty nomination have kindly consented to waive their claims in case my name is presented to the Republican Convention.

I make this statement with a profound appreciation of the friendliness which has been displayed for me by petitions, letters and in other ways, and with a feeling that the step which I am taking is a duty. I have received letters from President Roosevelt and Secretary Taft and have talked with Secretary Garfield, whose opinions have aided me in reaching a decision. At an early date the views of each of them may be made public."

Mr. Burton was nominated September 7, and the only part of his platform that it is necessary to consider here was the plank which dealt with the street railway question and read as follows:

"A settlement of the traction question at a rate of fare to be left to the determination of Mr. Burton on a basis which shall in no event be less favorable to the city than seven tickets for a quarter without zone restrictions, with universal transfers and sufficient cars and upon a grant to be limited to twenty years and conditioned upon a readjustment of rates of fares at the expiration of ten years, and subject to the right of the city to purchase the property at the end of twenty years at a price to be fixed by arbitration, the grant to provide also for securing the principle of but one system and one fare."

It was in this campaign that we nominated E. B. Haserodt, Republican councilman, at the Democratic primaries after he had failed of nomination by his own party. His defeat in the Republican primaries was his punishment for having voted with the administration on street railway matters. So we nominated and elected him on the Democratic ticket.

The Democratic Convention was held September 21 and besides myself the other candidates nominated were C. W. Lapp for vice mayor, Carl H. Nau for treasurer, Mr. Baker for solicitor, Springborn, Leslie and Cooley for board of public service. From the convention hall I sent a letter by messenger to Mr. Burton inviting him to engage in a series of joint debates. The first big campaign lie was already in circulation. Somebody had told somebody who had told somebody else who had told Burton that a certain man had been coerced into supporting the administration by the arbitrary refusal of a building permit. We sifted this story to the very bottom, proved that it wasn't true in a single particular, presented the proofs to Mr. Burton and his managers but never got a retraction from them. It wasn't a very auspicious beginning for a dignified campaign.

Mr. Burton refused to meet me in debate proposing instead that we fight out the issues through the columns of the daily press. Of course there was nothing for us to do but to accept this substitute.

Never perhaps was there a campaign anywhere in which the community as a whole took such an interest and in which such intense personal feeling was manifested.

Privilege was fighting with its back to the wall now and stopped at nothing in the way of abuse or persecution, not of me only but of the men associated with me. At their clubs our boys were treated with such open contempt, such obvious insult that many of them felt they could not endure it and stayed away altogether. They were cut on the street by men they had known for years. They were made to feel like aliens in their own city. And this treatment didn't stop with the men. It was extended to their wives and children. To be " for Johnson " was the cardinal social sin and society proceeded to mete out its punishment of ostracism. Everywhere the campaign was the town talk. In banks and factories, in offices and stores, on the cars, in the homes, in the schools. Women talked it to their domestics, to the butcher, the baker and the candlestick maker, to the clerks in the stores, to their dressmakers and their milliners. Even little children in the public schools engaged in the controversy. While the issues were being thus fought out among the people in personal ways public meetings were being held nightly attended by vast throngs.

Mr. Burton very early exhibited a surprising ignorance of local affairs. None of us had suspected that he was really so little informed on the questions at issue. Now the electorate of Cleveland had had a lot of education on many civic questions and on the street railway problem in particular. They commenced to ask Burton questions which he couldn't answer. They heckled him so mercilessly that we were in daily dread of the reaction which would probably result from this. The opposition newspapers persistently played up this feature of the campaign by reporting that it was " Johnson hoodlums " who disturbed the Burton meetings. Many people no doubt believed that our side was responsible for these disturbances but it wasn't true. The trouble was that Mr. Burton was trying to discuss matters which were strange and unfamiliar to him with men and women who knew all about them, and when they asked him questions he didn't tell them he couldn't answer, but tried to make believe that he could answer if he would, but that for some reason known only to himself he preferred not to do so. It wasn't unusual for him to promise at the beginning of a meeting to answer questions at its close, and then when he finished speaking to put on his coat and in the midst of a burst of music from the band hurry off to another meeting without giving a chance for questions. He couldn't fool those people. He complained that he couldn't keep order in his meetings. I sent him word that I would send the whole police force to take care of his meetings if he liked, or I would agree to come myself alone and guarantee to preserve order.

The Cleveland *Leader* sent for Homer Davenport, the celebrated cartoonist, and for weeks his cartoons appeared daily in that paper. Davenport's wonderful drawings had been a large factor in defeating the Cox crowd in Cincinnati at a previous election, and in other cities his services had been found invaluable in similar contests. Davenport hadn't much heart for his task. He came to see me and explained the nature of his connection with the *Leader* — as I remember it, his time was sold to the *Leader* by an Eastern paper to which he was under contract. At any rate he appeared greatly relieved when I told him that I appreciated his position and wouldn't bear him any personal grudge. " Go ahead and do your best for the *Leader*," I said to him, " I'll forgive you." " Well, my father never will," he answered, " I don't know how I am going to square this with him." His father like himself had for years been a single taxer.

And so the fight went on. The Republicans were sure they were going to win. They had all the money they wanted and they brought out brass bands and worked all the old-fashioned mechanical effects for all they were worth. Everything of this description had long been eliminated from our campaigns. They neglected no possible point of vantage in their efforts to influence people against our side and succeeded so well that it amounted almost to public disgrace for a business man to admit that he was for me. Everything that offered the slightest chance for attack was attacked. Cruel and malicious stories were circulated about Mr. Cooley's administration of his department. As fast as the enemy launched one of these unspeakable falsehoods we set about running it down.

Never before or since was the contest as bitter as in that campaign. But it had its humorous aspects too. Each campaign had its own particular slogan or catch phrase. In my first race for mayor my opponent W. J. Akers made frequent reference in his speeches to picking strawberries in Newburg when he was a boy. Harvey D. Goulder who ran against me in the second campaign spoke with feeling of the old town pump. William H. Boyd had something to say of " forging thunderbolts " to my undoing. And so in their turn we had rung the changes on picking strawberries in Newburg, on drinking at the old town pump, and on the forging of thunderbolts, but Mr. Burton furnished us with the most delightful phrase of all. In accepting his nomination he declared in classic Latin, " Jacta est alae," for Mr. Burton is a scholar. This expression, unfortunately for him, sent the man on the street into convulsions of mirth. One or two of our speakers paraphrased it in German and French, and I interpreted it for the Irish as " Let 'er go Gallagher."

Then Mr. Burton had an impressive way of beginning a speech by saying,

" I have spoken within the halls of Parliament in London, and in the Crystal Palace also in London, in Berlin, Germany, and with what poor French I could command in the south of France, in Brest, and once my voice was heard within the confines of the Arctic Circle, in the valley of the Yukon, Alaska, but kind friends, I am glad to be here with you to-night."

On the heels of this address Peter Witt arose in one of our tents and began his nightly speech with great solemnity,

"I have spoken in the corn fields of Ashtabula, in the stone quarries of Berea and at the town hall in Chardon, etc., etc."

There had been fifty-five injunctions against the low-fare companies now. Three times I had been elected on the same platform. The people had shown clearly by their votes that they wanted what we were standing for and the fifty-five injunctions indicated how hard the Cleveland Electric and its allied interests had tried to thwart their will. Would the people give up the fight now? Would they be fooled by Privilege?

I was elected by a majority of nine thousand while the city solicitor and the members of the board of public service were returned by majorities of several thousand more. It was a tremendous vindication coming as it did at the close of such a campaign. The east end, the rich and aristocratic section of the city voted solidly against me but contributed somewhat no doubt to the majorities of the candidates who ran ahead of me.

The newspapers were all agreed that the election was one of the most orderly ever held in Cleveland. That night the streets were a surging mass of humanity. The whole town seemed to be out. While some thousands were receiving election returns in the Armory and in the theaters, tens of thousands were swarming on the streets. They overflowed the sidewalks and spread out over the streets in such numbers that the street cars had to crawl at snail's pace in the down town region, and automobiles had difficulty in getting through at all. It was unmistakably a great common people's victory. The City Hall was packed with a happy, radiant crowd and Peter

Witt gave characteristic expression to his exuberance of spirit in a telegram to President Roosevelt reading, " Cleveland as usual went moral again. The next time you tell Theodore to run tell him which way." Poor Mr. Burton! He must have been sadly disillusioned and deeply wounded. He had nothing to say. He hurried off to Washington or somewhere without sending me the congratulatory message which is customary on such occasions.

On election night when the returns began to show beyond doubt that Burton was defeated the Concon issued orders to stop selling seven tickets for a quarter (this rate of fare having been in operation from October 2 to November 5), and go back to the old rate of a five-cent cash fare or eleven tickets for fifty cents.

XXV

LAST DAYS OF THE FIGHT

THE election occurred November fifth. On the seventh I sent the following letter to the Cleveland Electric Railway Company:

" GENTLEMEN:

The passage of various ordinances by the council within the past few months, and the legislation necessary to complete some of the grants already made, indicate that the council will, in the near future, be called upon to consider matters affecting the general street railroad situation. The approaching expiration of the franchises upon many of the lines operated by your company of course requires early action to provide for an uninterrupted continuance of public service.

These considerations lead me to suggest that I call a public meeting of the present members of the council and the councilmen-elect to consider any suggestions your company may have to offer either to insure against confusion or public inconvenience at the date of your franchise expirations, or looking to a general settlement of the entire street railroad question. I shall be very glad to call such a meeting for the council chamber at ten o'clock Saturday morning, unless you prefer a later date, in which case I shall be glad to know your preference at as early an hour to-morrow as is convenient, so that the persons who would attend such conference may be informed in time.

I am assured by members of the council, and I speak for them and the city administration, in saying that we have a common desire to bring about a settlement of this question which will be

276

At work on Pay Enter Fare Box

just and equitable to your company and upon terms that will
preserve fully the public right.

                    TOM L. JOHNSON, *Mayor."*

President Andrews accepted in behalf of his company
and once more we embarked on peace negotiations. Little was done at the Saturday meeting but the Concon
announced it would bring a proposition to council on the
following Thursday. It did — a proposition to make
a six months' trial of three-cent fare *after a twenty-five
year franchise had been granted.* The council rejected
this proposition and tried in vain at this and future meetings to have Mr. Andrews name a price at which his
company would lease its property on the holding company
plan.

During the election Concon stock had dropped to forty-
two, and later to thirty-seven, and by the middle of November to thirty-three dollars a share. Yet the company
instead of meeting council in a conciliatory spirit at first
exhibited all its old time obstinacy and a good deal of its
old time arrogance. Realizing at last that the city had
no intention of giving up, the Concon selected F. H.
Goff, a prominent attorney as well as a good business
man, a man of sterling qualities and one who inspired
confidence, as its representative, to arrange the details
of a settlement. At the conclusion of the negotiations
these characteristics of Mr. Goff were generally understood and appreciated by the public. He began by refusing all compensation for his work, and a lawyer of
his standing would have charged a private client a fortune
for such service.

The council appointed me to act in a similar capacity

for the city. So the administration and the council were finally put in the position for the first time of dealing with a single individual with power to act, and whose decisions the Cleveland Electric was bound to accept. Lawyers representing both sides of the contest were appointed to determine the exact date of the expiration of all unexpired franchises, engineers to appraise trackage and pavement claims, operating managers to get at the valuation of cars, rolling stock and miscellaneous equipment, and so on through the various classifications of the property. All valuations were made by a committee of two persons, and when they failed to agree Mr. Goff and myself were the arbitrators. The principal points to be agreed upon were physical and franchise values of the property, and that the management should be in the hands of a holding company which should manage the street railroad for the benefit of the car riders.

For four months the negotiations between Mr. Goff and the mayor were carried on in public meetings held almost daily in the council chamber. At the end of that time Mr. Goff recommended a valuation of sixty-five dollars per share on Cleveland Electric stock and I recommended a valuation of fifty dollars per share.

At about the close of these negotiations the State legislature passed the Schmidt bill which provides that property owners' consents are no longer needed for a new street railway franchise on a street where there is already a street car line; that new franchises may be given on such streets within one year after street car service has been abandoned or within two years prior to the expiration of a franchise; that if fifteen per cent. of the voters petition for an election within thirty days after the passage of a franchise ordinance, there must be an election, and the ordinance becomes invalid if a majority of the votes cast are against it.

If this law had been on the statutes when the Cleveland Electric's franchises expired on Central and Quincy avenues, it would have been impossible for the Concon to prevent the establishment of three-cent car service on those streets through the medium of a consent war.

Under the Schmidt law the council was enabled to grant to the Forest City Company certain franchises without property owners' consents, and it also made a grant to the Neutral Street Railway (another low fare company) for lines on Central and Quincy avenues.

Two or three weeks previous to this the stockholders of the Forest City had had their first meeting and I had been present by invitation, and had strongly advised them to consent to a consolidation with the Cleveland Electric under the name of the Cleveland Railway Company. I told them that in my opinion their company had served its purpose, that it had been organized to get lower fares for the people of Cleveland which was now practically accomplished, that the necessity for competition had passed and that the city's needs would be best served by one company.

Mr. Goff agreed to the holding company plan and he and I soon got together on a price of fifty-five dollars a share for the stock. Council made a security grant to the old company which was to become operative as a grant only in case the holding company failed to pay the stockholders six per cent. on the agreed value, and which gave the city the option of buying the stock at one hundred and ten dollars at any time. That the fare was to be three cents on the whole united system goes without saying.

On April 27, 1908, the Municipal Traction Company, the holding company, took charge of the lines, and inaugurated its operations by running the cars free for that one day. This free day was meant to serve as an object lesson of their victory to the people. Nothing like this had been done in any large city before — nor perhaps any place else except in Johnstown after the flood. It was like a holiday. Men and women and children rode and in spite of the crowds not a single accident happened to mar the happiness of the day.

Threefer employés were getting a cent an hour more than Concon employés so the wages of the latter were immediately raised one cent per hour, and all the men were provided with free uniforms. This made the maximum pay twenty-five cents per hour. Some of the old company's men showed a spirit of disloyalty and insubordination immediately the Municipal Traction Company commenced its operations, and a strike was early threatened. The labor union of Concon employés had, it seems, a contract with the old company which promised a wage increase of two cents an hour providing the Concon got a renewal of its franchise. The low-fare employés were also unionized, but their charter was revoked by the international body on the ground that some of them were stockholders in the company that employed them. The charter was revoked without notice to the low-fare company which had a contract with the union. Mr. du Pont declared the entire willingness of the Municipal Traction Company to arbitrate all differences and neither he nor I believed that a strike would be called, but on May 16 a strike was called. It affected the members of the old company's labor union only. The questions raised were:

1. Whether the agreement between the Municipal and the old Forest City union had any bearing on the agreement between the Cleveland Electric and the striking union.

2. Whether the international association had the right to revoke the charter of a local which had an agreement with the railway company without the company's consent.

3. Was the two-cent-an-hour agreement between the Cleveland Electric and the union binding on the Municipal as lessee of the Cleveland Electric?

Violence broke out at the very outset of the strike, cars were stoned, wires cut and dynamite placed on the tracks. The strike with its accompanying necessity of operating the cars with inexperienced men, and the expense occasioned by the destruction of property was just one of the things resorted to to make the operations of the holding company fail. Unfriendly newspapers abused the service, political organizations were formed to refuse to pay fares by giving conductors more work than they could do, these same men organized clubs to tender large bills in payment of fares in order to exhaust the conductors' change. It wasn't men with dinner-pails who offered five dollar bills in payment of three-cent fare, nor was it groups of labor unionists who crowded the cars at certain points and exerted themselves to make it impossible for conductors to collect fares, and it wasn't workingmen either who instigated conductors to overlook fares or persistently to refuse to collect them. But all these things were done — these and many more — by some of the people who were pledged to carry out the agreement which Mr. Goff had made in their behalf.

In spite of all past experiences with the Concon, we were unprepared for these attacks. We thought a gentleman's agreement meant a gentleman's agreement. We were mistaken.

The Municipal Traction Company, on the other hand, was not free from blame. Some bad moves must be charged to its account, but it can never truthfully be said that it dishonestly violated any agreement or maliciously refused to abide by its contracts. Its mistakes were those of judgment.

The strike finally died by reason of the weakness of its own case. It did not have the support of the labor unions of the city and strikes instigated and aided by Privilege are never very useful to the strikers themselves nor to the cause of labor.

Of course I was blamed for everything. If the cars were too cold it was my fault, if they were too hot it was my fault. If the rails were slippery or a trolley pole broke it was my fault. If the cars were late, if they stopped on the wrong corners, if they were held up at railroad crossings, if a conductor couldn't change a twenty-dollar bill it was my fault. It is even said that a man who fell off a car one night exclaimed as he went sprawling on the pavement, " Damn Tom Johnson."

Finally a referendum petition was circulated just in time to become operative before the end of the thirty-day period following the making of the grant. Republican organizations, business men's organizations and all the combinations that Privilege could bring to bear were enlisted against this grant. At the referendum election,

October 22, 1908, the grant was defeated by 605 votes out of the 75,893 votes cast. The people, in my opinion, made their biggest blunder in defeating this franchise. If they had been even half as patient with the Municipal Traction Company as they had been with the Concon all would have been well. The defects in the service of which they complained, and often justly, would have been remedied. But, as I have already pointed out the people insist on a higher degree of efficiency in a public company than they do in a private one.

There was a touch of the irony of fate in the defeat of the franchise. That the referendum should be invoked by the very interests which had always opposed it, and that the result of the first election under the law should be inimical to the people's movement was something of a blow. But people learn by their mistakes and the good effects that have come and will come from the referendum will largely outweigh any temporary disadvantages.

One stipulation of the agreement between Mr. Goff and myself was that should our plans fail the property which had passed into the hands of the Cleveland Railway Company should be restored to the original owners, that is that the old company should take back the Cleveland Electric property and that the original three-cent lines should be returned to the Forest City. The old company refused to comply with this agreement. Instead it sought by every means to embarrass the Municipal Traction Company, urging creditors to press claims, tying up the funds of the Municipal in court and finally succeeding in having receivers appointed, though the money tied up was more than sufficient to meet all obligations that were then due. The receivers took over all the street railroads in the city and under the direction of Judge Tayler who appointed them they operated the property from November 13, 1908, to March 1, 1910.

On February 1, 1909, the fare on some of the old lines was raised to five cents. Such a raise could not be made on the low-fare lines since their franchise provided for three-cent fare. I advised charging a penny for transfers rather than raising the fare, but Judge Tayler thought the additional revenue thus provided wouldn't be sufficient to meet immediate needs. The service was far from satisfactory and on February 6 this very significant comment appeared in the *Electric Traction Weekly,* a monopolistic organ:

"Altogether it is a safe guess that the inconvenience in routing and the heterogeneous system of transfers and tickets will so annoy the people of Cleveland that they will force their councilmen to over-ride Mayor Johnson and grant a franchise that the receivers and the Cleveland Railway Company will accept."

On February 27 the Federal Court at Cleveland, Judge Knappen of Michigan, sitting in place of Judge Tayler, decided that the franchise of the old company on the Woodland and West Side lines had expired February 10, 1908. This had been the city's contention and on the strength of it a three-cent-fare franchise had been granted a year before. The old interests insisted that the five-cent-fare franchise had been extended to July 1, 1914, or at least to January 26, 1910. The receivers therefore appealed to the court to know whether they could charge five cents on these lines or were restricted to three

Photo by L. Van Oeyen, Copyright, 1911

"The secret of a good executive is this—one who always acts quickly and is sometimes right."

cents as the city insisted. Under the decision the receivers had no authority to charge a higher rate of fare than the city had granted to the low-fare company.

Judge Tayler, Attorney John G. White and the mayor were a committee endeavoring to find a way to solve the whole problem. Frequent conferences were being held. On March 26, Judge Tayler addressed the city council, saying in part:

"The streets of a city belong to the community, and not to anybody else, and cannot be acquired by anybody else; and as an incident to that proprietary interest of the community in the streets, there must be easy methods of transportation in those streets, and you cannot accomplish their suitable transportation except by the investment of large sums of money, upon which, in order to obtain it, there must be a fair return. Now there is a perfectly simple proposition, grounded on fundamental right, in the people and in the persons who invest their money.

We have been going along here for a great many years on a certain theory of giving franchises for the operation of street railways in communities, all based upon a wrong view of the rights of both sides; so far as the people are concerned, the giving of a monopoly without suitable restraint; and on the other side such a condition of things that the necessities of their situation, the expiration of their grants at some time in the future, compelled them as business men to make the very best bargain they possibly could, with the result that scandal and injustice have from the beginning characterized a large number of street railway enterprises in all of the great communities of this country. It seems to me that the time has now come, and perhaps it never came until now, when we should reach a settlement on the foundation that the public own the streets, and that the people who furnish transportation are entitled to a fair return and a sure return, and nothing more than that. What this community wants is an ordinance that will settle this street railway trouble upon a basis which will mean that the people will get good service, and will have to pay for it not one copper more than it costs. There ought to be no grave difficulties in the way. An accommodating spirit, a spirit accommodating itself to that settlement, anxious to bring about that settlement, on both sides of this controversy, will necessarily result in a settlement of this controversy, because the differences can only arise over details which in and of themselves are not vital to the working out of a plan whereby this settlement can be reached.

Of course, we all know that if there is no settlement there must be what has been called war. But I have confidence in the purpose and in the ability of the gentlemen involved in these negotiations to come to an adjustment along those lines. It is strong because it is eternally right. How to express it in your legislation is for you to say. But I think that in the city of Cleveland we have left behind us the day when any fixed rate of fare shall be said to be the rate of fare which the people must pay. Any rate of fare may be too high, or any rate of fare may be too low. What we are entitled to is good service at the cost of service, whether it is one cent, or two cents, or three cents, or four cents. That is the only sound basis upon which a street railway settlement can rest."

On the mayor's suggestion the city solicitor was then instructed by council to prepare three ordinances as follows:

1. The Judge Tayler plan providing for a sliding scale of fares so as to limit profits to six per cent.

2. A three-cent fare grant to the Cleveland City Railway, subject to its acceptance.

3. A three-cent fare grant to the Forest City Company, subject to its acceptance.

The city solicitor prepared the ordinances as directed, John G. White preparing a counter ordinance which was proposed to the council by Horace Andrews. The differences in the two ordinances were, as was to be expected, largely in the quantity and quality of the control by the city over the street railway company. While the public conferences over the settlement proposition were being carried on, the council to be on the safe side in case no settlement should be reached had passed thirteen new street railway ordinances covering all the territory over which old franchises had expired or would expire by January, 1910. On May 18, bids for new franchises on four routes were received by council from two parties. The Cleveland Railway Company bid on all the routes at five-cent cash fare and free transfers with six tickets for twenty-five cents, but no deposit accompanied the bid. Herman Schmidt, a prosperous business man and a devoted friend of our movement, bid on one route, the Payne avenue, offering three-cent fare and making a deposit of eighteen thousand dollars.

The question of a revaluation of the railway property having come up, President Andrews insisted that all stock should be treated alike, while the mayor and the council were just as insistent that the Forest City stockholders must neither profit nor lose by such a revaluation. The people who had purchased Forest City stock had rendered the community a truly patriotic service. There was nothing speculative about this enterprise, and I was determined to fight to the last ditch rather than to see their interests placed in jeopardy. It is the greatest possible satisfaction to me that when the receivership was terminated they received their back dividends in full and have been receiving them regularly ever since.

The warring between the council and the old interests went on. A three-cent fare grant was made to Herman Schmidt. The Chamber of Commerce, business men, the newspapers and the Republican organization were against the Schmidt grant and it was defeated by 3,763 votes at a referendum election on August 3. Only 68,807 votes were cast out of 80,000 expected. The people were getting tired and being humbugged by special interests.

And the newspapers — every last one of them — were joining in the hue and cry of, " settle, settle, settle," which was raised by the representatives of Privilege. If even one newspaper had had the courage to hold out and to stand by the people to the end the result might have been different. But the influence of the counting-room is a thing mightily to be reckoned with. Newspapers at once preach the highest and practice the lowest morality. They set up the highest possible standards for everybody and everything but themselves. I am not blaming them — I am simply stating a fact.

Finally both sides in the street railway controversy agreed to leave to Judge Tayler the fixing of the physical and franchise value of the property, his judgment to be final. Almost every other point of the pending ordinance had been agreed to, but a few ordinance questions were arbitrated by him.

After a good many weeks of hearings in which I represented the city and the railroad company was represented by its president, each side now and then calling in lawyers, Judge Tayler made a slight reduction in the price fixed by Mr. Goff and myself, seeming to disregard all evidence that we had been at such pains to present to him showing that the Goff-Johnson valuation had been too high. The railroad company seemed to expect several millions increase, while I thought the company received five or six millions more than it should have had. Judge Tayler did not itemize his findings. The ordinance was approved by vote at a special election called for that purpose.

Its greatest defect is that the management is entrusted to hands that have a pecuniary interest in its failure. They can reap no profit above six per cent., and as the controlling stockholders have street railroad interests in other cities they would like the three-cent fare to fail on account of its effect on these other interests. This interest in failure however does not go to the extent of permitting them to earn less than six per cent. on the Tayler valuation for that loss would come out of the stockholders.

The traction question was practically settled before the fall election, so taxation was the paramount issue in that campaign. We directed our principal energies towards securing the election of our candidates for the board of quadrennial appraisers. This was the first election for such appraisers since the enactment of the law providing for them, and although I was defeated for mayor by 3,733 votes out of a total of 80,409, four out of five of our candidates for appraisers were elected, and Newton D. Baker was returned as city solicitor.

I had been mayor for so many years that many people had lost sight of conditions as they existed before that time. Thousands of young voters couldn't remember any other mayor, and there was a great deal of that feeling which is always manifesting itself in politics, that —
" Oh, he's had it long enough; let's have a change " feel-

ing, and so the wave of democracy receded and the enemies of the things we stood for were swept into power.

On December 18, 1909, after election but before I left
the mayor's chair, council passed and I signed the ordinance known as the Tayler grant with the understanding
that the same was to be submitted to referendum vote.   I
felt most strongly that the responsibility for the settlement must rest upon the people.   At the referendum election held in February, 1910, only 46,504 votes were cast,
27,307 for the ordinance and 19,197 against it.   The
ordinance provided for:

1. A franchise for twenty-five years with a maximum rate of
fare of four cents with one cent for transfers or seven tickets for
a quarter with one cent for transfers, and an immediate or initial
rate of fare of three cents with one cent for transfers;
2. Profits limited to six per cent. on actual capital (including
$22,923,749.53 for all existing property) ;
3. Rates of fare to be increased within the maximum if necessary to realize this profit, and to be reduced if not necessary;
4. The city to have complete and continuous supervisory control of operation;
5. After eight years the city may name a purchaser to take
over the system at $110 per share, or it may itself purchase the
property at this price at any time that the state laws permit;
6. Questions of rates of fare under the six per cent. proviso
to be arbitrated.

The ordinance contains a safety clause which was fixed
by an arbitration committee of lawyers of which City Solicitor Baker was one, and it provides that:

In the event that the section of the ordinance dealing
with rates of fare shall fail in the courts, including the
submission of the rates to arbitration, then the council

F. H. GOFF   A. B. DU PONT

shall have power from time to time to fix the rates, not exceeding the maximum.   This rate must not impair the ability of the company to earn sufficient money to meet all expenses and pay six per cent. dividends; and if the company refuses to turn its property over to a purchaser, when the city so decides, then the council is given power to forfeit the franchise.

After the Tayler grant was approved at the referendum election the receivers turned the property over to the old company and since March 1, 1910, it has been operated by them under the supervision of a street railway commissioner appointed by the mayor.   The man appointed to this position, Gerhard Dahl, was the Republican candidate for city solicitor defeated by Mr. Baker at the last municipal election.

The cars are still operating at the initial rate of fare provided in the Tayler grant, three cents with a penny for transfers.*   Any disposition on the part of the company to raise the fare has been promptly discouraged by the city.

The work of our quadrennial board of appraisers (the last work for the city in which I had any share) was the best of any in the State and is the beginning of a correction of one of the worst of taxation injustices.   Under the law the board was compelled to complete its labors prior to July 1, 1910.   Now, for the first time since we commenced the taxation fight in Cleveland in 1901, we had the machinery for a perfect performance of the task of assessing the real estate of the city, but we lacked the time.   The board was elected in the fall of 1909 and instead of waiting until the first of the year to begin its

* Appendix.

work it organized at once. W. A. Somers, who had furnished his system to us in 1901, was employed by the board as its chief clerk. The real estate duplicate as made in 1900, to which had been added the buildings erected since, was now about one hundred and eighty million dollars. When the board of appraisers got through with its labors the real estate duplicate, exclusive of such exempted property as churches and the holdings of federal, State and municipal governments, reached five hundred millions. For the first time since Cleveland had ceased to be a village was its property appraised with any degree of fairness between its owners.

To some who have followed this story, it may seem that we have achieved a comparatively small measure of success. I do not share this view. To have taken more than ten millions of dollars of fictitious value out of a capitalization of thirty millions, as we did in the street railway fight, to have established three-cent fare in the sixth city in size in the United States, and to see that rate of fare paying after two years of trial — this alone is worth all the fight has cost. Municipal ownership of street railways is not yet possible under the State laws, it is true, but the sentiment in favor of it is stronger than ever and an effort is being constantly made to have the legislature authorize cities on their own votes to own and operate their street railways. The Cleveland city council — a Republican body — has just adopted (February 20, 1911) by unanimous vote a resolution endorsing a street railway municipal ownership bill now pending in the State legislature. This resolution was offered by Mr.

Haserodt, one of our administration councilmen to whom previous reference has been made.

Add to these things the by-products of our fight, if we may so characterize the beneficent legislation which has resulted from our agitation, the development and training for practical service of men interested in economic justice and the influence of our movement on other States and other cities. But the biggest thing and the most far-reaching in its effects is the example we have given of how to fight Privilege. The same kind of a fight carried on in any other city under similar conditions will bring equally encouraging results.

But I would sound a note of warning here. There is very great danger of having the best of movements sidetracked by the calling of hard names and the personal abuse of individuals. Tactics of that kind will never get anywhere. Throughout the whole of our fight we adhered to our first plan, which was to attack institutions — Privilege, and not men. This is the first great thing to be kept in mind — that the battle is not a battle against persons, but against unnatural conditions, against a wrong social order! The next important thing is that the fighters be armed with patience, much patience. It takes as much patience to carry on this kind of a warfare as it takes stones to build the proverbial stone chimney.

" How much stone does it take to build a stone chimney? " asked someone of the man who had just built one, and he answered, " Haul and haul and haul until you *know* you've got enough, then haul twice that much more, and the chances are you'll have about half enough."

But with the object of the fight well defined, the line of action faithfully adhered to, and plenty of patience, there

is no reason for despair.   It is inevitable that those engaged in the great struggle should sometimes become discouraged.   Temporary losses assume an aspect entirely
out of proportion to their real importance.   The defeats
of the moment loom large and so obscure the vision of the
workers sometimes that they are not always able to see
that the direction of the general movement is invariably
forward.   But *it is a forward movement* and this is the
word of cheer I would send to those taking part in it.   It
is in the nature of Truth never to fail.

PETER WITT TOM L. JOHNSON NEWTON D. BAKER

1910

THE LAST CHAPTER

"Blessed the Land That Knoweth Its Prophets Before They Die"

MR. JOHNSON'S health was seriously impaired when the referendum election on the Schmidt grant was held in August of 1909, and while the beginning of his illness doubtless dates from a much earlier period he himself regarded this as the time of the fatal break. Yet he went through his fall campaign with much of the vigor, the fire and the good humor that had always characterized his work.

On election night when the returns showed beyond a doubt that he had been defeated he alone of the devoted group of men and women gathered at the City Hall was philosophical and brave and calm. For men who were to weep unashamed, no matter where they happened to be on the day their leader died, made no effort to conceal their emotions that night. Some of them swore, some of them cried, some of them became ill. Only the mayor was very still and very gentle and "sorry for the boys."

When it was known that he had been returned as city solicitor Mr. Baker came and stood beside his chief and gripped his hand and said in a voice tense with suppressed feeling, "I don't know how I can do it." Without a second's hesitation came the answer, "Do it? Of course you can do it. You've got to do it. The people want you."

The mayor insisted upon remaining in his office until early morning and when the last returns were in and he knew that four out of five of his candidates for the quadrennial board of appraisement had been elected, he construed this as an endorsement of the taxation principles on which the campaign had been fought.

He had trained his spirit never to know defeat and it harked back now, all unconsciously no doubt, to the lesson of the Noah's Ark incident of his childhood, and there were " two left anyhow."

When he relinquished his office to his successor, January 1, 1910, Mr. Johnson said, " I have served the people of Cleveland for nearly nine years. I have had more of misfortune in those nine years than in any other period of my life. As that is true, it is also true that I have had more of joy. In those nine years I have given the biggest and best part of me. I have served the people of Cleveland the best I knew how."

Almost immediately after this he went to New York for medical treatment, remaining there until February 6, when he returned to Cleveland. He spent five weeks at home all of that time under the care of a trained nurse. On the thirteenth of March he went back to New York, his mind fully made up to go abroad. He was no better; his physician's prognosis was unfavorable, he was slowly losing strength and for hours each day was the victim of severe pain. But he ceased consulting physicians, dismissed his nurse and proceeded with the arrangements for his voyage. By some supreme act of will he had resumed the mastery of himself.

One who was observing him closely at this time wrote to a friend, " A most remarkable thing has happened.

Tom seems to have struck rock bottom and then to have lifted himself by his own boot-straps out of the depression caused by his illness. His spirit is in complete ascendancy over his body. He is going to Europe. Nothing can stop him."

On March 23, in company with Mr. and Mrs. Joseph Fels, Mr. Johnson sailed on the *Mauretania* for London. He seemed reasonably well and enjoyed the voyage. Arriving in London he was met at Paddington station by a reporter, but he consistently stuck to the policy he had adopted upon going out of public office — that of refusing to be interviewed by the newspapers. Mr. Johnson had several rules of personal conduct from which he seldom swerved. One of these was never to speak at a meeting or gathering of any kind at which an admission fee was charged, and another was never to stop with friends in their homes, but always to put up at a hotel. By some magic Mr. and Mrs. Fels persuaded him to depart from this last named rule and be their guest during his stay in London.

On April 11, the United Committee for the Taxation of Land Values gave Mr. Johnson a dinner at the Trocadero, one of London's big restaurants. His address on that occasion was a fine one, at least half of it being devoted to an appreciation of the character of Mrs. Fels, who was, he said, half of her husband's work, giving to it not the mere old-fashioned inspiration of the heart, but thought.

Just as he had insisted upon going to England so Mr. Johnson now insisted upon a trip to the continent. Fearing that the contemplated journey might prove too fatiguing friends tried to dissuade him, but in vain. He was determined to go, so Mrs. Fels and John Paul, editor of *Land Values* and, next to Mrs. Fels, the closest friend Mr. Johnson made in Great Britain, accompanied him. They made a ten days' tour visiting Paris, Rouen, Brussels, Cologne and Frankfort. The change stimulated Mr. Johnson wonderfully. Following this trip Mr. Fels and Mr. Paul joined Mr. Johnson in a few days' visit to Glasgow, Belfast and Dublin. A reception was given them in Glasgow which afforded Mr. Johnson an opportunity of meeting many of the friends whom he had for years desired to know personally. He was especially attracted to those who had been friends of Henry George. " He suffered a great deal of pain at times, indeed almost constantly," writes John Paul, " but he was cheerful and enthusiastic over the evidence he witnessed on every hand here of the progress of the ideas and the policy he himself had done so much to promote in the United States."

On April twenty-seventh, the night the vote on the Budget was taken, a dinner was given to Mr. Johnson at the House of Parliament. He tells about this dinner in a speech in New York a month later, but fails to mention what an English correspondent tells us that " on this occasion all factions and conflicting opinions were harmonized, Mr. Johnson being the reconciling spirit. Josiah Wedgewood, M. P., presided, and speeches were made by Redmond, the hero of the Budget fight, Keir Hardie, T. P. O'Connor, Charles Trevelyan and Joseph Fels. Mr. Johnson's own speech was of the things nearest his heart. He talked but little of his work in Cleveland, dwelling rather on the outlook for the final triumph of truth and justice, and expressing his own profound faith in democracy. On the thirtieth of April he departed for

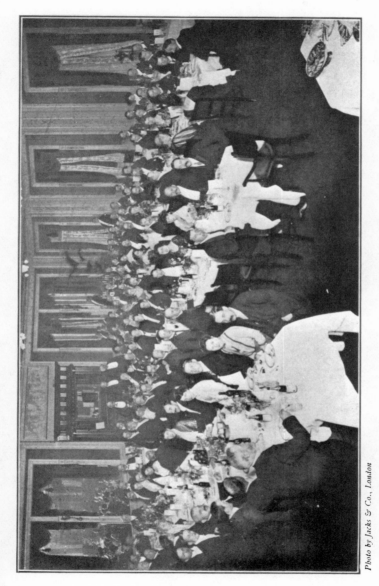

Photo by Jacks & Co., London

DINNER GIVEN TO MR. JOHNSON IN LONDON, APRIL, 1910

America, leaving behind him many new friends and a broadening of spirit to the single tax movement in England."

Mr. Johnson returned to New York on the *Mauretania*, arriving May 5. That he had benefited by his six weeks' holiday was with him a hope rather than a belief, but he was full of enthusiasm for the people's cause. " A political revolution is going on all over the world," he said, " and the next fifteen years are going to show great progress. I'd like to live to see it and I almost think I have an even chance."

For months a self-constituted committee composed of August Lewis, Bolton Hall, Joseph Fels, Lincoln Steffens, Frederic C. Howe and Daniel Kiefer, representing thousands of Mr. Johnson's friends, had been importuning him to permit a demonstration in his honor. They now refused to be put off longer and Mr. Johnson gave a reluctant consent to the public reception and dinner which took place at the Hotel Astor in New York City, the evening of May 31, 1910. The interval between his return from England and the time of the dinner he spent in Cleveland. The special feature of the testimonial banquet was the presentation to Mr. Johnson of a bronze medallion bearing the faces of Henry George and Tom L. Johnson in bas-relief — the work of Richard George, the sculptor and son of Henry George. Frederic C. Leubuscher, president of the Manhattan Single Tax Club, presided and addresses were made by Herbert S. Bigelow of Cincinnati; Henry George, Jr., and John DeWitt Warner of New York; Louis F. Post of Chicago; Newton D. Baker and Edmund Vance Cooke of Cleveland.

As Mr. Johnson ate nothing he must have found the

long dinner a tedious ordeal. It was nearly midnight when he was called upon to respond to the addresses which had been made in his honor. He spoke briefly, saying, in part:

" The friendly words that I have been listening to to-night might be more appropriate at a later time — when the struggle for me is closed. They are pleasant to hear, but it does not seem just fitting while I am still with you. The bronze medallion, too, in which I am associated with Henry George, seems more appropriate for that later time. I said to my friends when they first suggested this testimonial, that it seemed to me like a tribute to one who had completed his work, who had finished the game; but some of my friends said I was so near the end of the struggle that we might overlook the seeming inappropriateness. I don't believe we are at the end of the struggle. I don't believe we have been in our last fight together. But if I am mistaken I have no regrets — only that I might have been stronger, more powerful, more nearly deserving of the things that have been said about me to-night, for no man can deserve all those nice things * * * Since my return I have often been asked, ' Did the trip improve your health? ' I don't care whether it did or not. If by taking it I shortened my life by many years I should never regret that trip, for I met over there a set of men and women who have kept the fires burning all these years, who have never failed, and who have never compromised the truth. I would have made that trip to have met one of those men — John Paul. * * * It was my good fortune to meet and know this man in Great Britain, who, with Mr. Fels, has done so much to bring our movement to the center of the stage.

" One night John Paul said a suggestive thing. It was a sort of a fable, a dream — I don't know what he called it; but it has been ringing in my ears ever since and I am going to try to tell it to you.   *   *   *   John Paul said there was a certain river and that many human beings were in it, struggling to get to the shore. Some succeeded, some were pulled ashore by kind-hearted people on the banks. But many were carried down the stream and drowned. It is no doubt a wise thing, it is noble that under those conditions charitable people devote themselves to helping the victims out of the water. But John Paul said it would be better if some of those kindly people on the shore engaged in rescue work, would go up the stream and find out who was pushing the people into it. I could not help but follow that thought. We single taxers, while ready to help pull the struggling ones out, feel something urging us up the river to see who is pushing the people into the river to drown.

" It is in this way that I would answer those who ask us to help the poor. Let us help them, that they may at the last fight the battle of Privilege with more strength and courage; but let us never lose sight of our mission up the river to see who is pushing the people in.   *   *   *

" In London I found that they understood me. I did not know whether they would understand me or not, but they looked on me as one who had accomplished something — and I was a friend of Henry George. They understood that; and they loved me as you do, and of course that made me very happy. In Scotland, at Glasgow, at Number Thirteen Dundas street, they gave me a banquet, not at two dollars and a half a plate, but at ' ninepence a skull.'   *   *   *   Probably the most en-

joyable part of my trip was the dinner that took place under the House of Commons in Westminster the night the
Budget was passed.   It was attended by radicals in the
Liberal party in Parliament, by Irish members and by
Labor members.   During the banquet we went upstairs
while the Budget vote was taken, and then came back for
our speeches.   When we broke up it was to go again to
the House of Commons to hear the discussion of the Ver-
ney resolution; *our resolution,* we single taxers could say,
for it declared for our principles.   *   *   *   It was carried by forty-three majority.

"We of the United States are interested in that struggle over there, not as outsiders but as insiders.   *   *   *
The English fight seems to us a fight where we are making
the biggest headway.   But everywhere, all over the
world, our cause is moving, so that those of us who twenty-
five years ago thought it far off, have now the good fortune of seeing the realization of our dreams.   Privilege
has been caught, exposed; and there is but one way of putting it down, and that is by the doctrine of Henry George.
Abolish Privilege!   Give the people who make the wealth
of the world an opportunity to enjoy it.

"And now I come back from England and am invited
to this gathering.   I find here that same love and affection that I found abroad, that I have found in Cleveland.
But I am not taking it as a personal compliment.   I am
but an instrument, I am but an agent in promoting that
greater love, that love of big things, that love of justice
which at last must win the world."

About the middle of June Mr. Johnson went to Sias-
conset on Nantucket Island to spend the summer.   Here
he remained, except for two or three days spent in New

York on business, until late in August. He made a friend of every man, woman and child with whom he came in contact. Nearly every man in the village was soon known to him — from the rich owner of the cranberry meadows to the casual doer of odd jobs. The engineer on the little steam railroad, the fisherman, the sail and tent maker, the house painter, the carpenter, the dairyman, the butcher, the store keeper, the lawyer who came up from Boston for week ends, the actor who spends his summers in " Sconset "— he knew them all and liked them all and they all liked him. Declining physical strength did not seem to lessen the charm of manner which gave him such a hold on the minds and hearts of all who came his way.

The books on advanced mathematics, the games of chess, which he had employed at an earlier period of his illness to divert his mind were superseded now by poetry and fiction. He became very fond of several of Kipling's poems and these were read and re-read to him. He frequently quoted snatches of poems he had committed to memory years before. His enjoyment of Kipling's jungle stories was like the enjoyment of a child with a well-developed imagination. He delighted in the romances of Sir Walter Scott and every character in the story he was reading became to him a living person for the time being. He looked over the newspaper clippings which were sent him regularly from Cleveland and read a New York paper daily, but rather as a duty than otherwise.

He enjoyed the wonderful sunsets over the Nantucket moors, and on the " longest day in the year " arose at three o'clock in the morning to go out, accompanied by his attendant, James Tyler, to see the sun rise over the ocean. The flowers and the birds of the island interested him

He was on a little spot of earth at last where there were more jobs than men to do them, where health was the rule and where there was no poverty, where the jail had not been occupied within the memory of several generations, where there was one church at the service of all denominations, where by means of the yearly town meeting the people ruled. It was a good place for recreation for a man of Mr. Johnson's convictions.

His health improved somewhat under the stimulus of outdoor life, though he continued to suffer pain and was being gradually forced to a more and more restricted diet. Upon the advice of his physician he had given up smoking months before and he never resumed it. Though he had been an inveterate smoker for years no word of complaint on this account, nor, as one by one he was obliged to give up the things he liked to eat, escaped him then or afterwards. For long weeks before his death his diet of milk was varied only by an occasional egg or a few raw oysters. One of his attendants, seeing his suffering in spite of all this precaution, was moved to remark, "I wish I could bear it for you." He summoned a smile and answered with a bit of ever ready philosophy, "No Tomlinson in this." There was indeed no Tomlinson in him.

Mr. Johnson returned to Cleveland August 28, and on that day decided to give a favorable reply to the publishers of *Hampton's Magazine,* who were urging him to write for them a story of his Cleveland fight.

He went to New York the following week, arriving on Monday, September 5, Labor Day. "I don't like Labor Day," he said, "except as a holiday. These parades of working men seem to proclaim a difference between them and the rest of us which ought not to exist. It hurts me."

Mr. Johnson devoted a week or more to dictating a magazine article on the Cleveland movement and from this developed the plan to have him tell his whole story. He had this in mind when he returned again to Cleveland, October 8.

The evening of the eleventh he paid a brief visit to the Democratic headquarters. Commenting on this, the *Plain Dealer* said, "When Tom L. Johnson walked into Weber's Hall last night the ceiling did not go up because the floor above held it down." He spoke but a few sentences, concluding with this characteristic one: "While we are building this city on a hill let us never forget the one necessity — that we must deserve success."

The next few weeks were the most painful of Mr. Johnson's illness. He was not able to proceed with his writing for some time, though he had his secretary at his house daily and attended to his mail as usual and to various matters of business.

Regardless of the effort it cost he insisted upon going to a tent meeting at which Governor Harmon and others were speaking the evening of November 1. He was not expected. This is the way a local newspaper described that event: " For a second only there was a hush. Men who had followed Mr. Johnson for years with exceeding devotion leaned forward to make certain their eyes did not deceive them. Then as the former mayor mounted the platform there was a demonstration such as is seldom seen at any time. As the governor and Mr. Johnson clasped hands the tent fairly rocked with applause. Almost the entire crowd rose to its feet to cheer. Among

portions of the crowd the cheering nearly approached a
frenzy.   In the moment or two that the former mayor
spoke he showed his old time vigor.   The tent, the crowd
and the flood of recollections seemingly inspired him."

Governor Harmon said that night what he afterwards
repeated in substance to Mr. Johnson in a letter: "The
demonstration we have just witnessed has stirred me to the
depths of my soul.   I can only say that if at any time after
my service as governor has expired and I appear before
a body of citizens of my State and there, without the powers of office, without the possibility of bestowing favors,
I shall receive such a testimonial as you to-night have
given your old fighting leader, I will consider that life certainly has been well worth living."

On November 7, Mr. Johnson voted early and busied
himself for the remainder of the day much as he had been
wont to do in the days of his strength, receiving election
returns at his apartment in the Knickerbocker in the evening.   The next day he commenced to write his story.   He
did his last work on it March 14, 1911, the day before he
was attacked by the acute illness which was to terminate
in death.

Mr. Johnson left Cleveland but once after he returned
in October and that was to attend a meeting of the Fels
Fund Commission in New York in November.   Louis F.
Post's account of Mr. Johnson's participation in that meeting, written especially for this story, follows:

"To friends who had not seen Mr. Johnson since tne days of
his health and strength his wasted appearance was discouraging.
But to me the contrast was not with his days of. health.   It was
with periods in the course of his illness, and I thought the signs
were hopeful.   In no respect were they more manifestly so than

in the clearness of perception, and the responsibility and direct-
ness of utterance, with which he participated in the deliberations
of the Commission.   Here he was altogether, except in vim, at
his wisest and best.

"We met him in Cleveland, November 17, 1910.   Those who
gathered there were Daniel Kiefer (chairman of the Fels Fund),
Fenton Lawson of Cincinnati, Doctor Wm. P. Hill of St. Louis,
W. S. U'Ren and W. G. Eggleston of Oregon, George A. Briggs
(one of the commission) of Indiana, myself of Chicago, and
James W. Bucklin of Colorado.   A loyal friend of Tom L.
Johnson's for twenty years, Bucklin was formerly a state senator
of Colorado and a distinguished one; he has long been a leader
in the Henry George movement; he was an attendant at the
first single tax conference, in New York, and at the second, in
Chicago; and he was the father of the " Bucklin Bill " in Colorado (a single tax amendment) and of the Grand Junction plan
of commission government.   Mr. Johnson personally conducted
the party — which A. B. du Pont and Peter Witt had then joined
for the purpose,— through the du Pont subway.   He did it with
almost all the enthusiasm of his days of intensest interest in
mechanical inventions.

" On the railroad train that night he gathered us into his state-
room, as many of us at a time as it would hold (as James Tyler
can testify), for he wanted the companionship and the conversation.   He said very little, but he listened with manifest interest;
and what he did say showed his unabated hunger for news and
thought about the cause that had won his lifelong devotion nearly
thirty years before.

"Oregon had just voted upon the county-option-tax amendment, now in force in that State and which, thanks in part to the
Fels Fund, is to be utilized next year for a single tax campaign
in every county.   This measure had been proposed by Thomas G.
Shearman as early as 1888, and had been then embraced and
always afterward advocated by George and Johnson as the best
means for promoting the single tax cause in this country.   The

result of the Oregon vote was not yet known, but Mr. U'Ren's account of the campaign, which had been financed largely by the Fels Fund, was particularly interesting to Mr. Johnson. All the more, perhaps, because the introduction through friendly channels into the Oregon campaign of two nominally friendly but (under the local circumstances at that time) really inimical amendments, must have reminded him of a kind of Big Business method of opposition which he had encountered in his Ohio contests with Privilege. It was probably in part an identification in his mind of these subtle tactics in the two States as the same in origin that caused him to make the only speech I heard him make at the public meeting of the Fels Fund two or three days afterwards. His sustained interest in the result of the Oregon election on the county option tax amendment may be inferred from his message to Bucklin and me on our way home through Cleveland. Having heard in New York, as we all had, that the amendment had been defeated, but learning from Edward W. Doty on returning to Cleveland that there were vague newspaper reports to the contrary, he sent Arthur Fuller down to our train as it passed through Cleveland later than his own, to tell us what he had learned from Mr. Doty and to ask what we knew about it. We knew nothing then, but his news was soon confirmed. The county option tax amendment had carried. It was the other two that had been defeated.

" In committee consultations at his rooms in the Prince George Hotel after our arrival in New York, Mr. Johnson had little to say; but his mind was alert, and whenever he did say anything he went directly to the point and without irritation or personal feeling. In all our twenty-five years of coöperation in the same cause I never knew him to be irritable in conference or public speech, nor to be moved by personal animus, and in the Fels Fund conference he was in those respects his old-time self.

" When he spoke at the public meeting of the Fels Fund, in the rooms of the Liberal Club, he did so because matters had

taken a shape which in his judgment precluded his remaining
silent. He recognized obstructive influences of the same character and apparent origin as some he had encountered in his nine
years' fight against Privilege in Ohio. It was not a pleasant task
for him to speak of this, but as he saw the matter it was his
task if anyone's, and he did not shirk. There was no unkindness
toward individuals, either in what he said or in his way of saying
it. He made no accusation of bad faith against anyone immediately concerned. His suggestions, on the contrary, were of good
faith played upon from outside. Nor, on the other hand, was
there any weak holding back of facts he thought his associates
ought to know. He spoke deliberately, frankly, and without any
spirit of personal unfriendliness toward anybody, just as in public
speaking he had been accustomed to do; yet with the characteristic
force and clearness of statement which never left anyone in doubt
of what he meant. The parallels he drew, and which were of
the substance of his speech, were to the effect that whenever he
had encountered the outlying influence he mentioned, it came in
the form of a proposal of what he described as ' something different, just a little different,' from the movement it seemed to him
designed to obstruct or divert.

" Those who saw Tom L. Johnson as he made that speech,
having known him before his illness and seeing him then for the
first time since his health had broken, thought of him reasonably
enough as of one whose physical strength had hopelessly gone;
but no one who had ever known him well, could have heard him
then without realizing that the man himself was there in all his
mental and moral vigor. Had I closed my eyes so as to shut
out the emaciated body, and but listened to the voice and followed
the thought, I think he would have seemed unchanged to me.
In that speech I recognized as of old the vigor of voice and
thought and phrase and sense of responsibility, of the same Tom
L. Johnson who, coming over to Henry George in the early
eighties, followed him until death, and then good-humoredly but

relentlessly, regardless of friends, fearless of foes, irrespective of
fortune and of victory or defeat, took the lead in fighting Privilege in its varied moods, from subtle to ferocious, for nine memo-
rable years in Ohio."

On January 6, 1911, Mr. Fels and Mr. Kiefer visited
Cleveland as one of the points on their Western tour in
the interests of the single tax propaganda.   A public meeting was held in the Chamber of Commerce auditorium in
the evening.   Dr. Cooley presided and Mr. Fels, Dr.
Eggleston of Oregon, Newton D. Baker and Mr. Johnson were the speakers.   And so it happened that Mr.
Johnson's last participation in a public meeting was in behalf of the cause so near his heart.   The hall was crowded
and here in the very citadel of his old time enemy he received such an ovation as could not but gladden the heart
of anyone.   As he looked at the cheering crowd before
him he said, " This does not look like the old tent, but it
sounds like it."   He spoke simply and directly as usual,
and eloquently as he always did when the single tax was his
theme.   His voice was clear and distinct with a fullness of
tone that had been absent for a long time.   His closest
friends might well have been deceived by his apparent
strength, and those who knew that this was probably the
last time he would make a speech rejoiced exceedingly in
the nobility of the sentiments he enunciated that night and
in the power manifested in their utterance.

On February 6, owing to contagious illness in his own
family, Mr. Johnson was ordered by his physician to leave
the family apartment in the Knickerbocker until all danger of infection was past.   He therefore moved to Whitehall, an apartment hotel on the edge of one of Cleveland's
most beautiful parks.   He was suffering less at this time,

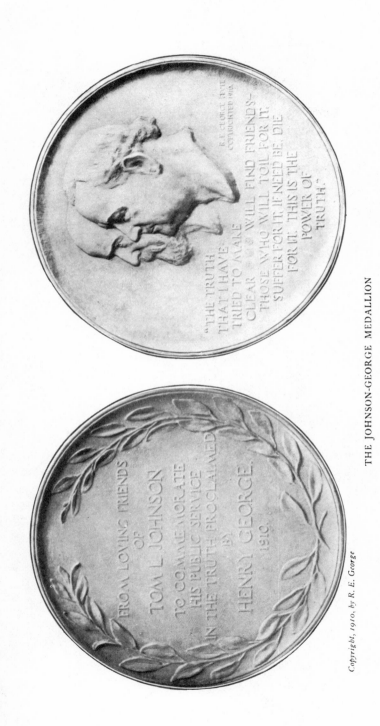

"THE TRUTH THAT I HAVE TRIED TO MAKE CLEAR ☙ ☙ WILL FIND FRIENDS— THOSE WHO WILL TOIL FOR IT, SUFFER FOR IT, IF NEED BE, DIE FOR IT. THIS IS THE POWER OF TRUTH."

R. E. GEORGE. FECIT COPYRIGHTED 1910.

FROM LOVING FRIENDS OF TOM L JOHNSON TO COMMEMORATE HIS PUBLIC SERVICE IN THE TRUTH PROCLAIMED BY HENRY GEORGE. 1910.

THE JOHNSON-GEORGE MEDALLION

Copyright, 1910, by R. E. George

the peritonitis which was said to be the cause of his pain having evidently subsided. Now, for the first time, he was under the constant care of a physician and the daily visits of his doctor, to whom he became greatly attached, added greatly to his comfort.

His interest in current happenings revived. He watched the newspapers for every bit of political news, especially that which had to do with the State legislature at Columbus. He looked forward with eagerness to the week-end visits of Senator Stockwell, who brought him details of activities which he could not get from the press. Magazine articles on social and political questions interested him as they never had done before. Book after book, short stories without number were read to him, and in the very last days Ernest Crosby's poems pleased him most of all. His correspondence with friends in Great Britain was one of his diversions, his interest in British politics never abating.

On March eleventh Mr. Johnson attended as a guest the annual meeting of the Nisi Prius Club, which is to Cleveland what the Gridiron Club is to Washington. Its membership is composed of the leading lawyers of the city. Mr. Johnson went down to the Hollenden hotel early in the day and took a room, where he rested until the time for the programme following the dinner arrived, and then he went to the banquet hall in another part of the hotel to enjoy the fun. His three closest friends, the men who were with him almost daily during the last two months of his life and who had been associated with him so intimately and for so long, A. B. du Pont, Newton Baker and Billy Stage, were there, but this was not an assemblage of Mr. Johnson's followers. It was a gathering of repre-

sentatives of the privileged interests of the community.
Men who had fought Mr. Johnson in the Chamber of
Commerce, on the stump, in court, through the newspapers
and on Cleveland's streets made up the majority of that
gathering. Yet with hardly an exception every man
present shook hands with Mr. Johnson that night and expressed his good will. Perhaps they understood, as they
saw him now, so sweet of spirit, so serene, so far removed
from the influences of human passion and worldly strife,
that after all he never had fought them, that the war he
had waged with such relentless power had been directed
not against individuals, but against " a wrong social order," an order which makes victims no less of the masters
than of the slaves. Perhaps they had a glimmer of that
larger understanding which had distinguished Mr. Johnson for so many years. He returned to his apartment at
Whitehall the next morning literally radiant with happiness. Once more and for the last time his body had been
subjugated to his all but invincible will.

He was attacked by acute nephritis the night of March
14, and though he had subsequent periods of rallying
death was galloping towards him now and he knew it.
His anxiety was not that it was approaching so fast, but
that it might be too long delayed. He was at peace with
the world. If it still held enemies for him he did not
know it. He had no regrets, for he had no hates. He
had fought a good fight, he had done a day's work, and
he was very tired. This extreme exhaustion mercifully
passed some hours before he became unconscious. A
night and a day of unconsciousness preceded the end. He
emerged from it once only long enough to say with a
smile and a sigh, " It's all right. I'm so happy." Heart

action and respiration ceased at the same instant at thirteen minutes before nine o'clock the evening of April 10, 1911.

The simplest of funeral rites were performed by his friends Harris R. Cooley and Herbert S. Bigelow two days later. " Two hundred thousand persons saw Tom L. Johnson's last journey through Cleveland," said the Cleveland *Leader*. " The heart of the city stopped for two hours while the simple cortege passed through the lines of silent, grief stricken men and women on its way from the Knickerbocker apartments to the Union station. * * * Flags were at half mast, buildings were decorated with crepe and pictures of the former mayor edged with mourning were displayed in most of the windows along the streets traversed by the procession. Public buildings and the Chamber of Commerce were closed. * * * Men, women and children from every walk of life comprised the vast assemblage who came to bid their former mayor a last farewell. That his friends were legion was evidenced by the respectful lifting of hats by all who were close to the passing cortege. It was not alone the women who wept. Tears flowed down the cheeks of many men who made no effort to wipe them away, but gazed with streaming eyes on the carriage containing *their friend*."

The next day all that was mortal of Tom L. Johnson was laid in a grave in Greenwood Cemetery, Brooklyn, beside that of his master teacher, Henry George.

APPENDIX

(Out of consideration for Mr. Johnson's freely expressed dislike of foot notes all such notes have been omitted from his book, the few which seemed necessary being assembled here instead.)

Chapter V, page 47. See *Congressional Record* of January 8, 1895 —" Honorable Tom L. Johnson of Ohio in the House of Representatives on The Money Question."

Chapter X, page 89. "During Tom Johnson's business life in steel his emphatic, radical beliefs and policies brought him frequently into trouble, and at times even into financial danger. I could speak of more than one close crisis where the choice practically lay between all the financial help he needed for his business enterprises, to be won by stultifying himself in his political faith, or, as an alternative, financial opposition which at the time looked as though it would be fatal."— *From a newspaper interview with Arthur J. Moxham of Wilmington, Delaware, April 11, 1911.*

Same chapter, page 90. "By 1895 the works were completed and put into operation at Lorain, Ohio. The location of the new plant at this point excited bitter comment on the part of Pittsburgh steel men, as it involved practically moving from the Pittsburgh district to the new location, a step that could only be justified by belief in the greater advantage of the lake shore as a steel center.

"Subsequent events, such as the contemplated construction of a large steel plant by the Carnegie interests at Conneaut, Ohio, one of the elements that determined in some measure at least the purchase of the Carnegie interests by the United States Steel Company; such as the location of the latest and largest plant of the United States Steel Company at Gary, Indiana, on the lake shore, and still more the success of the Lorain Steel Company,

315

now owned by the United States Steel Company, have confirmed the foresight and wisdom that prompted this step."— *Same interview.*

Same chapter, page 91. " In 1898 the steel plant and business were sold to the Federal Steel Company. The original holdings of the Federal Steel Company consisted of two plants, the Illinois Steel Company at Chicago, and the Lorain Steel Company at Lorain, Ohio, and properties on the lakes and the connecting railroads. As is known the Federal Steel Company was the precursor and practically the originator of the United States Steel Company."— *Same interview.*

Chapter XII, page 108. See *Congressional Record* of August 24, 1893 —" Honorable Tom L. Johnson of Ohio in the House of Representatives on Silver."

Chapter XIX, page 205. The following State laws in which Mr. Johnson was interested were enacted by the Ohio Assembly which adjourned in April, 1911:

Nonpartisan Judiciary — a bill providing that the names of nominees for all judicial offices shall appear on the ballot without party designation of any kind.

Direct Election of United States Senators — a bill embodying the Oregon plan which provides for the direct nomination and election of senators. Members of the legislature are required to sign one of two statements — the first, pledging them to vote for that man for senator who receives the most votes at the regular election, or the second, refusing to be so bound. Under this plan a Republican legislator may vote for a Democrat for senator, or a Democratic legislator for a Republican.

Nonpartisan Constitutional Convention — a bill requiring all delegates to the constitutional convention of 1912 to be nominated and elected on a strictly nonpartisan basis; nominations to be made by petition only.

Shorter Workday for Women — a bill limiting the hours of women employed to fifty-four hours a week, with not more than ten hours in any one day. (Amended from eight hours as provided in original bill.)

Workingmen's Compensation Act — a bill creating a State compensation fund, from which money shall be paid employés injured and dependents of employés killed at their work.

Municipal Initiative and Referendum — a measure requiring thirty per cent. of the voters of a municipality for the initiative and fifteen per cent. for the referendum. Covers " ordinances and resolutions granting a franchise, creating a right, involving the expenditure of money or exercising any other power delegated to a municipal corporation by the General Assembly."

Corrupt Practices Act — a measure regulating the amount of money a candidate may spend, and throwing other safeguards around elections.

Chapter XXV, page 291. On May 23, 1911, G. M. Dahl, street railway commissioner of Cleveland ordered the Cleveland Railway Company to stop charging passengers a penny for transfers. The order was given under the terms of the traction ordinance which require that whenever a balance in the interest fund, less proportionate accrued payment to be made therefrom, shall be more than $500,000 by the amount of $200,000 fares shall be reduced from the existing rate to the next lower rate provided by the ordinance. The street railway company resisted the order, but on May 29 the city council adopted a resolution compelling it to comply, and straight three-cent fare became effective June 1, 1911, less than two months after the death of Mr. Johnson.

INDEX

319

INDEX

Harrison, Benjamin, 64.

Harter, Representative, 63.

Harrison, Benjamin, 64.
Harter, Representative, 63.
Haserodt, E. B., 269; 293.
Hauser, Elizabeth J., editor. (See acknowledgment; introduction; last chapter.)
Henna, Dr., 52.
Herrick, Myron T., 134; 135; 200; 201; 206.
Hill, William P., 307.
Hindman, T. C., 2; 4.
Hodge, O. J., 62.
Hoefgen, J. B., 160; 161; grant to declared invalid, 162.
Hogsett, Thomas, 192; 194.
Howe, Frederic C., quoted, xxiv; 121; 204; 216; 224; 299.

Ingersoll, Robert G., 74–75.
Initiative, xvi; 119; 199.
Injunctions, record of in street railroad fight, 164–166.
Ivins, William M., 57; quoted, 58.

Johnson, Albert, brother of J., 3; 57; 86; 91; 98.
Johnson, Albert W., father of J., 1; service to Confederacy, 2; quarrels with Gen. Hindman and joins Gen. Breckinridge, 4; sympathy with North, 5; attempts to operate cotton plantation in Arkansas with free labor, 7; engages in business in Evansville, Ind., 7; superintendent of street railroad in Louisville, 11; chief of police, 11; president of street railway company in Indianapolis, 14; shares in profits of sale, 31; friendship with Henry George, 55; 123.
Johnson, Maggie J., J. marries, 13.
Johnson, Richard M., 59.
Johnson, Tom L., advocates initiative, referendum, recall, short ballot, woman suffrage, juster laws on taxation, municipal ownership and city home rule, xvi; interview with President Roosevelt, xvii; conversation with W. J. Bryan, xvii; applies merit system to city departments,

Johnson, Tom L. (*continued*). xviii; summary of improvements and reforms while mayor of Cleveland, xviii, xix; hissed in Brooklyn, xx, 56; manner and method before an audience, xx, xxi; accedes to strikers' demands, xxii; favors labor unions, xxii; invents pay-enter fare-box, xxii; enmity of newspapers, xxiii, xxiv; a friend's estimate of, xxvii, xxviii; "Slip-Slide," xxviii–xxxii; defines Privilege, xxxv; discusses monopolies, xxxv–xxxvii; judiciary and Privilege, xxxviii; public ownership of utilities, xxxix; parentage, birthplace, early recollections, 1; family moves to Little Rock, Ark., 3; to Atlanta and Milledgeville, Ga., 4; to Corner Springs, Withville, Natural Bridge and Staunton, Va., 5; typhoid fever, 5; first business venture, 5, 6; moves to Louisville, Ky., 6; early instruction, 6; moves to Arkansas, thence to Evansville, Ind., 7; return to Kentucky, 7; freedom from class feeling, 7; enters street railroad business in Louisville, 8; lives with Coleman family, 9; duties, learns bookkeeping, invents fare-box, 10; secretary of company, superintendent of road, 11; marries, 13; purchases control of Indianapolis street railways, 13; litigation and disputes with Wm. H. English, 13–16; bids for street railway grant in Cleveland, 17; buys Pearl street line, introduces transfer system, 19; contests with M. A. Hanna, 17–25; buys Jennings ave. line, 22; gets grant to build east side lines, 24; refuses Hanna's offer of partnership, 25; on private as against municipal ownership of public utilities, 25–27; goes into business at Johnstown, 29; establishes plant, 31; profits on

Johnson, Tom L. (*continued*).
sale of street railroad, 31; ventures in St. Louis and Brooklyn, 32; builds rolling-mill, 33; builds steam railroad and buys street railways in Johnstown, 34; removes bodies of victims of flood, 38; discusses free street cars, 39–40; blames Privilege for Johnstown flood, 43–44; substitute for currency during panic, 45–46; need for better currency system, 47; reads *Social Problems* and *Progress and Poverty,* 49; urged by Henry George to enter politics, 51; at George's death-bed, 52; first attempts at public speaking, 53; advocates change in Ohio tax laws, 54; backs Cleveland *Recorder,* 54; suffers in 1897 panic, 54; aids *The Public,* 55; manages George's campaign for mayor of New York in 1897, 56; nominated for Congress, 59; declares belief in free trade, 60; defeated by Burton, 61; again nominated, 61; debates with Burton, 62; elected, 62; again nominated and elected over O. J. Hodge, 62; votes for single tax bill, 63; approves "Reed rules," 63–64; acquaintance with Harrison, 64; with Bryan, 65; committee work in Congress, 65; reform in assessment and taxation in District of Columbia, 65–67; distributes *Protection or Free Trade* at government expense, 68–70; delegate to national convention, 70; visit to Grover Cleveland, 73; predicts defeat of Democratic party; defeated for reëlection by Burton, 74; replies to charge of insincerity, 75; credit to George for letter to Cleveland cloak-makers, 78; the letter, 79–81; tent meetings, 82–84; meets Peter Witt, 84–86; the Cleveland street railway situation, 86–88; sells street railway in-

Johnson, Tom L. (*continued*).
terests, 88; his social philosophy alienates friends, 89; expands scope of Johnstown mill, builds mill at Lorain, 90; sells out, 90; builds street railroad Lorain to Elyria, 91; manages Detroit street railways, 91; rebuilds them, 92; convinced of practicability of three-cent fare, 95; friendship with Pingree, 95–97; manages Brooklyn street railways, 98; litigation, 98–99; gets grant for Brooklyn Bridge line, 102; Harriman suggests alliance, 103; sale of Brooklyn roads, 103–105; interview with R. T. Wilson, 106; takes steps to quit business, 106–107; determines to devote energies to advancement of George's principles, 107; trip to Europe, 108; delegate to national convention, 108; opposed to "16 to 1," 108; views on the money question, 108; nominated for mayor, 109–110; standards of political morality, 111; declines to bargain for support, 111–112; platform, 112; the campaign, 112–116; sues to prevent consummation of corrupt council's grant of lake front, 113; elected mayor, 116; sworn in, 117; secures repeal of lake front grant, 118; his first two orders, 120; organizes better element of council for good government and chooses cabinet, 121; institutes reforms, 122–125; establishes Tax School, 125; its purpose and accomplishments, 126–131; tax valuation of steam railroads, 132–144; taxation of public utilities, 145–147; home rule, 147–149; source of railroads' power and remedy for its abuse, 149–155; invited to Columbus, 156; offers to buy street railways there and give three-cent fare, 156; makes charge against Judge Summers,

Standard Oil Company, 154; 195; 213; 214; 215; 216.
Steel Rail Pool, 76–78.
Steffens, J. Lincoln, estimate of J., xx; 299.
Stockwell, John N., quoted, xiv; 311.
Stone, William J., 68.
Summers, A. N., 157; 158.

Taft, William H., 267; 268.
Tammany Hall, 57.
Tariff, 33; 71; 73–75; 76–81.
Taussig, J. E., 134; 135.
Taxation of land values, discussion of in District of Columbia, 65–67. (See, also, Single Tax.)
Tax School, 125–131.
Tayler Grant, 290; 291.
Tayler, Robert W., 237; 284; address to city council quoted, 285–286; 288; 289.
Threefer, 225; 241; 250; 262; 280.
Tracey, Representative, 63.
Trevelyan, Charles, 298.
Tuckerman, Dr., 115.
Tyler, James, 303; 307.

Union Club, 171; 266.
United States Steel Company, 90.
U'Ren, W. S., 307.

Vilas, William F., 70; 72.
Vorhees, 104; 105.

Wadsworth, James, 65.
Warner, John DeWitt, 63; 299.
Warrington, John W., 237; 238; 247.
Washington, D. C. (See District of Columbia.)
Washington, Joseph E., 65; 68.
Watterson, Henry, 70; 72.
Wedgewood, Josiah, 298.
Wells, Representative, 197; 198.
Westenhaver, D. C., 247.
White, John G., 285; 287.
Whitlock, Brand, 207.
Whitney, William C., quoted, 73.
Widener-Elkins Syndicate, 196.
Wiebenson, Edward, 224.
Williams, Charles D., xxiii.
Wilson Bill, 73; 74; 75; 78.
Wilson, Richard T., 91; 92; 93; 98; quoted, 106; 108.
Wilson, William L., 72.
Witt, Peter, 75; 84–86; 115; 126; 181; 203; 218; 256; 257; 258; 259; 273; 274; 307.
Woman Suffrage, xvi.
Wright, Mr., 200.

Zmunt, J. B., 187.